RADICAL CHANGE RADICAL RESULTS

7 ACTIONS TO BECOME THE FORCE FOR CHANGE IN YOUR ORGANIZATION

KATE LUDEMAN, PH.D.
COAUTHOR OF *THE CORPORATE MYSTIC*

EDDIE ERLANDSON, M.D.

Dearborn™
Trade Publishing
A **Kaplan Professional** Company

This publication is designed to provide accurate and authoritative information in regard to the subject matter covered. It is sold with the understanding that the publisher is not engaged in rendering legal, accounting, or other professional service. If legal advice or other expert assistance is required, the services of a competent professional should be sought.

Vice President and Publisher: Cynthia A. Zigmund
Editorial Director: Donald J. Hull
Senior Project Editor: Trey Thoelcke
Interior Design: Lucy Jenkins
Cover Design: Design Solutions
Typesetting: the dotted i

© 2003 by Kate Ludeman and Eddie Erlandson

Published by Dearborn Trade Publishing, a Kaplan Professional Company

Printed in the United States of America

03 04 05   10 9 8 7 6 5 4 3 2 1

Library of Congress Cataloging-in-Publication Data

Ludeman, Kate.
    Radical change, radical results : 7 actions to become the force for change in your organization / Kate Ludeman and Eddie Erlandson.
      p.   cm.
    Includes index.
    ISBN 0-7931-7363-9 (6x9 hardback)
    1. Organizational change. I. Erlandson, Eddie. II. Title.
HD58.8 .L835 2003
658.4′013—dc21

            2002155112

Dearborn Trade books are available at special quantity discounts to use for sales promotions, employee premiums, or educational purposes. Please call our special sales department, to order or for more information, at 800-621-9621, ext. 4404, or write to Dearborn Financial Publishing, 30 South Wacker Drive, Suite 2500, Chicago, IL 60606-7481.

Advanced Praise for *Radical Change, Radical Results*

"Kate's coaching causes a huge 'ah-ha' in people she works with. These new insights drive visible change in the workplace. A must-read for anyone seeking to be authentic in today's complex business environment."
—**Glenn Gienko,** Senior Vice President, Motorola

"Traditionally strong and independent, physicians have been slow to embrace management practices used successfully in the business world. Drs. Ludeman and Erlandson have written an essential and effective prescription for radical change. Go to your bookstore and fill it!"
—**Jack L. Cronenwett, MD,** Professor, Dartmouth-Hitchcock Medical Center and President, Society for Vascular Surgery

"I loved this book! Any leader in business today would benefit greatly from the tools, techniques, and strategies offered in this book. Kate and Eddie lay out a clear and compelling roadmap to help leaders create lasting impact, the kind that separates good leaders from great ones."
—**Donna Kindl,** Former Senior Vice-President, Monsanto

"For healthcare providers to compete in these chaotic times, we must accept that constant change is the number one business challenge today, and we must abandon outdated leadership habits as fast as we can. Use this guidebook to step up to new, exhilarating levels of leadership adventure."
—**Don Hutton,** Former CEO, Brooks Health System

"Kate and Eddie remind us that to transform our companies, we must first transform ourselves. If you want the essential tools for successfully navigating the turbulent waters of modern business, the seven actions in *Radical Change, Radical Results* will guide you to your chosen destination. A seminal work!"
—**Jim Strohecker,** President, HealthWorld Online

"Learn from Kate Ludeman and Eddie Erlandson, whose exceptional perspective comes from years of successful work with top-level executives in major corporations. This book presents radical approaches—both inner and outer—to accelerate the evolution of people in organizations. Expect your organization to thrive!"
—**Lee Kaiser, Ph.D.,** President, Kaiser Institute

"Today any business decision based on reliable information and made quickly is a good one, and any decision made too slowly is a bad one. These seven powerful actions optimize information gathering and streamline decision making."
—**Dennis Cagan,** Chairman and CEO, Santa Barbara Technology Group

FOR
GAY AND KATHLYN HENDRICKS

Our mentors, our teachers, our closest friends,
Whose devotion to the truth has
Unleashed our creativity,
Expanded our love,
And magnified our connection
With each other and everyone in our lives.

CONTENTS

7 ACTIONS
To Become the Force for Change in Your Organization

1. Curiosity: Learn on the run. Dropping your defenses and taking in all feedback has become the critical difference between success and failure, but many people prefer being right to being successful, or even to feeling good. As long as you stay stuck in, "That's just the way I am and that's just the way *they* are," you increase the inertia in your company and guarantee that you both fail to live up to your potential. When you become truly open to learning, you feel surprised by your problems, which will constantly change.

2. Awareness: Tap your bodymind intelligence. To make the wisest, most transformative decisions, learn to use the multidimensional intelligence and intuition you carry around with you wherever you go. Your bodymind invites you to slow down to go fast, leading you to deeper truth in deal making and decisions of all kinds. It also helps in anticipating future trends and recovering more quickly from upsets. The two most powerful ways to tap into bodymind wisdom are by feeling your feelings and by taking several deep, centered breaths.

3. Authenticity: Drop the roles that bind you. Become authentic at work, and you'll joyfully thrive at whatever you do, regardless of the challenges that come your way. As long as we cling to personas like Victim (complaining), Villain (blaming), and Hero (saving the day), the same problems keep showing up again and again. Learn to catch yourself the moment you start to feel a familiar murky, mucky, flattening of energy you can't quite name.

Then get real. One person's commitment and skills for authentic behavior will empower everyone else to make a shift.

4. Accountability: Take responsibility. Many people seem to feel more responsible for *explaining* their results than for *achieving* them. Accountable individuals, on the other hand, make solid agreements and take 100% responsibility for their experiences and commitments. They look inside themselves, wondering about their contribution to problems, rather than making them somebody else's fault. They communicate frequently with updates, they're reliable on tight deadlines, and they rarely drop the ball. If they must change an agreement, they let those who will be affected know and renegotiate that agreement.

5. Candor: Tell the truth. Lies occur at epidemic levels in companies. About 95 percent of the time, we lie because we want to control the uncontrollable: others' reactions or emotions. If you mislead someone, address it immediately. Truth instantly gets all the information out on the table so everyone involved can quickly make the right decisions with the benefit of all details and opinions. True power and enormous speed result when people deal directly with the truth and with one another.

6. Genius: Awaken your sleeping giant. Most companies focus their time and energy on improving employee weaknesses rather than capitalizing on their talents and strengths. Truly successful people get "good enough" at basic skills, then optimize their natural gifts, their areas of genius. They also recognize where they don't need to be a genius and delegate those areas to others. When you align your purpose and genius with your jobs and your company's genius, your efficiency, productivity, satisfaction, and joy skyrocket.

7. Appreciation: Express your gratitude. As much as 80 percent of conversations at work contain critical comments because most people tend to notice what's missing, rather than what's working well. You may incorrectly assume your coworkers feel appreciated because they haven't received negative feedback, but vibrant, sustainable, collaborative relationships require a ratio of 5:1 positive experiences to negative ones. Appreciating a personal quality rather than a skill usually touches people more deeply than appreciating contributions, behaviors, or abilities anyone could provide.

ACKNOWLEDGMENTS

We feel deeply thankful to our editor Winnie Shows for transforming our ideas into a readable and entertaining book and for her impeccable commitment to practicing the principles in this book throughout the writing process. Her ongoing insight and humor kept us energized and on schedule.

We also feel fortunate to be represented by Bonnie Solow, our miracle-working agent, who nurtured the book through countless iterations. She played an essential role in bringing the book into the world, and in helping us grow as writers.

Kate's daughter Catherine Ludeman-Hall joined our company during the final phase of working on this book and gave us the *space* to complete it, as she reliably handled all the day-to-day details of our business. Marisa Huston rode herd on the myriad crucial details that can skitter out of control when bringing these ideas into the form you now hold in your hand. Along the way, we were greatly helped by Erin Miller, Kerrie Nanni, Kathryn Sutton, and Marjorie McIntosh.

This book could never have been written without the personal support, friendship, and teaching tools lovingly handed to us by Gay and Kathlyn Hendricks. Working and playing with them for the last 20 years has been a highlight of Kate's life and a relatively recent gift to Eddie that keeps on giving. They have also given us the opportunity to observe firsthand one of the richest and healthiest marriages on the planet.

Finally, we feel deeply honored to work with our clients, who share their stories and teach us every day. Their courage and commitment to learning is changing the face of business and, ultimately, the world.

INTRODUCTION
Inside Actions, Outside Results

Speed matters. And speed keeps speeding up. As business accelerates, the ability to easily and quickly respond to constant change becomes increasingly valuable. Today we must quickly and easily understand ourselves and others so that our businesses and our teams can morph as needed in the new business environment. But few companies or leaders seem to know how to reduce the unpleasant fear-based stickiness that gums up the work and slows things to a crawl.

Thinking all our problems are "out there"—caused by other people and events—creates enormous drag on both individuals and corporations because it leads to rumors, complaining, and blaming, and fosters accountability gaps. Companies must invest their time and energy where it will pay off exponentially—on the subtle internal shifts that unleash huge, high-leveraged changes out in the world. These changes start with individuals like you, who are willing to take the necessary steps.

I (Eddie) have had a lifelong fascination with transformational change. During my 25-year career as a vascular surgeon, I've been able to create a significant shift in a patient's physiology, but many times they got well only to get sick again. I began to realize that sustaining the change is as important as the change itself. A true surgeon, impatient with myself and others, I wanted the changes and shifts to occur quickly and be easily maintained. I've learned that life doesn't always happen that way. Change is organic and follows natural laws and rhythms, despite our best efforts to harness and control it.

I became fascinated by the biology of change as well as the biology of leadership and put this "art and science" to work in multiple leadership roles in the Michigan Heart and Vascular Institute and at the Saint Joseph Mercy Hospital, where I served as Chief of the Medical Staff. As I worked with my colleagues in healthcare to tackle the outside challenges of resources and technology, I connected with the inside challenges of comfortable identities and familiar styles of interaction. I've always loved being the "answer man" (my nickname when I taught anatomy at the University of Michigan), and today I realize that the best answers come not from command and control but from an organic, inside-out process with daunting challenges and miraculous results.

Most of us know how to transform our company's business plans, our strategies, and our processes, and this works with the stuff of business. Now if we'll learn a new approach to *people* (starting with ourselves), we'll be able to truly harness the capital of this new era. We must master skills that until now seemed like options or luxuries or qualities we only see in movies: telling the whole truth, taking the time to feel and express appreciation, being totally committed to learning, and sidestepping natural tendencies toward defensiveness. These relating and connecting skills will enable each of us to move forward in a flash, unencumbered by politics, fear, or bureaucracy. We'll reap the rewards of our work faster, too.

Many of us equate speed with hurry up, and efficiency with a kind of stingy streamlining—minus the fun. When a company knows how to make the choices that sustain instantaneous change, speed is coupled with ease, and humor and joy count as much as efficiency.

I (Kate) have had a lifelong fascination with how to get from here to there more quickly, and by the time I was 20 years old, my interest in speed and efficiency resulted in a lot more tickets and car accidents than I'd like to own up to. As I moved into my 30s I began to look for a better way to enjoy that edge without such a big downside. I started to explore the "inner speed" that would accelerate every part of life. This was a lot faster and way more fun! As the years passed, my career ultimately took shape around a particular issue: *Which attitudes and capabilities most help people move swiftly and gracefully through rapid business change?*

As executive coaches, we constantly remind our clients that to lead change, they must both embrace and embody it, viewing even unexpected downturns as opportunities to drop their defenses and open wide to learning—especially about themselves. If one person changes, it reverberates throughout their companies that have become flat, webbed organisms. Our clients, like you and me, tend to see the problems as "out there" and focus on others' resistance, instead of looking at their own. *So the real issue becomes: How do you come to realize that the chronic problems around you have something to do with* you?

In the late '70s, '80s, and early '90s when I had an initial meeting with a new client, I often described myself as an expert in transforming "jerks" into "nice guys." And I do mean *guys* because 95 percent of my clientele were men. These hard-hitting, super drivers treated people like machines, and companies had operated in fact like machines until then. Because these guys were smart, they made brilliant decisions, then pounded on their people to accomplish these goals. My business enjoyed a strong start because these executives had been a visible nuisance in their companies. They were too strong in their business and technical skills to terminate, yet everyone, in their heart, believed they had what I referred to as "interpersonal BO." I feel grateful to all those men who helped launch my career. Their willingness to change meant that I had some early wins—tangible proof of the difference a new mindset and these steps could make.

I had value because I'd found a way to do what few people could: get these tough guys to make obvious changes, behaving more humanely, listening, engaging others, and actually feeling interested in others, not just pretending to be. It wasn't hard. All I did was match their energy and talk straight—truly straight. When they saw how much faster their careers and their companies could move, they jumped at the chance to change.

It reminded me of herding cattle, which I'd often seen as a kid growing up on a South Texas ranch. I was unrelenting in my focus and determination to shut off the various passes to get them into the corral. Once there, they'd be branded and turned into leaders of the herd, instead of the stud loner, drifting farther and farther away from the people they wanted to lead. They had energy and they had power, and I loved my work with them.

And it *was* work. Hard work. I don't know if you've ever sweated in the hot Texas sun on the back of a tired horse or herded cattle in a jeep bouncing across a ridged, plowed field, but working with difficult people is like this—hot and sweaty. You have to get right down there in their stuff with them and through sheer will and confrontation take them to a higher level.

One day I decided I wanted to work on the peaks, not the bullpens, and two extraordinary events paved the way.

The first was encountering the work of Gay Hendricks in 1974 when I (Kate) read *Learning to Love Yourself* in one sitting. It dramatically shifted my perspective on life and on work. Shortly after that I met Gay and his wife Katie and began a friendship that has lasted nearly 20 years. We've learned from them an approach that's elegant in its simplicity and profound in impact. Their work reached hundreds of thousands of people from every walk of life, including several thousand therapists. We consider the Hendricks global experts in the art of living consciously for creative relationships at home and at work.

The second key event was consulting with Dell Computer's top executives during the five years of its greatest growth and during its remarkable emergence following the economic slump of 2001–2002. The Dell culture has a passion for doing things in a way that saves time. The senior management team shared my same passion for speed and efficiency, and I got to see the impact of this commitment in a whole company. Dell was the first company that embodied the agility in operations and personal relationships I'd imagined was possible. Even better, the top 20 people were unbelievably coachable and wide open to learning, and their growth and earnings reflected that.

The significant turning points for me (Eddie) spanned all parts of my life: First, I began running marathons in 1976 and expanded to triathlons and bicycle century rides. Along the way I learned how my attitudes, assumptions, and habit patterns colored my results. The second turning point came when I met Kate Ludeman, a visionary leadership coach, when she was a faculty member in a Kaiser Institute program on Medical Leadership. I had read *Conscious Loving* by Gay and Kathlyn Hendricks the year before and was curious about their work. My marriage to Kate and our business partnership created profound changes in my life, both personally and professionally at levels I never imagined were possible. I have added the groundbreaking work of both Kate and Gay and Kathlyn Hendricks to my "black bag" for my patients, my physician and healthcare-leader clients, and myself.

The third turning point for both of us was working with the Defense Logistics Agency after 9-11. The agency believed that high-level management changes could achieve bottom-line savings in its mission as the Department of Defense supplier of consumable items to America's military services around the world. Agency leaders saw that high-level trust could result in a more efficient workforce and yield an increase in productivity. The leaders and their executive team were willing to invest the vast amounts of time necessary to learn about and apply to their business the tools we taught them during the course of our sessions together.

These experiences have helped us create a breakthrough methodology we've used with thousands of clients. Our approach consists of the following seven actions:

1. *Curiosity.* Learning on the run

2. *Awareness.* Tapping the bodymind intelligence

3. *Authenticity.* Dropping the roles that bind us

4. *Accountability.* Creating a culture of commitment

5. *Candor.* Telling the truth and turning the tide

6. *Genius.* Awakening the sleeping giant

7. *Appreciation.* Seeing gifts everywhere

These seven inner moves will help you keep pace, no matter how quickly your business and the world morph into their next amazing forms.

Taking these actions, day in and day out, is a lifelong process that yields both immediate and long-term rewards. In the first chapter we'll look at how business is today and how it might be. Then we'll explore each of the seven choices in depth and wrap up with suggestions of how to implement all you've learned. We describe here a way of work most of us have only dreamed of and all of us must create to prosper in the new form of business that's birthing now. Keep an open mind. Take a deep breath, and enjoy the ride!

CHAPTER ONE

COURAGE
Committing to Conscious Change

*How can I transform our people
resources into the greatest
competitive advantage?*

*How can I get people to make
needed changes faster?*

*How can I eliminate politics,
bureaucracy, and the rumor mill?*

Let us show you a genuinely exciting phenomenon, an example of a new way of work:

Every morning 1,000 or so people who don't need to work get in their cars and come to jobs at Dell. There, they work side-by-side with 36,000 other employees. Why don't they need to go to work? Because they're multimillionaires. Due to the run-up in Dell stock over the years, even with more recent drops, people at many levels of the company have become millionaires. And yet, they still show up for work. Something gets them out of bed, puts them behind the wheel of their cars, and inspires them to go to the office—even though they could easily be at home behind the remote control or the fishing pole.

When you walk in the door at Dell, everywhere you look, someone is contributing, making exciting changes in projects—and having fun! Sit in on a meeting, and you'll see people smiling. Walk down the hall, and you'll feel engagement and commitment on all sides. Everyone contributes high-impact ideas, and everyone focuses on success and excellence. People log long hours, yet enjoy astonishingly high energy levels. Although I (Kate) have worked as a consultant to Dell for a number of years, I still feel moved by the tangible spirit of Dell whenever I walk through their front door.

I could feel the spirit the first day I started consulting with Dell in 1995. I wouldn't describe the company as wealthy then— I definitely arrived in their salad days. Their stock was, to put it mildly, in the tank, and with 8,000 employees, this was no start-up company. Here's what was odd, though: People radiated happiness. I heard and saw learning occur at every level in every moment. A day didn't go by where I wouldn't hear people sorting out a problem, clarifying a challenge, sharing what they know—and admitting what they don't know—without defensiveness. I also heard a lot of laughter. I felt instantly fascinated. Dell had created a culture that viewed constant change as new opportunity. The company seemed filled with delight, despite the skimping, saving, and struggling that was obviously going on in this very low-margin business. Dell enjoyed unprecedented rise in stock valuation and growth over the next five years and retained its intellectual capital through dark economic times in 2001 and 2002, enabling the company to gobble up its competitors. The bottom-line testimony: Whatever they were doing, it worked. They had created a cocommitment contract in which all managers and all employees agreed to take 100% responsibility for work, and one of the remarkable benefits was loyalty.

At Dell and other companies where high-speed change is the order of the day, you've got to learn faster and faster just to keep up. We call it "learning on the run." This means being able to get the message quickly, regardless of how it comes in, and to act on it without delay. We used to value thinking on your feet, but now even this seems like crawling. In their recent book, *Creative Destruction: Why Companies That Are Built to Last Are*

Underperforming the Market—And How to Successfully Transform Them, Richard Foster and Sarah Kaplan point out that many of the "visionary companies" cited in *Creative Destruction* have underperformed largely because of their inability to respond quickly enough to change. These days you have to think while your feet are running, dancing, and dodging. Now you learn to dance on running water or drown.

This fast-moving, stimulating, and fun culture bursts into bloom when everyone in a company operates accountably, sensing what's next, then making it happen. Learning, direct communications, and personal responsibility become an integral part of the workplace environment. You glow inside with an inner freedom and self-assurance that makes it easy for you to bring your best to work, regardless of what you're doing or how much you're paid.

To ease you into this exciting environment, we are going to make the same request we make of our clients: Put what you think you know about change on hold for a little while. We want you to create an open space—free of prior learnings and experiences—to take a fresh look at what these times require. We have found that only radical shifts do the job. Why do we harp on this word *radical?* If you look it up in a good dictionary, you'll see that it's based on a Latin word that means "root" or "core." When you make a radical shift, you change yourself and your company at the very core. We have not found that lesser change goes to the depth necessary to get the job of transformation done.

Think of any time you made a radical, positive shift in your life. You know it's a radical shift because it shakes you to your roots—usually stirring up huge resistance—and then reorganizes you from the depths of yourself out to the visible surface. This requires courage and reminds us of watching figure skaters who choose to become Olympians. This means practicing their complex routines so many times that their footwork becomes automatic. They can do it in their sleep. In the heat of the games, the right response comes instinctively.

Executing the inner changes in this book is a lot like the commitment required to win a gold medal. These actions will transform you into a quick, easy, adaptable character, working with this same automatic ease instead of the spirit-squelching patterns we often habitually slip into. There's something magical about companies who've caught this wave and its essential underpinning of trust. They creatively redirect energy once spent job-hopping, salary negotiating, complaining about turf wars, and dodging responsibility for problems. When this new kind of culture change takes hold, everyone benefits. Momentum gathers. Shareholders, employees, and customers alike experience a synergistic connection where everyone wins, including your very own 401(k).

You might assume that changing yourself and your company involves some mystery or requires huge capitalization, rare genius, or even a booming economy. On the contrary, the essential change strategies resemble shareware, easily available and simple to understand. Acquiring the "secret" amounts to the committed application of these seven actions that anyone—you, your new hires, your direct reports, your fast trackers, and your executives—can master.

And when you do master them, you'll feel exhilarated and fulfilled at work every day. Sound like an outrageous promise? Here's another one: The challenges and decisions that delight and energize *you* will catalyze your company, bringing it unprecedented success. The daily commitment of both managers and employees to these seven actions will mark a revolution in our interactions with people—a revolution in what we do and say and how we do and say it.

Figure 1.1 shows a preview of these seven powerful actions that will transform both your company and you. To appreciate

FIGURE 1.1   The Seven Transforming Actions

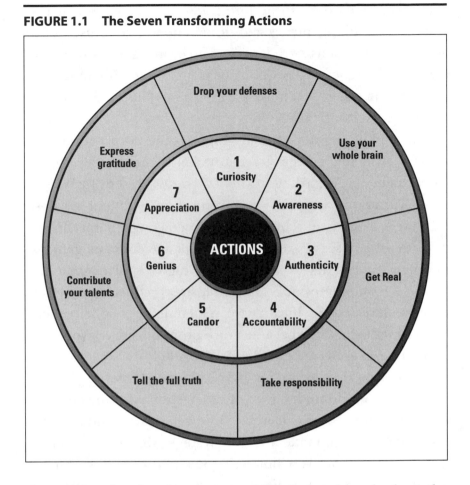

the need today for these seven skills, let's take a look at the changing face of business.

BUSINESS TODAY—HANGING TEN IN HIGH TIDE

What businesses used to need most from their people was reliability. Today, they need brilliance. Now that we're webbed and linked, the breakthroughs of the few can become the shared experience of the many. The market values companies by their brain trusts, not their inventories, because a top engineer and a few peers can outperform hundreds of average engineers. Today, *failure* simply means additional knowledge to use in the next iteration of sensing, adapting, and evolving. Energy has become our currency and people, not plants and equipment, have become our assets. We must acquire new skills as parameters mutate on an hourly basis.

The public demise of many high-profile corporations has made it clear that integrity, accountability, and courage count more than ever. According to *WorkUSA 2000**, a study by Watson Wyatt Worldwide, shareholders' returns of companies whose employees trust top executives were 42 percentage points higher than those whose workers lack confidence in management. International Survey Research of Chicago reported that the number of employees indicating that stress reduces their effectiveness increased significantly to an all-time high of 38 percent in the year 2000, which became more pronounced as layoffs and hiring freezes continued into 2001 and 2002.

As we quickly become an entire planet of Internet surfers, clicking our way to undreamed of connection and convenience, we do it within an intricate web of interrelatedness and extreme expectation. We've made a huge paradigm shift in our view of technology and the Web, how we shop and do our tasks, but we haven't made the same shifts in ourselves or in the way our companies work with people. When the world and every aspect of our lives are changing faster than ever before, our normal resistance to change can become a huge stumbling block. It will require courage to shift the paradigms for how we work.

When Columbus didn't fall off the end of the earth as he sailed west, people could no longer sustain the old paradigm of a flat world, but this worldview didn't change overnight.

---

*Watson Wyatt Worldwide. *WorkUSA 2000.*

Corporate America must similarly drop its belief that improved processes will change people or that we can downsize and ask people to "do more with less."

We stand on the verge of a genuine renaissance in how we work and why we work. Business today requires that we get products to the marketplace faster and with fewer people. Yet many of us have an uneasy relationship with speed, because we think it means stress or hurry. We equate speed with pushing people, walking over them, and squelching their ideas, but that's part of the old way of navigating, where speed was used to justify domineering behaviors, premature product launches, and other unfortunate decisions. We have a choice. We can "speed up," attempting to do more in less time, as we careen along the business highway. Or we can move nimbly over the metamorphosing business terrain, covering more ground with a lighthearted energy and far less hard work and effort. Do you want to drive or fly?

For more passion and productivity, individuals and teams must make two commitments: (1) to construct a workplace built around authentic communication and (2) to deconstruct the endless politics, fed by gossip, defensiveness, and blame. Everyone must have permission to speak the truth and to make their highest contribution. Business as usual must mean a deep grasp of people's internal motivations, the courage to make new choices, and the ability to create rich and meaningful collaborations. Decisions will then come faster and execution will happen at the speed of light.

We've witnessed this phenomenon from Silicon Valley to Silicon Alley, and in the Asian equivalents from Bangalore to Singapore. As human potential experts for the past 20 years, we would almost classify it as one of the wonders of the world. We dream of such things.

WE HAVE SEEN THE ENEMY OF CHANGE AND HE IS US

Companies invest lots of time and money in change programs, but these are mostly ineffective. People also invest personal resources to change. They work out, take graduate courses, make amazon.com one of their favorite shopping sites. And yet most change projects, on both corporate and individual bases, fail. Notice if anything in Figure 1.2 sounds familiar.

Living and working successfully today means replacing some comfortable and predictable old habits. But we identify with them: "That's the way I am." We get stuck: "You can't teach an old dog new tricks." We prefer Mark Twain's view: "Old habits can't be thrown out the upstairs window. But they can be coaxed down the stairs one step at a time."

The great business leaders we've worked with have become a modern breed of alchemists who continually search for the optimal blend of heart, soul, and skills in the laboratory of corporate culture. With the right combination, the human equivalent of gold appears, and we never stop feeling awestruck. When it happens with enough frequency, we want to shout it from the rooftops. Or take some time out to write a book about it.

Let us introduce you to some real-life examples you'll meet later:

- Dell Executive VP Ro Parra tells Steve Price, his director of HR about the wall he puts up and Steve coaches him in taking it down. As a result, their unit shifts from a bunch of driven individual executives to a team with incredible cadence and rhythm. Later, Michael Dell acknowledges Ro and the unit as the feeder pool for a large number of talent transfers to other groups. (Chapter 4, Authenticity)

FIGURE 1.2   How to Prevent Radical Change

Look Upward:	Focus your energy on changing people up the organization. It's up to them to make your life better.
Just Hope:	Spend most of your waking hours in the land of wishful thinking. Who needs to take action?
Accommodate:	Make agreements you know you won't keep, then live down to your expectations.
Pretend:	Fake it till you make it. After you make it, continue to fake it. Don't let anyone know what you feel.
Deny:	Problem? What problem? Ignore them and maybe they'll go away.
Blame or Gossip:	Constantly complain that some person, organization, or situation is responsible for your pain.
Get Buzzed:	Seize on today's buzzword. Set up a "program" for change. Give it a name. Assume it works. When it doesn't, start a new one.
Give Up:	Expect perfection, then give up at the first sign of resistance or of a need to modify the approach.

- The executive team at the Defense Logistics Agency (DLA) agrees to do its best to create the high trust their rapidly changing organization needs to hum. Some of them curious, some perhaps nervous, but all of them willing, they gather together to take the first step, clearing the air, sharing the accumulated criticisms, judgments, and irritations they've withheld from one another, sometimes for years. Two months later, they implement the first phase of a $700 million systems change that impacts across the 23,000–employee organization. They openly and honestly discuss the successes and the glitches of this first phase of the implementation. Their truthful discussion lays some groundwork for the next implementation phase. (Chapter 6, Candor)

- Bill Kimpton leverages his genius and brings in Tom LaTour, who's gifted in areas Bill doesn't enjoy. Bill's job becomes more fun and his company grows from 2 hotels and 1 restaurant to 35 hotels and 29 restaurants. (Chapter 7, Genius)

- Michael Dell, founder and chief executive officer (CEO) of Dell, spontaneously expresses his appreciation to a vice president (VP) for having the courage to disagree with him during a high-pressure meeting. Michael, who had expressed strong opinions in the meeting, becomes open to a contrary view. The stress evaporates, and the group reaches easy agreement about their approach to a business challenge less than an hour later. (Chapter 8, Appreciation)

Today, optimizing the human resources who do the work has become priority one. Creativity explodes because employees contribute in their zones of genius, and integrity ensures that people tell the truth and keep commitments.

WE ARE ALL CONNECTED

Everyone pays when we refuse to change. If our clogged and compromised companies don't work, neither do our communities or countries. Every person affects the whole. Everything matters. And organizations that move at the speed of light know this. Anything's possible, with no fixed future. We create new possibilities in each moment.

Take a few seconds and breathe that statement in.

Individuals and companies have become a lot like underwater ecosystems, or corporate supply chains, or the Internet—intricately webbed together—and one person's actions impact others more and more quickly. Have you ever unwittingly passed along one of those virus hoaxes that multiplied into unnecessary e-mail for hundreds or thousands of others? Ever taken a moment to adjust your attitude and immediately turned a situation around? Then you understand—you've experienced the power of the connection.

"Shift happens." I (Kate) laughed out loud the first time I spotted this parody of a popular bumper sticker. At the same time I realized that, besides being a clever 180° twist on a familiar phrase, these two words describe our new world. An idea takes hold and transmits around the globe, because information fields contain unseen forces and connection that directly influence our experience and our behavior. These fields affect physical, mental, and social forms the way the vibration of a tuning fork stimulates a similar tuning fork without touching it.

New research by leading physicists points toward a reality in which we are one being. Amazingly, in some studies, when a person in one room feels an electric shock, it registers in the polygraph readings of a person in another room. Even the blood volume of a test subject's finger changes when a "sender" in another room encounters the name of someone familiar while reading a list composed mainly of names unknown to them.*

Numerous studies have shown that by focusing their attention, individuals can reliably influence mechanical systems such

---

*Talbot, Michael. *The Holographic Universe*. New York, NY: HarperCollins Publishers, 1995.

as random-number generators. In an extensive series of research studies by Robert Jahn and Brenda Dunne at Princeton University's School of Engineering* the groups affected the generators so much that the probability of the output occurring by chance was only 5,000 to one. Neurologists, physicists, engineers, psychologists, biologists, physiologists, and systems theorists equally confirm the existence of physical *fields* that influence consciousness and behavior, based on research in their respective disciplines. This gives a whole new meaning to the phrase, "He's well connected."

We know you may find this notion of interconnectedness too hard to believe, but hang in there.

To detect the presence of a field, quite often we must first observe its consequences. W. McDougall studied 50 generations of rats over 20 years and reported that once a rat learns a new behavior, any subsequent rat reared under similar conditions learns the same behavior more quickly. The larger the number of rats that learn the task, the more easily similar rats learn it, wherever they live. This occurs in the absence of any known type of physical connection or communication between the rats who were first trained and those who learned the task later.** This implies people in the late twentieth century learned to drive a car more easily than our parents did, even if the design and operating systems were the same. It would also apply to our grandchildren learning to use computers in the twenty-first century.

A department with high turnover may have a field that feels discouraging. We all feel the effect of others' thoughts and judgments. Our often-unsubstantiated beliefs about a coworker influ-

---

*Jahn, Robert and Brenda Dunne. "Princeton Engineering Anomalies Research (PEAR)" Princeton University, 1979.
**Sheldrake, Rupert. *7 Experiments That Could Change the World.* New York: Riverheads (Berkley), 1995.

ence how he feels about us and the trust he has that we are "for him." All the busy, judgmental, and critical minds at work do a lot to dampen our spirits and slow things down, even if we're not consciously aware of it. We also pick up the fear in the air at work more quickly than any contagious disease. Think of the supersonic speed that might become available to our organizations if we redirected all the energy we invest in negative thoughts into something more constructive, like making our numbers this quarter and having fun while we're at it.

Andrew Foss, President of Northern California Operations and Market Development for Spirent, understands that any unspoken judgment hurts the whole team and the company. He declared it off limits in his organization to refer to coworkers as "B" players, because this expression implies inferiority. He wants people to speak directly to each other about perceived limits and performance shortfalls to fix the problems, not label them as "A" or "B" players. The focus becomes connection, collaboration, and contribution—not judging and evaluating—for the biggest possible benefit.

WELCOME TO THE FEAR-FREE ZONE

Most companies could double their margins if they eliminated fear. Fear creates paralysis and more checking in and approvals. All the typical "cover your assets" (CYA) behaviors increase fear and therefore the time it takes to get anything done by as much as 50 percent, in our estimation. This means payroll costs have to increase to add enough people to get work done. Fearful companies trade alchemy for acquiescence. Fear keeps people from speaking up with the truly weird ideas that stimulate discussions leading to breakthroughs for a new product or process.

To be able to turn on a dime with the next change, you must find the courage to act with integrity instead of fear 24/7. Integrity means our actions and attitudes match our words and demands that we dig inside daily for our own learning edge, using an automatic "curiosity reflex." As a result, we avoid burnout, endless politics, and job-hopping. We transform our work culture in the process. When we've made this commitment, we don't delay decisions to see what others want or change decisions to keep others happy, then complain about it behind their backs. Instead, executives, managers, and employees take more personal responsibility for problems, communicate more directly and more promptly, and create quicker and easier alignment. We watch imbedded bureaucracy morph into easier and faster change—in our corporate culture, in our products, and in our business partners.

CORPORATE SLUDGE AND THE LAND OF DILBERT

What causes the time-draining and energy-sapping relationships most of us experience in our companies? *Poor communication, dishonesty, and fear characterize business as usual today and create the by-product we call "corporate sludge."* Our two default modes of operation—protectiveness and pleasing people—create interpersonal muck and mire that slow progress to a crawl and snuff out any movement toward change. We don't think you'll experience any surprises at the recipe in Figure 1.3.

Sludge includes anything that slows us down—from rigid attitudes to overly complex procedures, time spent in turf battles, and energy expended not being real. Many of us with mud lines along our ankles from working in corporate sludge long to rekindle our hope in a transformed future, but we have no idea what to do. The problems look so large and so beyond our individual ability to solve, we sit by, doing nothing. The future seems to spin out of con-

FIGURE 1.3   The Seven Ingredients of Corporate Sludge

1. Time pressure and business complexity lead to packed meeting agendas, which attempt too much in too little time; also known as conning yourself.

2. The same predictable people comment in meetings, discussions drift into rat holes, opinionated people push for their way, while several key players withhold their ideas and pretend to agree; aka fail to tell the whole truth.

3. Time pressure leads to snap decisions with fuzzy follow-up actions or no actions; aka set up low accountability.

4. After meetings, people complain and vent in the hallways; aka gossip.

5. People bring personal agendas to top executives and lobby for change; aka politics.

6. The manager listens, changes the decision in private, and communicates the change by osmosis; aka the rumor mill. People complain when the decision is changed, but no one mentions this directly to the manager; aka more gossip.

7. No one takes responsibility for the communications lapse and for implementing the decision across work teams. People complain that they heard about the decision by accident, instead of figuring out how to get into the communications loop; aka blame.

trol, as we struggle to find a place to start. We find ourselves in a "catch 22." If we ignore these problems, they may get worse; and if we see their enormity, we're likely to believe there's little we can do to avoid eventual burnout.

Corporate sludge slows our ride on the river of progress, erodes motivation, and snuffs out inspiration, creating workers unable to make their highest and best contribution. But only if they buy into sludge and make limited choices. Does any of the following in Figure 1.4 sound familiar?

FIGURE 1.4   Sludge Strategies

Scared Chitless:	To build your portfolio of skills, you have to cozy up to your manager. You make managers above you look good, supporting them whether or not you agree. Disagree, and you use up a chit, and you don't get many per manager. With some, you don't get any chits at all.
Bite Your Tongue:	You cannot talk to your manager's manager about ideas your manager doesn't support. Viewed as disloyal, this will hamper your chances of promotion and opportunities to develop your skills through juicy job assignments and lateral moves.
Home Court Disadvantage:	Sometimes you have to align with your manager to beat another team or product line in your company. This can seem more important than actually producing a better product or delivering a better service.
Stealth Bomber:	You need to spend much of your time working behind the scenes to influence people. You must become a lobbyist rather than a creative thinker.
Toe Jam:	Not stepping on toes or disrupting the political balance becomes your main focus because your career advances more by who you know than by what you accomplish. The flow of innovation becomes jammed with fear.

In organizations that successfully ride the change rapids, people do it differently. They get coaching when these human dramas start to bog them down. I (Kate) once worked with the CEO and chief operating officer (COO) of a well-known major corporation who respected each other and enjoyed working together, yet each felt thwarted by the other's very different style. They complained to other people but were unwilling to face their problem directly, fearing they would damage their relationship, which they valued a lot. I've always found it ironic that we talk about people we respect behind their backs, rather than tell them the truth because we don't want to hurt our relationship!

The CEO, a warm, friendly guy, wished the COO wouldn't behave so harshly with people—yet he realized he got to act like the nice guy only because the COO took on the tough and demanding role. The COO wished the CEO would make quicker decisions, especially about a complex new factory needed for 3,000 new employees to meet the anticipated demand a year out. They scarcely had time to order the equipment and build the building.

This exemplifies the sludge we all deal with, day in and day out. It consumes our emotional energy, takes our time to manage, and never leaves us feeling fully satisfied. We always seem to want "somebody" to do something. The radical change is to realize that *we are that somebody!* To figure out your next steps, look first at what you complain about.

I met individually with both men and got them to share their complaints about one another with me. I then showed each of them how to take responsibility for his contribution to the problems and brought them together. They spoke their truth to one another and broke through this logjam. The whole endeavor took less than three hours—quick and easy in process, profound in effect. The new building was up and running in time, and the two executives continue to appreciate their relationship and the lightning-fast communication now possible between them.

An environment of corporate sludge doesn't foster direct communication. Any bit of space or quiet we create to invite the self-reflection that taps our true human potential (and, of course, reduces corporate sludge) is immediately filled by the opinions, gossip, and "he said, she said" dialogues of coworkers. It seems as if many of us have made the pledge found in Figure 1.5.

Consider the seven actions described in this book a form of personal coaching for making the inner changes that will help your company cut the sludge. Practice them every day to keep the sludge at bay.

CHANGES INSIDE, CHANGES OUTSIDE

One of the first courageous changes you may want to make is to put the gossip mill out of business. *Gossip*—"talking about people not present"—fuels mistrust, fear, and endless soap opera dramas. Most of us were taught it's not polite to gossip.

FIGURE 1.5   My Commitment to Corporate Sludge

1. I commit to blaming everyone else for my problems.

2. I commit to ignoring the truth, no matter what the cost.

3. I commit to focusing only on *my* success.

4. I commit to being right, even if it prevents me from getting what I want.

5. I commit to stifling my creativity and hindering the creativity of others.

6. I commit to working in a job that only uses a fraction of my skills.

We may do our best to avoid it in our personal lives but still engage in casual conversations by the water cooler or latte machine and post mortems in the hallway after a difficult meeting. Gossip also includes the complaining and blaming we justify as "venting" and "letting off steam." We're not referring to a moral issue but to something that simply doesn't work.

Gossip poisons the work environment. The insidious, virus-like nature of gossip fuels defensiveness and can derail projects and careers. When you eliminate gossip and all its mutations and replace it with direct, truthful communication, problems dissipate, tensions evaporate, and trust grows faster than you can speed-dial your best friend with the latest dirt.

Perhaps you don't believe you gossip because that's for busy-bodies. Your coworkers and you "debrief" and share what happened in meetings that some people didn't attend. Think about conversations you've had. Would the same critical comments or implications have been kicked back and forth like a Hackey Sac if the subjects of those remarks were present? If not, that's gossip.

When we say a critical thing, we also plant the first seed of fear. If we talk about others in this moment, what do they say about us in another moment? In our experience, these kinds of conversations go on continually in most companies. What's the risk, you might ask? The risks are wasted time and depleted emotional energy, and an unwillingness to expose yourself to being criticized behind your back. *What's more draining than a bunch of people complaining about a manager or a company initiative no one agrees with, but no one will do anything about it?*

Our culture—especially the media—wholeheartedly supports complaining, blaming, and gossiping. Try going one day without talking about anyone who's not present. We suspect most of us would have very little to say. If you're committed to cleaning up corporate sludge in your organization, be on the lookout for the patterns in Figure 1.6 and apply the suggested antidotes.

FIGURE 1.6   Sludge Patterns and Their Antidotes

Patterns	Antidotes
Defensiveness:	Identify escalation into defensiveness and shift into learning. (Chapter 2, Curiosity)
Complaining:	Discover and heal the problem at the source. (Chapter 4, Authenticity)
Criticism:	Take 100% responsibility for problems. (Chapter 5, Accountability)
Blaming:	Make clear requests for changes. (Chapter 5, Accountability)
Gossip:	Speak directly to people about issues. (Chapter 6, Candor)

THE ROOT SYSTEM FOR CORPORATE SLUDGE

The roots of corporate sludge go back to our educational system that originated with the early Industrial Revolution. Industry demanded large numbers of workers to mind machines and mind their business, neither complaining nor questioning. The model for that system was, literally, the Prussian army. The driving thought behind the education and training of the Prussian army: 20 percent of the recruits would become officers and 80 percent would become troops (or cannon fodder!). We see the result today—a factory model of education with large classes designed to teach basic skills.

Although our school system influences our people and our companies, it has not kept up with the needs of business. Consider these research findings from a variety of studies by Harvard educators Howard Gardner and David Perkins, World Bank leader Richard Barrett, widely recognized child development psychiatrist Jean Piaget, educational psychiatrist Georgi Lozanov, and Nobel laureates and neuroscientists Roger Sperry and Gerald Edelman:

- At age five children, on average, ask thirty questions an hour; at age seven the number drops to two or three. Children grow into adults who don't ask the necessary questions to fully understand their jobs, many times out of a fear of looking stupid to others.

- At age five, 82 percent of children have a positive view of their ability to learn; by age sixteen, only 18 percent have a positive view of their learning ability. Four out of five adults feel inadequate when they start a new learning experience—a handicap in a world where knowledge doubles every two years to three years.

- At age three years to five years, 95 percent of the children display creative genius, which drops to 63 percent by age ten, to 32 percent by age fifteen, and to less than 10 percent by age twenty.

- Intuition drops dramatically when kids enter the first grade and continues to decline at an accelerating rate, becoming negligible by fifth grade. Intuition, combined with creative thinking, provides the bridge to safely carry us over the countless discontinuities our businesses face today.

Unfortunately, schools focus on what children should learn and what (not how) they should think. In subtle ways most companies continue this pattern. *In a time of such radical change, we must make it our top priority to teach employees* how *to learn and* how *to think.* Our wealth and security, as a nation and a world, live in the sum of the brains of our people—their creativity and skills.

Our collective ability to learn fast and to adapt thoughtfully to situations we can't predict emerges as our strongest asset.

CONSCIOUS OR NOT, HERE I COME!

Your intentions broadcast themselves loud and clear in the results you produce. Whenever I say I want one thing, such as a balanced life or supportive clients, and I get something else, I know I have an unconscious operating assumption. *Unconscious intentions contradict our conscious ones in "sneak attacks" because we're not aware of them.* We glimpse this when we make an impetuous decision or when words fly out of our mouths that we later regret. Have you ever wanted to do well in a situation, yet blew it in some way and just couldn't figure out what happened? Have you noticed similar challenges as you move from job to job or spouse to spouse? That's a signal to wonder about your underlying intentions.

Intention means "having a desired outcome in mind." The Latin roots of the word mean, "to stretch out, direct, aim at." Intentions act as homing devices for our dreams and the joy and ease we create in our day-to-day lives. We all have unconscious beliefs, fears, and assumptions that influence our lives. In fact, psychologists tell us the 80/20 rule applies here: *80 percent of our actions are governed by our unconscious. We rarely feel upset for the reason we think.* And the more upset we feel, the less likely it is for the reason we think. We learn early, often before we can speak, to create particular patterns in our life and we continue to spit these out. Like a manufacturing line, we spit out what we were programmed early to produce. *We're like pattern-making machines; we unconsciously perpetuate the same patterns that helped us survive and get needed attention and nourishment when we were young.* The outside look of these patterns changes to fit our adult lives, but the deep echo feels similar, and year after year, job after job, we create the same patterns with this same familiar echo, even if unpleasant.

When I (Kate) entered the corporate world, I couldn't stand my first three managers. On the surface, they were all different: One was very controlling; another acted like a jerk; the third was extremely passive. When I stopped blaming them and looked at my own patterns, I realized I had an issue with authority figures (surprise!), so of course I brought this into every position. Once I took responsibility for my view of the world, my managers seemed to change. In fact, I thrived while working for the next four.

We recently worked with an extremely talented technical guru who was convinced his manager was out to get him. When he talked about his work experiences in other companies, they were dramatic and awful—including nasty notes left in his cube and a peer threatening him one night with a large knife. But he didn't see the connection. He didn't see the common element—himself. His insistence on making the other person the culprit fed his own drama-machine mechanism. Based on some childhood information he shared, we could see he went through life as rejection waiting to happen, and his victim-shuffle and willingness to feel slighted and hurt set it up the day he walked in the door of any company. Completely unaware of this, he described himself as someone who worked hard to get along with everyone. He had, perhaps, more drama in his life than you or I, but the message is the same: To unearth your unconscious intentions, become an observer of your life—especially of repeating patterns.

Our inner worlds are laced with old, unresolved emotional content that spills out at most unwelcome moments. Think of the huge implications. Your manager may secretly remind you of your childhood piano teacher in whose intimidating presence you always cowered, and to whom you never told the full truth about how much time you really spent practicing. You therefore may very likely feel anxiety whenever your manager confronts you with even the tiniest complaint about your work. Your manager can't help it that you were traumatized by piano lessons! But you can.

Unconscious intentions usually reflect our beliefs about life, and we form them at an early age to survive. For example, a child whose parents divorce may believe that if he had behaved perfectly, this wouldn't have happened. He attempts the impossible—to impose unachievable standards on himself and others, which results in repeated failures.

Naturally, we see unconscious intentions in others more easily than we see them in ourselves, and we often project our motives onto others, rather than see our part. Ed wanted to retire wealthy by age 50, but he kept repeating the same pattern: joining the founding team of a Silicon Valley start-up firm as a VP of marketing then being ousted after the successful initial product launch, a painful loss for both Ed and the company. But he refused to see his own self-sabotaging patterns that sprung from growing up competing with a younger brother who seemed to succeed effortlessly. Ed did retire at 50, angry and bitter. He left the computer industry without the benefit of his range of talents, lost the chance to apply his creativity in his own zones of contribution, and walked away with far less cash than he'd hoped.

When we become aware enough, we don't blame other people or events for our emotions. We learn we have each, on a very individual basis, tied certain emotions to certain "threats." Hearing a sarcastic remark during a presentation, one person interprets it as an insult and says, "How dare he talk to me like that!" Another person might muse, "That reminds me of how my dad treated me." A different person might comment with compassion, "He seems to lack information." Someone else might wonder, with detachment, "What's going on with him? This seems like unusually negative behavior." Or another might leap at the chance to learn with, "I wonder why he gets sarcastic when I disagree with his ideas. I wonder if there's something *I* could do differently."

These old core issues got anchored in us in the distant past. Our dilemma becomes how to efficiently step out of them in the present—and especially how to stimulate and nurture that process in the workplace without doing deep psychotherapy or infringing in any way upon another person's privacy. That's a radical change.

The limiting lens of "out there" thinking focuses on your re-actions to what others are doing to you. Viewing life through the "in here" lens, you focus on the qualities, intentions, and re-quirements *you bring* to the situation. The question is: *How do my unconscious intentions and my conditioning contribute to my present situation?* See Figure 1.7.

Here's how we untangle and release these beliefs in real life: When I (Eddie) was the staff vascular surgeon at the University of Michigan Medical Center in Ann Arbor, I confronted two senior-level surgical residents who often erupted into loud dis-agreements about medications, tests, and specific procedures for patients. Jeff said that Tom wasn't meticulous enough in his assessment of laboratory data and diagnostic information. He didn't tell the patients enough about the risks and possible com-plications of procedures but instead reassured them that every-thing would be fine. Tom said that Jeff drove him crazy with his obsessiveness and fussing over the details. Tom said Jeff went over and over things without coming to a decision about any-thing in a timely fashion.

As they talked more, each one realized the other reminded him of his brother, and that's why they'd been reacting the way they were. Suddenly they had a bond and saw the chance to blend their gifts as they reviewed cases, which they did for sev-eral hours, ending with dinner at a local watering hole. Tom and

---

FIGURE 1.7   How Our Beliefs Create a Home in Our Psyches

- A series of unpleasant or scary events happen, typically early in life.

- We respond to the events as best we can at the time.

- The intensity of the experience makes our response into a pattern that we replicate throughout life.

- This pattern gets us attention or ensures our survival, and shapes our interpretation of the world.

- Our interpretation becomes a core belief about "the way things are."

- We then forget how we came to our beliefs.

- These beliefs drive our emotions, behavior, and results, and they become our unconscious intentions.

Jeff remain fast friends, moving through postgraduate training together and last I heard were working on the same surgical faculty together.

Unless you've experienced this yourself, you may find it hard to believe that others will change effortlessly, as soon as you change. Most people find this a huge leap. Rather than try to understand how this works, make the commitment, experiment with it, and watch what happens. You'll delight in this new way of working—quickly and with far less effort than getting others to make changes that will probably never happen.

UNLEASHING OUR LIMITED BELIEFS

By observing the results we create, we expose our underlying beliefs and glimpse the intentions that operate unconsciously and shape so much of our behavior and actions. Beliefs act like the mind's operating software that can hinder us the same way out-of-date software does. Beliefs can run us on autopilot, or we can consciously choose frequent upgrades.

Read the following statements based on limiting beliefs. Identify those beliefs you see in yourself when conditions become difficult. Add your own statements to reflect other limiting beliefs at the end of each section. Focus on beliefs pertaining to the following:

- How you try to get people to work at their best

- How you attempt to get the most from yourself

Agree to honestly look at your own limiting beliefs. This important commitment helps you unearth the ideas you inadvertently reinforce and keep alive in your life and your work group, courtesy of your unconscious intentions. Study Figure 1.8, identify your limiting beliefs, then replace each one with the suggested empowering belief or one of your own creation.

Did you notice any patterns? Experience any surprises? As we move through the upcoming chapters, you may want to return to Figure 1.8 to see if any of your beliefs have changed.

CREATING CONSCIOUS RESULTS

In this valorous new world we're hatching, these limiting beliefs and behaviors disappear because heart and soul stand front and center. The order of the day demands shucking off tired, cumbersome, soon-to-be-obsolete cultures of resistance and habits that no longer work. The radicals out there know the spine-tingling rush of tossing the tea into the harbor, overthrowing the hierarchies and corporate kingdoms, and declaring a new economic order, and it's contagious.

Just like the remarkable mushrooms you may have read about that consume toxic waste, people and organizations that

---

FIGURE 1.8   Limiting Beliefs and Powerful Replacement

CURIOSITY (Chapter 2)

Limiting Beliefs:	**Empowering Beliefs:**
It's hard to change.	Change is fun, especially changing my habits and behavior.
If someone feels angry, their feedback isn't worth taking seriously; it's just their stuff.	I can hear the lesson, no matter how it's packaged.

AWARENESS (Chapter 3)

Limiting Beliefs:	**Empowering Beliefs:**
Emotions don't belong at work.	Emotions can lead to breakthroughs in thinking.
I am in control of my body.	My body partners with me to bring me guidance and wisdom.

AUTHENTICITY (Chapter 4)

Limiting Beliefs:	**Empowering Beliefs:**
I can't change my personality.	I can radically change my thinking and my behavior, if I want to.
It's my job to ride people and also come to their rescue if they can't fulfill their responsibilities.	It's my job to be authentic, to stay free of old roles, and to focus on my own learning.

ACCOUNTABILITY (Chapter 5)

Limiting Beliefs:	**Empowering Beliefs:**
It's important to have a solid reason why I can't always meet my responsibilities.	I see my shortfalls in taking responsibility as opportunities for my own personal learning.
Sometimes I have to make agreements I can't keep to get people off my back.	I consciously make agreements that I have the time and resources to keep.

CANDOR (Chapter 6)

Limiting Beliefs:	**Empowering Beliefs:**
Telling the truth most often damages relationships.	The truth heals and strengthens relationships.
Critical feedback feels painful. Why go out of your way to hurt people?	The truth creates new learning and supports people in growing.

GENIUS (Chapter 7)

Limiting Beliefs:	**Empowering Beliefs:**
Work is work—not fun. That's why you get paid.	I can have fun at work every day.
If everyone did only what they love to do, the company would fall apart.	My company will thrive when we all work in our areas of genius.

APPRECIATION (Chapter 8)

Limiting Beliefs:	**Empowering Beliefs:**
Appreciation works if you give it in measured doses, and not too often.	The more I express appreciation, the better life works.
Others will take advantage of me if I express too much appreciation.	The more I express my genuine appreciation, the more people thrive.

have the courage to radically change find they can quickly dissolve corporate sludge, outdated beliefs, and other obstacles to success. They unearth and solve problems faster, within budget and on time. People feel happier and inspired. There's more joy at work, and companies become more profitable. Are you and your organization ready for change? Check out Figure 1.9.

If you want your organization to say "yes" to more of the attributes listed in Figure 1.9, congratulations. You've just taken the first magic step.

We breathe life into what we imagine and make it real. At the simplest level, hundreds of research experiments show that events typically turn out just as we expected, not because of a mysterious knowledge of the future but because our behavior tends to make the prediction come true.* The flavor of commitment required today begins, as Jaworsky says, "not with will, but with willingness,"** and the belief that we have the power to alter our future.

Many of the ideas in this book will require a leap of faith, then the courage to full-heartedly commit to action. You've probably gotten where you are by using your amazing, analytical left brain. The commitment to radical change requires mastery of the other side of the brain. Some of these ideas will sound more like poetry or ethics than proven business principles. This book isn't about a quantifiable prescription for leadership, but it is about experiencing some dramatic results that make work far easier and workers far happier. If you muster the courage and willingness to embrace radical change in yourself and your organization, you'll reap every reward we've described. Wait for no one. Take the lead. Begin to usher in a new era in business.

---

*Sheldrake, Rupert. *7 Experiments That Could Change the World,* New York: Riverhead Books (Berkley), 1995.
**Jaworski, Joseph. *Synchronicity,* San Francisco: Berrett Koehler, 1998.

FIGURE 1.9   Diagnostic: Is Your Company Committed to Radical Change?

How many of the following do you see as true for your company?

- **Meetings:** Energizing, satisfying, and fun.

- **Gossip:** Not tolerated.

- **Bureaucracy:** Nonexistent.

- **Decisive Dialogue:** Conversations move action forward.

- **Truth:** The rule, rather than the exception.

- **Recurring Problems:** Seldom happen; issues dealt with directly.

- **Enthusiasm:** Employees feel eager to come to work each day.

- **Laughter:** Heard regularly.

- **Vibrance:** Employees sparkle and generate energy.

SUMMARY

- Making conscious change requires courage.

- Society has made a huge paradigm shift in our view of technology, where we get knowledge, how we shop and do our tasks, and we can bring to our professional lives the same degree of change if we shift how we work with people.

- Every person affects the whole. Everything matters. That's because today, more than ever, we as individuals and companies have become a lot like the Internet—all connected—and one person's actions impact others more and more quickly.

- Most companies could double their profit margin by eliminating fear, because fear creates sluggishness that comes from unnecessary checks and approvals.

- Fear, dishonesty, and poor communication create a toxic by-product—corporate sludge. Sludge includes anything that slows us down—from rigid attitudes to overly complex procedures; from time spent in turf battles to energy expended not being real.

- Continuous learning, direct communications, and personal responsibility characterize companies that easily navigate the rapids of change. They use the very best we each have to offer in a way that demands we dig daily for our own learning edge, using an automatic "curiosity reflex." As a result, we'll avoid burnout, endless politics, and job-hopping.

- The "out there" view asks: What people or events caused this problem? The "in here" view asks: How are my present unconscious intentions and my past conditioning contributing to creating my present situation?

- Your world mirrors your underlying intentions. Unconscious intentions can and do contradict our conscious ones in "sneak attacks" because we're not aware of them. To unearth your unconscious intentions, become an observer of your life—especially of your results and your repeating patterns.

TAKE ACTION

- Think of those times when you've easily moved through radical change. What were the circumstances? What kind of work were you doing? What characteristics of your manager contribute to the ability of you and your team to change?

- When does your team naturally operate with speed and ease? What prevents them from working in this zone more of the time?

- What does corporate sludge look like in your company? Identify one step you can take to help reduce it in your work team. What radical changes can you make to reduce or eliminate the corporate sludge among your peers and throughout the company?

- Can you go a whole day without gossiping? If so, extend this experiment to two days, then to a week. How can you eliminate gossip in your one-on-one and team meetings?

- How can you reduce or eliminate your own fear at work? In your team?

- What specific changes can you get an even broader group to make, so these changes begin to permeate your whole company?

- List some of your own examples of "out there" thinking and the results. In what ways has this limited you? Have you ever used "in here" thinking? What were the results? Identify one problem with which you're willing to experiment.

- Can you identify any patterns of recurring unsatisfactory results? What unconscious intentions might create these results? What old beliefs prevent you from changing?

- Does your company seem to operate under some unconscious beliefs? What do these appear to be, based on disappointing results in turnover, product quality, or financial growth? What first step can you take to turn these beliefs around?

CHAPTER TWO

CURIOSITY
Learning on the Run

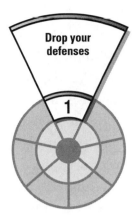

Drop your defenses

1

How can I eliminate chronic problems?

How can I become less defensive when I'm getting critical feedback?

How can I create more openness to learning in others?

Learning on the run—dropping our defenses and taking in all feedback—has become the critical difference between success and failure. If you want to stop repeating the same problems at work, make the radical change from defensiveness to learning, whenever and wherever you can. Embrace *all* feedback, whether it takes the form of unasked-for advice, a failed project, or a life that feels less vibrant than you'd hoped. Drink in the learning. Savor it. Splash it all over like a favorite fragrance— and learn. By dropping your defenses you will stop any unproductive and tiresome cycles in their tracks.

Ever notice how your problems have an "oh, so familiar" feeling to them? We have, and if you take a close look at your life, we bet you have, too. The same problems follow us from job to job and relationship to relationship, taking on the personalities of our coworkers, family members, and significant others. *Ah, you again.*

Most of us think we want to learn. Some would even say we live to continuously learn and grow. We enlist mentors, subscribe to newsletters, and read best-selling business books in a quest to be all we can. We notice others' defensiveness when receiving advice and feedback, and sometimes we perceive our own. But we certainly don't see ourselves as defended against learning as a survivalist's cabin.

We don't think of ourselves as overly attached to our own point of view and closed to new perspectives. We think of ourselves as right, and we're proud of it. By being right we don't mean confident and self-assured. We mean closed down and stuck.

Curiosity is a 180° about-face whirl from defended to willing. You take this action the moment you shift from fear to wonder, from explaining and justifying, to wondering how you can change. Chances are, if you commuted to work this morning, you already had a learning opportunity. Instead of raging about the person who cut in front of you, did you notice what you might do differently tomorrow? Curiosity makes lightning-fast organizations even faster because it ensures that everyone works at their best and gets better every day—at an ever-faster rate. Each bump in the road offers a chance to learn in the moment, instead of from the school of hard knocks, which is what happens when we insist on hanging on to what we are convinced is *the* answer.

I COMPLAIN, THEREFORE I AM (NOT LEARNING)

So how do we morph from defensiveness into curiosity and learn on the run? One way is to compare today's litany of complaints with the ones you had last year. Or last decade. Ready to say, "Amen!"? When you spend even a moment complaining, venting, blaming, or talking about someone else's problems and what they ought to do differently, you've missed a moment to learn. If you catch yourself complaining about the same things over and over at work, ask yourself if you're open to learning. If your complaints sound the same, you obviously aren't.

People truly open to learning feel surprised by their problems, which constantly change. We always find it interesting and a bit amusing that at the end of a 360° assessment, where people get feedback on their work behavior from managers, direct reports, and peers to gauge their effectiveness, the recipients proudly remark that they weren't surprised by any of the feedback. If these people aren't surprised by the problems their colleagues have highlighted with 1,000-watt lights, I have little hope they will change this time around. They somehow continue to see the problems as belonging to someone else (or else assume they themselves can't change) instead of stepping into learning and seeing what they might do differently. If you're ready to expand, listen to the complaints others make about you. I call that "learning for the asking," and people who want to excel willingly enroll in this form of continuing education.

My first executive coaching client 15 years ago put it best. Upon getting feedback that he was a Bulldozer (see Chapter 4) who constantly talked over people, he said, "I've heard I'm a poor listener since my first performance review 20 years ago. I just never understood my lack of listening was like having interpersonal BO!"

WARNING: "THAT'S JUST THE WAY I AM"

Other people we've worked with through the years have justified their 360° feedback about not wanting to confront performance problems, not speaking up directly with their opinions, and getting overly stressed when the pressure's on at work with variations of this same theme. "That's just the way I am," implies particular qualities or capabilities permanently embedded in their genetic code—a personal version of corporate sludge. We all have places like this, often more annoying than we'd care to admit to our coworkers and family, and yet we persist, attached to the "way we are." We fail to acknowledge these poignant and painful examples of our failure to learn, to grow from the feedback life gives us, and to make even a small change, much less a radical one. When we commit to curiosity, it opens the space for change. If you hear yourself saying or thinking, "That's just the way I am," sound the alarms and know you've identified an opportunity for instant learning.

Erik, the chief technology officer (CTO) and software guru at a client's company, liked to refer to himself as "the bomb." Like many people, Erik let his feelings build up, then would routinely "go off" on people. In this mode, his feedback was so direct and blunt, people tuned him out, creating a series of unresolved problems that brought—naturally—more explosions. Erik thought the company had gotten very political, that problems didn't get solved until he blew up, and he resented the fact that he "had" to get upset to make a difference. His coworkers had a different perception. They believed the best way to get a problem solved was to exclude Erik.

American psychologist Abraham Maslow said that when the only tool we possess is a hammer, there's a tendency to treat everything like a nail. Wherever Erik had worked, he got upset. His temper was fundamentally a hammer looking for a nail. Erik came to see that he needed a toolbox of influence capabilities so that his ability to impact people wasn't limited to his default "hammer" setting. By overusing "the bomb," which had worked to get his way as a child, he had failed to develop a more expansive repertoire of influence skills.

Our recurring problems remind me (Kate) of the roaches I grew up with in Texas, where I had more experience with these pests than I would have liked. Then, later, in my early 20s in Southeast Asia I got the delightful experience of giant flying roaches. They seemed prehistoric to me and absolutely impossible to eliminate—a lot like the persistent habits I struggled to eliminate in myself. "That's just the way I am."

It was easy to get rid of roaches in the short-term, but they invariably returned. What ultimately worked was a regular program of extermination using something simple: salt, instead of insecticides. The roaches left on their own. What helps eliminate personal habits that hold you back is also simple, though not always easy: facing your problems squarely. This may feel like salt on a wound at times, but you'll reap the rewards instantaneously. We typically try to kill our annoying habits instead of facing them fully and getting our full learning. When we attempt to see into their dark corners and embrace these foibles with love, they tend to go away on their own.

As long as we stay stuck in "That's just the way I am and that's just the way they are," we increase the sludge in our company and guarantee that the company fails to live up to its potential. Meetings last longer, decisions get made, unmade, and remade, and organizational changes are postponed and delayed. People work at less than their all-time best. The business moves slower toward goals and grows less rapidly and less easily than it might.

When learning doesn't happen, individually and collectively, we stay stuck in old patterns. We guarantee that our companies become collections of mediocre people who look "out there," blaming, complaining, and criticizing, instead of making course corrections and moving forward at full speed.

A venture capitalist who wanted one of his portfolio companies to move forward at full speed asked me (Kate) to meet with its founder and CEO. The company had more than 200 employees, and it planned an initial public offering (IPO) in six months. I chose not to work with the CEO because he did not seem coachable, even though he was a brilliant technologist.

At age 28 he had already built one company, and when they brought in an outside CEO, he became so irritated at what he saw as an overly controlling CEO, he took several undermining actions and ultimately left with all the technical talent to found another company. When the board of the second company brought in an outside CEO, the same shenanigans began again.

It looked like this guy had the bad luck to attract and hire CEOs who turned out to be jerks in disguise, and he certainly experienced this as true. In reality some part of him needed to rebel against someone. As I dug into his history, I could see that he hired in anger each time and then created the same kind of relationship with his CEOs that he had had with his father. He will repeat this pattern until he becomes coachable.

Remember Boris Becker? At the age of 17 he won Wimbledon—one of the most important tennis tournaments in the world—but the next year he didn't get much farther than the parking lot. Guess what this extraordinarily talented youngster did after he became the youngest winner of the fabled tournament? He fired the coach who got him there! Unbelievable as it may seem, that's just what he did. Remember your humility at age 17? We do, too.

Boris got tangled up in his ego. We'd hazard a guess that he got scared of his power and decided he wasn't worthy of so much positive energy. He swapped his power for a power struggle. He'd probably been angry with his coach for some little offense for a long time, and suddenly his ego kicked in and said, "I won Wimbledon! I don't need some jerk yelling at me all the time! How dare he talk to me like that!" So he canned the coach. I'm sure lots of people tried to talk him out of this action, and we're sure he had a "Yes, but" for each reason they gave. Life then proceeded to kick his "yes-butt" around the court a few times.

FEEDBACK FEEDING FRENZY

When we receive a piece of feedback—or any piece of information that shakes up our status quo—we get scared. That's human. Fear involves loss of control—it's our bodymind's frantic search for a solution to a problem we weren't prepared for, which can even mean an unexpected level of success.

We learn through feedback, especially from people and events that don't live up to our expectations. *When we revert to blaming or feeling victimized, we miss out on life's feedback, a lesson custom-designed for our own learning.* But who among us ever took a class called "How to Receive Feedback Gracefully and Put It to Use?" It's not easy, especially the first time, to go out in search of people's reactions to you and your leadership. In fact, we'd guess you probably feel fed up, rather than fed by feedback. Many of us desperately try to avoid finding out what other people think about us; others get upset with anyone who tries.

The issue isn't to be nondefensive every moment. Few of us can do that. Just make it a goal to catch yourself when you aren't listening and get back on track. It's somewhat like steering an airplane that constantly moves minutely off course but is always headed toward its destination. If you set the intention to bypass defensiveness, you'll notice when you deviate from that path and you'll easily get back on track. Look at Figure 2.1 with a curious mind to determine how you react to feedback.

Pretend you've set up every instance of feedback so you can learn. Shift away from indignation and into genuine curiosity. Nothing speeds up learning so much as experiencing every bump in the road, every single moment that's not blissful at work, as an opportunity for learning that helps us drop unneeded baggage and speeds growth. Become a feedback magnet.

Remember that successful companies regularly let go of everything they've known to be true so they can clear the sludge

---

FIGURE 2.1   When Confronted with Feedback ...

Unhappy, Unsuccessful People:

- Create a story of nonownership

- Ignore it

- Misperceive it as an attack on their being and get defensive

- As a smokescreen, fire a barrage of complaints they've withheld

- Find fault with the way the message was delivered

- Compound the lapse by lying

- Execute the messenger

Happy, Successful People:

- Appreciate the message and the messenger

- Acknowledge the lapse

- Find out what needs to be done to fix it (feelings, communication, actions)

- Do it

and transform themselves for today as well as tomorrow. Feedback acts like the rocket fuel of learning. Consider Chapter 2 the instruction manual.

AN ATTITUDE, NOT A TRAIT

Don't think of curiosity as a quality you have or don't have—instead think of it as a mindset. When you look at it this way, it becomes a personal decision, something you can control. And you'll improve with practice. We've seen hundreds of people change their lives and careers dramatically by even a little bit of improvement in their ability to shift into curiosity. Any improvement pays off. Remember, you don't have to be perfect. Who is? We aren't. And neither is Michael Dell. Or you. But what Michael Dell sure as heck wants for his employees and what we want for you is a willingness to increase your curiosity velocity. Eliminate any habits that block your forward movement, starting with defensiveness. Become a high-speed master of curiosity.

This action can take just a moment. When you think about it, business, sports, and life all work the same way: The players who win games usually take only a few seconds and create momentum by focusing time, energy, and talent on moving forward, as in the following examples:

- A sprinting youngster skids to a halt, takes a jump shot at the buzzer, and ices the game.

- A punter tunes out the roaring crowd, puts toe to pigskin, and clinches victory.

- A businessperson takes a deep breath and commits funds to a vision.

Everything comes down to those windows of opportunity where you execute or you don't. How much energy and creativity would be released in your company if it changed into a culture of curiosity? How might this translate to the bottom line if everyone listened and learned on the run instead of investing precious time and talent defending themselves against learning? And how would that impact loyalty and retention?

Kevin Rollins, COO and president of Dell, faced head-on the dilemma most leaders grapple with: openly confronting problems without demotivating his team. Some executives prevent embarrassment and hurt feelings by not discussing problems in meetings, but this has the distinct disadvantage of slowing down the resolution of problems.

Kevin wanted to retain Dell's nimble, direct culture as he visited the various global business units, and he also wanted the staff at the various sites to be comfortable openly discussing issues with him without feeling hammered or bruised by direct and public exploration of problems. He began to frame the meetings in a new way, describing the meeting objective as learning about problems faster. At the end of meetings, he asked each person to summarize their key learnings and their plans to act on these learnings. That simple yet radical change has made all the difference. Now his job is to stimulate learning, instead of metaphorically giving them a slap on the wrist.

THE POWER OF BEING COACHABLE

We all need to know what will allow us to execute successfully in our windows of chance. Natural gifts help, but they're not enough. Plenty of people have natural gifts galore—and they're sitting on their naturally gifted haunches along the curbsides of life. Luck helps, too. But even though you may get lucky sometimes or a lot of times, you'd better not bank on it, because luck can't be produced reliably.

Then there's old-fashioned hard work. Hard work really helps a lot. We also wouldn't be having this dialogue without having worked hard to get here. And we all know plenty of people who work themselves into the ground and don't contribute much value to the world. What's the secret, then?

If you want to succeed beyond your wildest dreams, become coachable. Listen to these comments about Michael Dell from his executive team:

- "He's one of the most successful businessmen in the past 50 years, and yet he works hard to change things that are uncomfortable for him. I find it inspiring that he works so hard to improve and grow, when he's independently wealthy and the company has his name on it." John Hamlin, VP, Consumer Business, Dell

- "After getting his 360°, Michael talked very frankly at an executive committee meeting about his leadership style and his commitment to emotionally connect with people. He later videotaped this talk and it's been shown to over a thousand managers, as a part of our culture change initiative. I continue to be impressed by his openness and his willingness to be vulnerable. He's a powerful role model for learning and for openly talking about and confronting his own imperfections." Bill Amelio, senior vice president (SVP) Asia-Pacific, Dell

- "He was open and forthright in sharing his 360°. He came across as somewhat uncomfortable, which made him seem more human. I so appreciated his willingness to venture into the zone of the unknown and to go full out for whatever changes he needs to make." Ro Parra, SVP Americas, Dell

- "Michael is a pleasure to work with because he's so clearly a learner. He took hold of the issues identified in his 360°, and promptly addressed them." Paul McKinnon, SVP, Human Resources, Dell

If you want to succeed and keep succeeding over the long haul, there's only one way to do it. You certainly have to be talented and get lucky and work hard, but above all, you have to be *coachable.*

Curiosity doesn't cost a cent, takes very little time, and profoundly enhances every aspect of your life. In two decades of working with incredibly successful people, we have felt deeply moved by their agility in making the radical move into curiosity and learning. And we have felt deeply saddened by watching people with great potential blow it by staying defensive.

Stay open in every moment to learning what you need to learn. Every event in life must be greeted and embraced with a wide-open mind asking the essential question: "What can I learn from this?" Start every day by reaffirming your willingness to learn from every bit of coaching that comes your way. This may seem like quite a stretch, but we don't get to know what we need to learn until we open ourselves to learning it. In other words, the moment we move into curiosity and open ourselves to learning, we find out what we need to learn.

How do you view the ups and downs and in-between times of life? Through the lens of "my way or the highway" or one of openness and wonder? With a commitment to blame and revenge or to gratitude and learning? When we view everything as an opportunity to learn, grow, and enjoy life even more, the resulting gratitude directs each of our steps along the right path.

But often the next opportunity looks like an obstacle and gratitude is the last thing that springs to mind. Recently I (Kate) was asked to help a company struggling with a scientific breakthrough. They were bogged down by a conflict between Scientist A, perceived by the management to be the problem, and Scientist B, the apparent victim. When I asked Scientist A how he thought he was perceived in the company, he said his team saw him as crabby when goals weren't met, and he hoped the rest of the company saw him as a nightmare. I allowed as how he was probably succeeding. I asked if he wanted to learn other techniques for getting what he wanted, and he said, "Yes, of course." He was coachable.

When I met with Scientist B, he spent most of his time establishing his victim position. When I asked if he wanted to learn new ways to resolve the problem, his voice got higher and he broke eye contact as he responded, "Well, I read an article . . ." Instead of learning, he spent the next couple of days following up with increasingly long e-mails expanding on his story of how he'd been wronged by Scientist A.

Why do you think this sort of thing occurs? And before we dismiss it as something that occurs to other people, let's think again. I haven't found anyone yet, including myself, who didn't have a mild dose of this particular allergy to coachability. The reason: *Many people prefer being right to being successful or even to feeling good.* Perhaps worse, many people prefer being right to having joyful, supportive relationships with others. People with an extreme case of this problem prefer being right to having a job.

While most of us don't have the problem to such an extreme degree, we've all got it, and it keeps us from self-understanding. We've watched closely as bright, capable people made the choice to become coachable. We've watched most of them decide being successful and contributing to others was more important than being right. We've watched a bunch of people go the other direction, too, and we feel sad about it. We feel sad about the times we've gone that way ourselves, too.

We don't want to make that mistake again. You probably don't either. We have no guarantees it won't happen, but there's a highly effective action you can take that continually speeds up your learning. Each time you make a mistake, use it as an opportunity to deepen your commitment. Make a commitment to learn faster next time, and then keep your eye on your reaction time. That's the magic moment, the moment when learning hangs in the balance. It's never too late to go back and eliminate the defensive moves—and it's also never too soon to bring in their replacements. The change starts with you, spreads to your department, transforming your whole company, moving faster and faster—as the time it takes to move from defensiveness to learning approaches zero.

THE WONDER OF WONDER QUESTIONS

Wonder questions take only a few seconds and provide a powerful means for making curiosity a way of life. They halt criticism, blame, and "out there" thinking. Their very existence expands our repertoire of reactions to feedback and sticky, sludgy situations. Ask a wonder question (without attempting to think of an answer) and you instantly open the way for a wider palette of possible solutions than our thinking minds could have created.

Here's an excellent general purpose wonder question: "I wonder what I need to see in this situation?" When noticing the shift into defensiveness, ask, "I wonder how I might listen more openly when I hear negative feedback?" When things don't go the way we want, instead of looking for someone to blame, say, "I wonder what I can learn from this situation?" To get the most from the rest of this book, ask yourself right now, "I wonder how I can add more value to my company and advance my career." Then sit back and enjoy the read.

When our friend and editor Winnie Shows had a public relations firm in Silicon Valley, she experimented with wonder questions and enjoyed a huge return on the investment. If a team member missed a deadline or didn't execute a project the way she'd expected, she began to routinely ask, "I wonder how I helped create this situation?" Her learning came quickly.

"At first I asked this question while mentally gritting my teeth. It certainly looked as if the other person caused the problem. Almost immediately, however, a pattern began to emerge: I had not been communicating clearly with my staff. Over several months, my willingness to be curious took my leadership up two levels, from feeling irritated with others for not delivering, to wondering about my part, to taking responsibility for it and making an effective change. What I learned made me more patient and responsible, and my company transformed into a happier and more efficient workplace."

Many of us approach learning backwards—we make the mistake of taking an attitude that says, "Prove you've got something to teach me, then maybe I'll open myself to learning." Consider Winnie Shows in the above example. How normal and human it would have been to resist learning from people who missed their deadlines. That very attitude, however, causes us to slam shut those valuable split-second windows of learning.

GETTING OFF OUR YES-BUTS

As a species, we suffer from a singular problem: Life tries to teach us lessons, and we typically respond with a yes-but: "Yes, but I don't want to learn that right now." "Yes, but I like my lessons delivered more gently." Don't feel bad about this tendency. I (Kate) have seen it in myself, and from Vermont to Vietnam.

Everyone has a blind spot, or two or three. What's blind to you often seems glaringly obvious to others. Some of the most gifted and talented people we've ever worked with had some of the biggest blind spots. It makes sense that great people have great blind spots. The brighter the light, the darker the shadow. Everyone has defensive flinches.

I (Eddie) met with Jerry, an emergency room physician executive who hired the emergency room (ER) physicians and monitored their quality and performance. Jerry felt frustrated that the people he hired seemed to develop problems within the first couple of months because of the way they interacted with patients, with staff, and with one other. Although a successful physician, he was not succeeding as an executive, and he felt blind-sided, angry, and confused.

I shared with him some interview selection and assessments skills from the corporate world, which I had used over time with good results. Jerry launched into a relatively long analytical explanation of why they wouldn't work with physicians. When I showed him a list of interviewing questions aimed at openness and defensiveness, he grinned sheepishly and admitted that he was more defensive and stuck in his view than he had appreciated, and he possibly overlooked that trait in his applicants. Although he could see that the analysis and skepticism that make great physicians can become huge obstacles for them as executives, Jerry was not interested in changing his approach. As we parted, I felt sad that so many in my own profession were unwilling to learn.

What gets rid of your blind spot—what gives you 360° vision— is openness to learning. When you walk through the door at work or when you go home—with kids, mate, dog, major appliances— you either demonstrate openness to learning or you don't. And the extent of your openness determines whether you'll feel happy as well as productive. Your employees' openness to learning becomes a reliable predictor of the time it will take to implement anything new, from rolling out your next product to rolling out the barrel to celebrating a successful IPO.

If we can get our yes-buts out of the way, we learn. After 20-plus years of coaching people to be more effective, we feel incredibly optimistic about human beings. I (Kate) became an optimist the day I realized I'm not stupid—just defensive. There turned out to be nothing wrong with me that curiosity and openness to learning couldn't fix. Once I learned to take this crucial action, life began to work smoothly. We guarantee success to any company in which people learn reliably to get yes-buts out of the way.

You might find the acronym FACE helpful as a guide to the change cycle:

- **F**eedback

- **A**cceptance

- **C**ommunication

- **E**xecution

Learning starts by getting feedback, then accepting that you need to change. Many people get stuck in denial and don't face the fact that they need to change. If they get past this step, then they have to communicate about the change that they plan to make. The final step is to consistently execute on the ideas they have shared with others. Is there some change you're grappling with right now that you're overdue to F-A-C-E?

RATE YOUR DEFENSIVENESS IN REAL TIME

Chances are, this chapter is asking you to change long-held behaviors. Take a moment to notice your attitude about what we've shared so far, then read the chart in Figure 2.2. Here's an opportunity to measure your defensiveness or curiosity. Keep the chart handy and see if you're open to learning or defending as you read further chapters.

Everyone slips into defensiveness. It's the American way. *The issue isn't whether or not you become defensive, but rather how fast you shift out of it.* When you notice you've slipped below the line, stop

FIGURE 2.2   Rate Your Level of Defensiveness as You Read This Book

- 1 Noticing slight boredom, while inwardly clinging to my opinions.

- 2 Criticizing the writing style and telling myself I'd pay more attention if the authors spiced it up a little and named more names.

- 3 Realizing I haven't absorbed the last 12 pages because I'm fretting about things I should be doing differently at work and worrying about radical changes I should be making, instead of moving into action.

- 4 Evaluating and comparing the content to what I know is correct. Hanging on to my perceptions; doing the mental marenge, sidestepping all temptation to wonder what I might learn.

- 5 Having a conversation in my mind with the authors, explaining how they got it wrong. Justifying my perspective, based on my experience and knowledge. Creating a PowerPoint presentation of key issues to send them.

- 6 Interpreting what the authors say as an attack on how I've behaved in the past. Feeling misunderstood for all my good intentions. Whining loud enough that the person in the next cube peeks to see what's up.

- 7 Knocking something over and spilling it on the book. Expressing my exasperation. Extra points for hands on hips or other body language of consternation.

- 8 Flipping to the back of the book to reread the authors' credentials. Attempting to verify their degrees.

- 9 Throwing the book away with a bit of an "attitude."

- 10 Complaining to someone else about how little I got out of the book, then eating more than I should at dinner.

and wonder, "What can I learn from this?" For help in doing this, see Figure 2.3.

Rate your level of defensiveness as you read each chapter. Then, no matter what the rating, learn on the run by trying on each of the actions as you read about them. By becoming conscious of your defensiveness, your score on openness to learning will increase in no time.

FIGURE 2.3   To Shift from Defensiveness to Learning . . .

+ 1   Noticing you feel a little bored and asking yourself if this might be a sign of defensiveness. Congratulate yourself that you noticed.

+ 2   Registering genuine curiosity about the content or asking a wonder question.

+ 3   Summarizing and paraphrasing the authors' points as a way to absorb and work with the information.

+ 4   Reflecting about past situations for a new interpretation of what really occurred.

+ 5   Thinking out loud and taking notes to apply the information to your specific situation today at work.

+ 6   Exploring specific things you can do differently in your job.

+ 7   Taking the tools back to your job and using them.

+ 8   Teaching the tools to your team and encouraging them when you see these in action.

+ 9   Telling someone else how much you're enjoying the book.

+10   Buying copies of the book for your team at work and asking them to read it.

PARDON ME—A WORD ON APOLOGIES

As we take off the blinders, we learn how we've been getting in our own way and in the way of everyone else. It's not unusual to want to apologize, once we've recovered from the shock of the havoc we've wrought. The urge to apologize comes from an awareness that something could have been done differently. It's a valuable starting point, but most people leave it there, instead of taking it to the next level.

Look up the word *apology*. The primary definition is "a formal justification, defense, or excuse." We don't believe in apology most of the time. We believe in change instead. Most people say "I'm sorry" or "I apologize" 20 times a day. That in itself isn't a problem; in fact it would be terrific—if the problems never recurred. After all, if you're sincere when you apologize, you don't do it again—right?

But most often the apology acts as the speaker's way of trying to "make nice" and placate upset people and smooth over the situation. This does not truly invite their higher selves to noticeable change. In fact, nine times out of ten, an apology more likely predicts repeated behavior. Contrast this with someone who doesn't apologize but who looks for her learning, then communicates it, and acts on it. "Sorry for taking the last of the coffee and not making more," versus "Sometimes I finish off the coffee and don't make a new pot. I just realized I've felt entitled to having someone make coffee for me, and I'll do my share from now on." The full pots of java say the rest.

IT'S VELOCITY THAT COUNTS

On-the-job-training (OJT) has morphed into on-the-job-learning (OJL). In an ideal world, we'd get a piece of feedback, weigh it carefully, make our correction, and get on with the job.

In the real world, though, we often resist feedback; we get so busy defending ourselves, we don't get the benefit. To get the goodies sooner, focus on velocity. The speed at which you take this action means everything. Do you spot your defensiveness quickly and drop it like a hot potato? Or do you take your own sweet time?

Persistent defensiveness can and should get you fired. That's what being defensive means in high-speed learning environments like Dell. They can't afford the drag of defensiveness or the snail's pace of sludge, and you can't either. In fact, we want you to beg your manager or your board or your spouse or your coach to fire you if you cling to your defensive postures. Tell them: "Unless you see me improving quickly in my ability to take feedback, learn from it, and make changes based on it, put me out of my misery! Fire me before I infect others with my defensiveness!"

Keep your eye on your reaction time. Don't worry about perfection. We're happy if we're a second faster dropping our defenses than last time. We want to catch feedback as it's coming in. We want to extract the useful juicy parts from it and put it to work in our lives as quickly as possible. Maybe someday we'll have the ability to do it instantaneously and flawlessly. Maybe you will, too. Until then, let's keep our eye on reaction time.

ENJOYING OUR COURSE CORRECTIONS

Our ancestors dealt with survival of the fittest and won, enabling us to be here now to deal with survival of the fastest. Remember, all of life—and evolution itself—operates on feedback. Luckily, you won't be eliminated for not learning, but let's do more than survive our careers. *Put yourself in the moment when you first receive feedback—especially feedback of a critical nature.* It's almost unnecessary, by the way, for us to specify feedback as "critical." If we aren't feeling defensive, we call someone's observations an "idea"; if we feel defensive, we call it "criticism";

and if we're feeling reasonably balanced, "feedback." Maybe you recognize the tendency? We sure do! We also recognize the very human tendency to swiftly move into planning a retort when we hear something critical or challenging—instead of truly listening to what's said. "Ah ha! What you just said can't possibly be true because . . ." and off you go, mentally building a case against the feedback as if you've got a legal dream team permanently on retainer in your own mind, always at the ready with an alibi or defense.

Naturally, if you're occupying your mind this way, you aren't learning much. Instead, you're just tightening the grip on your own point of view—while the person giving you the feedback tries, to no avail, to expand your perspective by investing valuable time and precious energy. At this point, as the defensiveness pattern escalates, you may cling more and more tightly to defensive behaviors, often prompting more powerful attempts on the other's part to break through the walls you're constructing. As the other person intensifies the feedback, you feel personally attacked.

We've described a typical pattern, and a common response from the "transmitter" of the feedback, especially from managers, because managers want to ensure you get the message. If you're heavily invested in explaining your point of view—in other words, if you're heavily invested in being defensive—it tends to require fairly intense feedback to get your attention, to get you to "shut up and listen," if not to change.

Sometimes life itself gives us feedback. If we say we've made a commitment to one thing but continue to manifest or experience something else, the wise person will pause to wonder about this and make course corrections. The action you take in that essential moment following feedback affects the learning, ease, and joy you experience—both in the workplace and far beyond. *That's a powerful act.*

Figure 2.4 illustrates the continuous cycle we experience when we receive feedback, react, drift into defensiveness, then recommit to learning. The faster we shift from defensiveness to learning, the less wasted time and fewer distractions we experience. The issue isn't *avoiding* defensiveness; it's how quickly we can shift *into* learning. Will it take us one minute, a day, a month, or a lifetime?

IGNORE THE PACKAGING—GET TO THE GIFT

Sometimes we pass up a great product because the packaging seems humble; other times, we plunk down lots of money for fabulous packaging, but there's no substance inside. We pay

FIGURE 2.4   The Feedback-to-Learning Cycle

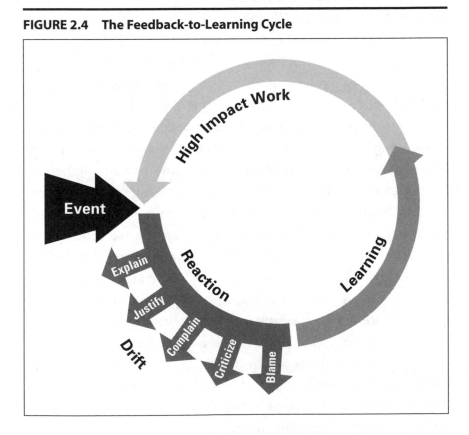

a similarly high price if we neglect to hear a message because we find fault with the way it's packaged. We see this negative and extremely ineffectual defensive reaction with unfortunate frequency. This particular defensive response implies that if only you'd given me the feedback better, if you'd spoken more softly or gently, then I'd listen and act on your input. We're employing just one more strategy to avoid getting the message, by convincing the person who gave the feedback she has wasted her breath (and, in fact, she has).

You have to drop the belief that information must be delivered to you in any particular way. Sure, it would be nice if we always got feedback delivered in a gentle, humane manner. We understand the Queen of England gets her messages from Parliament in purple velvet boxes, handed to her by a white-gloved butler. Wouldn't you love that sometimes? We suspect, though, she, too, might want to scream, every now and then, "Please give me one straight piece of information that's not filtered through all this ritual!"

Talented people commonly blow their potential by receiving feedback with a sarcastic, "Thanks a lot! Why did you have to tell me that right now?" Or "Did you have to tell me in such an obnoxious way?" They imply they might listen to feedback if it were delivered better. The problem: By the time you've stopped to get righteously indignant about how the message was delivered, the big bus of life has left you standing by the side of the road, shaking your fist at it. You can congratulate yourself the rest of your life that you were right and they were wrong, but you're still back there in that cloud of soot as the bus roars off.

Back when I (Kate) held a tight requirement that people give me feedback in a kindly fashion, they seemed to give it to me harshly or they didn't give it to me at all. Paradoxically, once I dropped the purple-box requirement, the feedback has come constantly and usually in kindly ways. Drop your requirement that feedback be presented to you in velvet boxes and your reaction time speeds up enormously.

Our advice—to ourselves, to nearly 1,000 executives, to our friends and family: *Take feedback any way you can get it.* If your manager delivers it at high volume, frothing at the mouth and sputtering obnoxious words, extract what's useful and move forward. Maybe later you can tell him how you'd like it delivered next time. Maybe he was in a bad mood. Maybe it's the way he's always behaved in life and always will. None of that matters. Notice instead how long it took you to extract the pearl and get on with the treasure hunt of your career—even faster now because of this new action.

PUT UP YOUR HANDS AND DROP YOUR DEFENSES

I (Kate) make my living giving people critical feedback. For years I assumed resistance and defensiveness came with the territory. I therefore became highly skilled at helping people unwind from their defenses so they could squarely face problems. Over time I developed an array of tools that ranged from straight reporting, to humorous "in your face" melodrama, to a whack on the head with a 2 × 4. For me, the process was tedious, time consuming, and as you can imagine, not much fun for anyone. One day I expanded my horizon by wondering if there were some way I could bypass that part of the feedback process while still helping them get their lessons.

As soon as this question came to mind, I saw a solution. But until that moment, I believed the problem lived "out there"— that just as sure as Starbucks sells coffee beans, people resist taking responsibility for their part of the problem, and my responsibility was to help them get past it. My curiosity resulted in a new tool: I began to teach clients to self-monitor their defensiveness and shift out of it. This allowed me to turn over the watchfulness and control to my clients. I merely taught them to shift into a learning mode if they observed their defensiveness. As a result, I provided greater value in the sessions for everyone.

In less than ten minutes I introduce them to the Defensiveness Learning Chart, seen in Figure 2.5, explain my own defensiveness escalation pathway, and then ask them to trace theirs, using a rating scale. I leave the chart out on the table while they read their 360° assessment results and we discuss their feedback. Then when I notice them becoming defensive, I ask them to look at the chart and point out what they're doing. I get sheepish smiles and "caught-in-the-act" gestures, and we have a lot of good laughs. Defensiveness—meeting critical feedback with resistance—ceases being a barrier and often becomes a rich connecting point for mutual chuckling at the lengths we sometimes go to be right and avoid facing the honest-to-gosh truth!

Figure 2.5 contains ten points along the scale that represent defensive behaviors when we get feedback and ten points that represent learning behaviors we may choose instead. The midpoint on the scale represents the essential action required to shift out of defensiveness and into learning. A person can enter the scale at any point or place. In other words, sometimes people get feedback and they respond by immediately feeling attacked; for others, defensiveness occurs later in the process. Yet others catch themselves instantly and shift into openness.

HIGH CURIOSITY AND HIGH LEARNING

What's *your* defensiveness pattern? I (Kate) get quiet and *pretend* to listen, while I'm mentally rubbing my hands together, preparing my retort that will sound logical and be delivered in a clear, sequential manner, designed to convince the

FIGURE 2.5   Shifting from Defensiveness and Low Learning to Curiosity

Defensiveness: Low Curiosity and Low Learning

− **1** *Direct:* Ask about the speaker's intention in bringing up this situation.

  Indirect: Show polite interest, while inwardly clinging to your opinions.

− **2** *Direct:* Point out that the other person seems to be missing some information.

  Indirect: Feel confused. Withdraw.

− **3** *Direct:* Explain how the person has misperceived the situation; provide a lot of supporting details to make sure they understand.

  Indirect: Feel misunderstood and unappreciated for your efforts. Worry about how you're perceived, instead of taking action.

− **4** *Direct:* Interrupt, then give a different perspective.

  Indirect: Get silent and still; provide cryptic answers and act as if you feel put upon.

− **5** *Direct:* Interpret what the person says as an attack.

  Indirect: Criticize the way the person delivers the message by thinking you'd feel less defensive, if only they had spoken to you more respectfully.

− **6** *Direct:* Provide an animated and long-winded justification for your behavior and why you're right and the other person is wrong.

  Indirect: Knock something over, drop things, spill a cup of coffee. Nonverbal displays of anger, irritation, and exasperation.

− **7** *Direct:* Communicate with a tone of righteous indignation; demand evidence in a hostile manner.

  Indirect: Get edgy, sharp, brusque, snappy, or nonverbally show your frustration in some other obvious way.

− 8	*Direct:*	Blame someone or something else.
	Indirect:	Pretend you agree when you don't.
− 9	*Direct:*	Attack or threaten the messenger, verbally or otherwise.
	Indirect:	Commit to do something when you don't plan to do it or don't have the time or resources to do it.
−10	*Direct:*	Create an uproar by making an abrupt departure.
	Indirect:	After you leave the meeting, complain to others about people or decisions; talk critically about people who aren't in the room; gossip.

The Key Transition Action:
Choose Curiosity over Defending

Genuinely wonder about the issue with an open body posture.
"I wonder what I could do differently to address
this issue successfully."

+ 1   Look interested; breathe; demonstrate an open posture.

+ 2   Express genuine curiosity about the issue.

+ 3   Listen generously (paraphrase others' points without interjecting your own).

+ 4   Express appreciation for the messenger and the message, regardless of delivery.

+ 5   Openly wonder about your role in creating the issue.

+ 6   Request information and examples about the issue.

+ 7   Take full responsibility for the issue and the results.

+ 8   Think out loud, making new associations about the issue.

+ 9   Feel and show a genuine enthusiasm about the possibilities.

+10   Implement (plan action, request support for follow-up).

other person they are wrong and I am right. If that doesn't work (i.e., if the other person doesn't agree with me), my voice gets a bit more clipped and definite. Somewhere along the way—maybe when I start climbing up on the soapbox clenching a megaphone—my logical explanations degenerate into justifications of my point of view (POV).

I know I'm hooked into a defensive pattern when I get so animated I talk over the other person. When I start feeling like they will never get it, that they're too dense to ever understand, I know I'm a momentary "goner"! This extreme response gets my attention and nudges me into learning.

The lights go on, the music begins, and the curtain pulls back to reveal a stage set for genuine listening and learning when I restate the other's point of view and their biggest, most noble intentions. More often than not, they're aligned with mine. If you find yourself stuck in a state of defensiveness and resistance, however, you'll find yourself far more focused on disagreeing than learning, more on saying the lines right than on creating art. You'll seal off any vulnerability, deny any weaknesses, argue vociferously against any wrongdoing or character flaws the feedback surely must imply—and the moment for learning will have passed. See Figure 2.6 for one way of seizing the learning moment.

FIGURE 2.6   How to Shift from Defensiveness to Curiosity

- Live in wonder rather than fear.

- Make learning more important than protecting your ego.

- Appreciate those who give you feedback, regardless of how they deliver it.

Early in my (Kate's) corporate career I got into some big trouble with a SVP for sharing some information with my manager that I didn't realize was confidential. Instead of feeling unfairly accused by him, or blaming him for not telling me the information was confidential, I asked myself what I needed to do differently. The lessons I learned from that one experience have served me for the past 30 years. There's usually a 10:1 ratio of learning to discomfort. In this particular incident, I definitely came out ahead.

If you're not learning on the run, you're dying on the vine. You die on the vine by asking questions like: "What's wrong with me?" or "What's wrong with those people?" because the answers don't move you forward. If you ask, "What's wrong with me?" or "What's wrong with her?" your mind gets busy coming up with answers all day and all night. It'll tell you plenty about what's wrong with you and with anyone else, but what's the point? If you ask, "What can I learn right now?" you fire up a different part of your mental machinery—one that's not hooked up to your ego and therefore needs no defending.

There's a phrase (and a tone) we hear a lot from people and companies dying on the vine. It's the self-righteous, misunderstood, doing-my-best-and-this-is-what-I-get-for-it whine, "Can you believe he said that to me?" Your self-righteous reaction to something takes about the same amount of time as learning from whatever it was the person was communicating. It will guarantee you a place on the bench at the next bus stop, where you will get to have animated conversations about how badly you have been treated. Unfortunately, you will be forced to have those conversations with people who are only watching your lips move until they have the chance to tell you how badly *they've* been treated and meanwhile life (and opportunity) move on. Listen for that tone. It signals a chance to learn.

CHAPTER SIX

TRAVELING FROM PLACE TO PLACE

Migrants could come West on the famous trails, many of which were built by the government to encourage migration. Those not coming in their own wagons often took a stagecoach, which was costly and slow. By 1869, however, the Union Pacific Railroad linked up with the Central Pacific making a transcontinental line and offering a form of transportation that was fast and relatively inexpensive. Only three years later, two railroad lines came into Boulder City: the Colorado Central and the Denver and Boulder Valley Line. Once in the city, a passenger could hop a streetcar or an overhead electric trolley, which was the chief mode of transportation within cities and towns before the automobile.

As the railroads and streetcars became more popular, road care declined. Maintenance grew slack. No one seemed to mind until the bicycle craze hit. Transportation changed radically in 1880—the same year that Billy the Kid was killed at the OK Corral—with the invention of the "safety bicycle." When the price of this two equal-sized wheel device came down to an affordable eighty dollars per bike, everyone wanted to own one. Riding was not easy, however, because the streets were in disrepair. Bicyclists pressured town and state governments to improve the roads; in fact, they fought for hard surfaces similar to those being built in Europe. By the time the craze peaked in 1896, the citizenry coveted individual transportation and smooth roads. The United States was ready for the "Model T." In 1893 the first gasoline-powered vehicle was invented, and by 1913 Model T Fords were produced on an assembly line, making automobiles affordable for the average person. As the number of people who owned cars increased, the demand for paved streets grew. By 1924, national highways spread across the country competing with the railroads for travelers and migrants.

Horse Power

You see, in the early days, they didn't take the water out of the river, ... and they had a stage stop over there. Sometimes they had to take people across in boats. It's hard to believe, but they did. [Edmund Darby]

There's an old tree as you go out of Erie on the north side of Erie with a big limb hanging over. My father and I was coming along there one day ... and he was tellin' me—and these old timers used to whisper some of these stories almost, when you were out on the prairies, because I couldn't decide whether he had taken part or somebody's family had. But ... a man murdered a couple up at Golden; stole what they had, stole their horse. The vigilante committee had wind of it. They caught him at Erie, and they hung him to the tree. That limb is still hanging down there by Erie where they hung this fella. They didn't hang him for murderin' the two people; they hung him for stealin' a horse. Now that was how important horses were at that time. [Frank Miller]

Stage stop and hotel? Well, that was put there by Tommy Jones as a stage stop and a hotel for the people coming through here. And he was their first man. ... probably was the first building in Valmont. It was, I forget how many rooms, it had in it, but least ways it was accommodation for stages, and ... he run this stage hotel and boardinghouse and like that. [George Sawhill]

They had a stagecoach out south of you know where Stern's Dairy used to be. They had a stagecoach [stop] there. The stage would come up from Denver from Sand Creek out to there and stop, I suppose they'd lay over night, and leave there and go on to St. Vrain about Berthoud or Loveland, the next stop. ... I think [it came through] either once or twice a week. Maybe it wasn't quite that often. But they had a ... station there for quite a long time. ... I remember my grandmother tellin' once about the military, the cavalry came through, and they stayed overnight. ... I remember her tellin' us she stayed at the kitchen range and baked a hundred pies for them militia men. A dollar a pie. As fast as she could get 'em made. She grossed a hundred dollars a sack [of flour]. I remember that so plain, she used to tell about it. [Ralph Miller]

Us stage drivers, we didn't have to pay for our meals at all, 'cause wherever we went, why, our passengers went with us, you see, so us drivers, we didn't have to pay for any meals. [Martin Parsons]

Before Longmont started to really growin' there was a little settlement there named Burlington. And then the stages and everything came from there directly to Boulder, and so they had to cross Gunbarrel Hill over here. The sayin' is that the road was so straight and the two tracks like a double-barrel shotgun [that] it was called Gunbarrel Hill. [George Sawhill]

- If you hear yourself saying or thinking, "That's just the way I am," you know you've identified an opportunity for instant learning.

- Defensiveness and blame are never the most useful responses to a critical input. They halt all learning and increase corporate sludge.

- Take feedback in any form and learn from it, no matter what its packaging.

- Focus on the speed at which you shift to curiosity rather than doing it perfectly.

TAKE ACTION

- What's the big learning you're trying to avoid? Explore people's most common complaints about you to find the likely answer.

- Look at your pattern of defensiveness and your particular pattern of escalation. When do you usually notice you're behaving defensively? What one step can you take to catch yourself in the act sooner and make the shift into learning? What specific ideas in this chapter make it the easiest for you to shift into learning?

- How do you respond to defensiveness when you see it in your team? Do you feed the escalation process by getting defensive yourself? If so, what's your escalation pattern with specific employees who seem to slip into defensiveness with you? What can you do with each of these people to create learning for you and for them?

- Are you willing to use the defensiveness scale the next time you give a team member feedback? If so, introduce it, point out your defensive pattern, then ask your coworker to indicate his level of defensiveness as you discuss the feedback.

- What sort of defensiveness does your company tolerate in meetings? What's the noble intention underlying this tolerance?

- Many times people erroneously believe if someone gets defensive in a group, we should spare them the embarrassment of having that pointed out. Which would you prefer: feeling embarrassed about slipping into a few moments of defensiveness or feeling embarrassed later about failing to perform because you didn't step promptly into curiosity and learn from the experience?

- How can you change the tone of the meetings you lead and encourage participants to drop their defenses? How can you do this in a way that people experience as supportive, instead of harshly confrontive?

- What about the meetings you attend as a participant? What active role can you play in setting the stage for learning and making defensive behavior something of the past?

CHAPTER THREE

AWARENESS
Tapping the Bodymind Intelligence

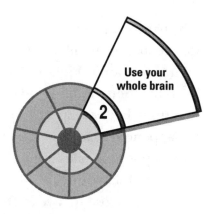

Use your whole brain

2

Do my emotions ever belong at work?

How can I develop my intuition even more?

How can I tap my emotional intelligence and all the rest of my capabilities?

To make the wisest, most transformative decisions, commit right now to awareness—to using the multidimensional intelligence and intuition you carry around with you wherever you go. To reap all of life's rewards, you must access and use your whole being to process information and make decisions. Your logical brain with its massive cerebral cortex has great value, but you have a full bodymind. Employing only the mind is like owning a three-dimensional wide-screen digital TV with the latest surround-sound system—and dimming the screen. You need both body and mind to navigate all the dimensions of our changing business world.

Make a radical change: Learn to think with your whole body. If you want to know the truth, ask your body. If what you think you feel doesn't match up with what you're experiencing in your

---

See also, Hendricks, Gay. *Conscious Living*, San Francisco: Harper, 2000, and *Conscious Breathing*, Bantam, 1995.

body, trust your body. Ask yourself: "Self, what's happening inside me at this moment?" Close your eyes if you wish. Breathe and notice. Don't think or analyze.

I once thought this mind/body connection was intellectually interesting, but not especially practical. Then something fascinating happened. I had a serious automobile accident that resulted in a complicated, painful case of whiplash. Migraine and cluster headaches followed. The whiplash healed, but the headaches persisted for close to a year. Determined to avoid chronic medication, I experimented with biofeedback to learn enough about my body that I could begin to have some influence over it (okay, to control it better). I realized that cluster headaches, located at the base of my skull, had to do with feeling mildly irritated.

It wasn't yet clear to me what caused the cluster pain to become a full-blown migraine until one Tuesday when our chairman asked me to get on a plane the next day and interview all the executives in a company we were thinking of acquiring. It would be a major business move for us, and I would be the first person from our company to visit. As he stressed how much he was counting on me, my rising irritation at the last-minute plans masked deeper, unfelt fears that I was totally unqualified to have a deciding go/no-go vote about this acquisition. I experienced a wave of nausea followed almost instantaneously by a migraine, triggered by my fear. Although in pain, I felt delighted at making this connection because it turned out to be useful on my trip.

As my plane took off early the next day I thought the butterflies in my stomach might give it extra lift. I so wanted to do a great job. I could have made this a nerve-wracking experience for myself, but instead decided to use it as an opportunity to stretch.

The people at the new company seemed bright. The acquisition seemed right. But my stomach churned every time the head of marketing spoke. I had such a bad stomachache (extremely unusual for me) that I took a long walk at lunch to clear my mind and allow my body to speak. I concluded that something unsaid was stimulating fear in me. I had a gut feeling it had to do with emerging technologies. So I asked him questions, dug in, and ultimately became convinced he was withholding information that posed a significant risk to our company.

Based on all I saw, felt, and heard, I suggested our general manager visit the company and meet with a multilevel team of marketing directors and technology leaders. Not surprisingly, the potential risk surfaced in the discussions. We ultimately backed away from the acquisition—a decision we all appreciated when the company toppled within 18 months due to a technology turn they had missed.

Awareness invites us to slow down to go fast. To pause, moment by moment, to tune into our whole being, to replace our love affair with the mind with a broader awareness that includes mind, body, intuition, and feelings. To stop using only our brains and learn even more deeply. To show up, 100 percent present, wherever we are. Awareness functions as a prerequisite for every action in this book.

Our culture seems to have a love affair with the cerebral cortex, the thick outer layer of the brain that handles thinking, problem solving, and decision making. Inside are the much larger structures of the limbic system, our rapid-response gut-level intelligence. Evolutionarily very old and very wise, it not only senses quickly and accurately but also elicits the right response from the body before we are aware of the problem. It sends its messages in sensations, heat, pain, tightness, shallow breaths, heartbeat, and sweatiness. Our jaw clenches, our throat feels tight, our back aches, and our stomach cramps. If we ignore these messages, they become louder and more bothersome until they get our attention. Scanning our bodies, including our breathing, is the best access to the limbic brain and its wisdom.

The thinking brain often depreciates the feelings of the lightning fast microsecond communications of the limbic brain, which is awake and functioning long before we wake up or become conscious of thoughts, ideas, or plans. We in western cultures generally override this highly developed intelligence system in favor of the slower and less accurate thinking brain. Denying feelings, hunches, and intuitions limits the creativity that we are capable of and in some cases can be disastrous.

DECIPHERING OUR BODYMIND'S MESSAGES

Our bodymind's messages can lead us to deeper truth in deal making and decisions of all kinds. They can help us quickly sense problems that can be much more significant down the line. It's no accident that phrases such as "gut-wrenching," "cold feet," "breathtaking," "heart-stopping," "hot-headed," "tight-fisted," "nose out of joint," "ears were burning," and "pain in the neck" have become part of our everyday language.

You only operate at peak efficiency when you're using your whole body to think. Listen to your body. It speaks volumes. Start by noticing when your energy goes up or down when you consider various decisions or interact with different coworkers.

Translate a stuttered reply, cough, or sneeze as possible resistance to an idea. I know you may be scratching your head in disbelief, and this may sound somewhat hard to swallow, but if you'll keep an open mind (all the way to the limbic system), just a few experiences of this rich resource will make you a believer.

Notice when someone says something positive while shaking his head no. We recently worked with a small team of four executives who were entangled in a major conflict. We listened for about 30 minutes to each person's view of the problem. We introduced the defensiveness and learning scale (presented in

Chapter 2), then one at a time, we asked each one if they were willing to do whatever it took to resolve the problem. The CEO and the first two VPs gave me a clear "yes." The last VP emphatically said, "Yes!" while shaking his head left to right. We pointed this out to him and, like hundreds of people before him, he predictably denied that he felt any resistance. In fact, he became downright defensive.

When we got out the defensiveness chart, he launched into a long explanation of why he was so committed and why we were stupid for not thinking so because he had invested the day in flying to Santa Barbara to work with us. Then he jumped to self-righteous indignation, as if we had personally attacked him. We continued to calmly point out that he seemed resistant to doing what it took to resolve the problem. Finally, after five long and emotional minutes, he said that he didn't believe he was in any way "wrong" or that he needed to change. He was willing to see the problem resolved, but only if *other* people changed. Everyone literally breathed a sigh of relief at having the truth on the table—a big step forward in resolving the conflict. No resolution was going to occur with his mindset operating as a hidden belief. This never would have surfaced had we not been attuned to the discrepancy between what he was saying and what his body was communicating.

EINSTEIN AND MICHELANGELO IN OUR BODIES

When we don't listen to the signals from our bodies or the signals of other people, we warp our intuition and limit our ability to make our biggest and best contribution. We also stifle our own satisfaction and joy. When you don't know what to do, when you don't know whether you want to do this or that, quiet yourself and listen to that still, small voice. The hush and spaciousness of tuning into our body wisdom takes us into the neighborhood of great inventors. The quiet acts as the canvas on which a technological leap or strategic breakthrough emerges. Einstein, Salk, and many other great scientists testified that their brilliant leaps occurred when their minds were quiet, not actively thinking.

Whenever you need an answer, a solution, or a creative idea, stop thinking and return to your body. When you think again, your thinking will feel fresher and more creative. In any creative activity (i.e., all of life), make it a habit to pulse back and forth every few minutes between thinking and inner listening. When you get overly attached to your ideas and feel angry others aren't buying in, you miss the subtle flurry in your gut that's trying to communicate something scary buried underneath—some nuance that could ultimately mean the difference between a great idea and a flop. In these situations, when we have strong opinions and others do, too, our body sensations carry especially important express mail messages for us, if we will just heed them.

One of our friends got a vivid lesson about the downside of becoming overly attached to an idea or position when she was a child. She took her baby sister's toy with a suction cup on the bottom and pressed it onto her own forehead to see if it would stick. It did. Then she couldn't pull it off. Seven-year-olds do things like that. She walked around for a week after that with a Band-Aid over the large circular bruise that resulted. Sometimes our minds get as attached as that suction cup to a point of view or to being right. As a result, we misperceive situations and can get embarrassingly bruised in the process.

When we do stop—in the midst of shouting down the other person or bulldozing our idea over the assembled group—we immediately open up the possibility of change because we've become *conscious*. It's in that moment when we've landed once again, fully here, that intuition and all forms of deep insight occur. *The ability to be completely, totally present largely determines our ability to anticipate future trends.*

Most of us have very active voices in our heads that rattle on all day, leaving little space for noticing how we feel, what our body is attempting to communicate to us, and what's actually occurring in the subtle messages in the people around us. This inner voice goes by many different names—gut instinct, experience, wisdom, intuition, inner guidance. We may not agree on what to call it, but we all sense that not using our whole brain is as limiting as doing research in books at the library whenever we have time to drive over there, instead of instantly accessing the rich array of Internet help right on our desktop.

Consider, for example, the number of people you hire into your work group, the number of suppliers and vendors you interview and select, or the number of acquisitions you target this year. Think about the more subtle decisions you make about whom to assign to projects, how long to wait for a struggling employee to improve before letting him go, what sales target to set for your team, whether or not project milestones will be reached. Imagine how your spirit would soar if you could somehow double your success rate in *all* of your decisions. What about even a 50 percent increase in your hit rate? That would certainly leverage your time and add ease to your work.

The mean time to collect sufficient information is getting longer than the mean time available for making a timely decision, and the gap is widening as you read these words. Is lack of time the real culprit here? If we can find ten seconds to slip into our bodies, we can access the intelligent equivalent of leaping tall buildings in a single bound. We need this talent more than ever right now. We're missing important information because we look to our inner equivalent of Star Trek's superlogical Mr. Spock and ignore the organic and intuitive wisdom of Counselor Troi. We focus on data and action for the answers instead of turning our attention inside. Like the various newsgroups to which we may subscribe, every second of the day our bodymind automatically delivers a complex web of feedback to us. We must learn to pay attention and decipher it, instead of ignoring it as we usually do.

WINNERS MUST BE PRESENT

Few of us have ever had lessons in staying present enough to hear the bodymind's suggestions. Our cultural messages—especially from the media—endorse lots of flash, quick fixes, and continuous action. Give the greatest gift you can to your company, your career, and yourself by living in the present moment, completely in your body. Do it now if your body and mind are handy. Set this book aside, breathe deeply, and take as long as you need to notice your thoughts and feel any body sensations or emotions. Describe them to yourself in detail. If you like, close your eyes. You may feel as if you're encountering a long-lost friend. You are.

Like virus-tracking software that takes a few seconds to do a scan before it lets us open a file, we often must pause and take a breath to register which emotions we're actually feeling—especially in settings like work. Both on our computers and in our jobs, the wait is worth it because the information that follows is "clean" and authentic. I (Kate) moved away from my computer just now, closed my eyes, and noticed some tightness under both my shoulder blades and a bit of tingling numbness running down my right arm. I had the thought, "I feel so frustrated that I'm not a better writer! I don't have the skills to get this across powerfully enough. I'm out on the skinny branches, and people will think these ideas are weird. Business readers aren't going to see how much information they miss by being *oblivious* to the massive data their bodymind constantly delivers. Of the seven, this feels like the most important action in the book, but I don't know how to get using it across."

I took a deep breath and tuned in again. Now I noticed my shoulders felt more relaxed and I felt excitement and energy coursing through my body. Everything changed in just a minute or two, and I felt the words coming more easily. What did you notice about yourself in this exercise? What thoughts emerged? What body sensations did you feel? Tightness across your shoulders? A clenched jaw? A swinging leg that wants to be in motion? A craving for chips and salsa? Did you suddenly remember something you'd forgotten to do? Feel fatigue? Antsy? Was there some emotion or other sensation going on in your body you didn't notice till now? (By the way, welcome back. Glad you're here.)

THE AWARENESS HALL OF FAME

Sometimes we don't feel present on the job because of outside concerns, and the way to help move these feelings along is to stop and acknowledge them. After the 9-11 attack on the World Trade Center, millions of people had trouble focusing on work. During the following week, Kevin Rollins, Dell's president and COO, and Michael Dell met with 400 to 500 VPs and directors around the company to talk about their emotional reactions to the bombings. People initially felt surprised and uncomfortable, as did Kevin and Michael. Dell's culture, like so many others, is focused on talking about work, not feelings.

Both Michael and Kevin talked about the importance of facing the emotions everyone was dealing with. They also shared that they felt awkward talking about this, just as they imagined some of the people in the room felt. They said this was an important learning for each of them personally and an important change in their culture. At some point, one of them said, "Consider us all 'touchy-feelies' in progress." One of Dell's particularly tough SVPs remarked to me later how much he appreciated that comment. He said this event helped him realize how much more there is to doing a job. Imagine how this rippled out from the senior staff into the whole company.

Michael Hammer, author of *The Agenda: What Every Business Must Do to Dominate the Decade,* believes the new business leader must be someone to whom others can relate and can have a sense of "empathic identification." Hammer, who's well-known for books like *Reengineering the Corporation,* indicates that "further reengineering ultimately depends on qualities that emanate from the right side of the brain: devotion, trust, empathy, and all of their touchy-feely cousins. And that calls for a new style of leadership."

TUNING IN AND TUNING OUT

I (Kate) once caught myself in a series of yawns, feeling as if I were pushing a river uphill, while delivering highly critical feedback to an unusually resistant executive. I experimented with a new approach and discovered a goldmine. As her defensiveness escalated, I communicated my authentic truth without any filtering: "I notice I'm feeling sad and I'm getting a tight feeling in my gut. I'm afraid what I'm saying is hurting you, and that's not my intention." She immediately opened up, tensions relaxed, and a reassuring bond formed in support of our work together.

Awareness of our emotions and honest communication about them create better listening, especially when people seem defensive. Most of us only experience fleeting moments of tapping our bodymind intelligence: when we're out in nature, in times of love, during emergencies, and in extreme sports. In fact, I think that's what makes these activities so popular—we're completely present and engaged, every molecule focused and exhilarated. The response we need arises out of that state of consciousness. People commonly report that in crises they're fully present and so much more effective than usual, they accomplish feats not possible in ordinary reality.

Many of us confuse *paying* attention with *being* attentive. One involves activity—paying attention—and the other involves our state of mind—being attentive. Because we don't understand this distinction, we attempt to muscle and mimic the heightened state of present moment awareness by *focusing*. We make our to-do lists, turn off the phone, close the door, and remove any other distractions like e-mail. This helps us focus, but differs from being fully present and receptive to information from our full being. We focus so fully on engaging our thinking brain that, like a headphoned teenager dazed by an amped-up CD of his favorite hip hop singer, we can tune out our body's feedback entirely.

I (Kate) once got so engaged working on a report on my computer that I didn't change position for six unbroken hours. When I suddenly moved my body to stand up, my back couldn't do it. I had become so intensely mentally focused that I completely overrode all signals from my body to get up and move around. As a result, I seriously put out my back.

Even though I'm someone who encourages others to look within, I reacted like so many of us do. I first looked "out there" and blamed it on the chair, and I actually went out and spent over a thousand dollars on the world's best office chair. But the real solution, I knew even then, was to remain aware, moment-by-moment, of my body. I saw what had happened as unarguable proof that I had successfully tuned out all body feedback for a significant chunk of my workday, and the best way I could "learn my lesson" was for a big dose of pain to get my attention.

Mastering awareness means both that you practice it minute by minute and that you become able to tune in during the toughest of circumstances. Awareness helps you recover from out-of-the-blue emotional blows and other ways we get whacked around. Your biggest client changes strategic direction and will no longer use your company as a vendor. One of your strongest team members leaves because a competitor has doubled his or her salary. Your company announces a major layoff. Your retirement portfolio loses half its value within three months. World events take a turn you couldn't have imagined. Tapping your bodymind intelligence lets you reboot. *Your response and recovery to upsets and losses indicate how successfully you stay in present-moment awareness.*

Sometimes you'll have such a reserve of connectedness and such a sense of bodily peace that you roll easily with the punches; at other times you'll need to take the action consciously. If possible, find a place to be alone quietly. Take a few deep breaths and notice any body sensations and emotions. Notice what deeper information becomes available. Take it in. Take a few more deep breaths and appreciate your awareness. Float back into the fray and spread some of that serenity around.

THINKING AND THE MIND BARRIER

We are not just our mind—the voice in our heads that prattles on and on. Once we reach the age of reason, we seem to make reason a way of life. Talk. Talk. Talk. We explain to ourselves why we're feeling what we're feeling, or judge what others are doing, or justify our behavior or someone else's. All this internal and external jabbering takes us away from our own inner experience.

Thinking also keeps unrewarding repetitive patterns in place. Analyzing why your manager interrupts people, you focus "out there," on something you can't change or control. Instead, report your own experience to yourself: "When I made a suggestion at the meeting, my manager talked over me to ask the opinion of a new team member. I feel as if I'm invisible. I feel sad. I feel a burning in my chest." Feeling your own sadness at not being listened to puts your attention on yourself and what's going on this very minute.

Instead of explaining why you missed a deadline, first stop to notice what feelings this brings up. Take a breath or two and listen to what your body says. Perhaps you're experiencing a deep feeling of disappointment and even a sense of failure. Perhaps this feeling seems familiar. Acknowledge what is—that you feel disappointed in yourself for missing a deadline. Then keep your commitment to turn the project in at another agreed-upon time. That's more effective than a detailed story of why you didn't come through.

Instead of using the mind as a tool, as needed, we let it stay on, cranking out repetitive and often negative ideas. According to David Nichol and Bill Birchard in *The One-Minute Meditator*,[*] more than 90 percent of the movies in our minds are reruns of the classics: our own repetitive stories and patterns.

We vigorously resist quieting the mind, so we miss the bodymind's sage advice. I (Kate) recently worked with Todd, a highly intellectual and conceptually brilliant CEO. He eagerly explored his feelings and his body sensations, but as intellectual concepts. He wanted to analyze them, not *feel* them. As we dug into this issue, what emerged was his own fear of failure. He so wanted to "do it right" that he focused all his attention on getting to the "right" answer. Inside this very successful 50-year-old executive was a 10-year-old boy, eager to please his parents and his teachers and especially to show up his older

---

[*]Nichol, David and Bill Birchard. *The One-Minute Meditator.* Cambridge, MA: Perseus Publishing, 2001.

brother. All of these old performance patterns (that took him like an express elevator straight to his head) got in his way each time he attempted to tune in to what he was experiencing. It's hard to answer the question, "What am I feeling right now?" if you're looking for the "right" answer. Like many of us, Todd had a biting inner critic, pointing out all his shortcomings and how he *should* be performing.

Danielle thought her stomachaches resulted from a promotion requiring more public speaking. While working with me (Eddie), she put her full attention on the stomachache and realized she felt afraid. As she stayed present with the body feelings, she realized she'd had a lifelong fear of feeling inadequate no matter what the task. She also had a harsh inner critic that lambasted her. In fact, her inner critic was lashing out at her at that very moment for being stupid enough to feel afraid. It also added that she was really stupid to have actually shared that with me. The problem wasn't fear of speaking, but this harsh inner voice. When she made that connection, the stomachaches disappeared.

Review the list in Figure 3.1. Do any of the refrains listed there sound like the voice of your own inner critic?

FIGURE 3.1   Favorite Refrains of Our Inner Critic

▪ Why in the world did I say that?	▪ How many times does it take me?
▪ Oh, no. I did it again.	▪ I can't believe it! I goofed up again.
▪ How could I do that?	▪ Where are my brains?
▪ Can't I do anything right?	▪ And why did I wear that today?

This lifelong inner critical acid drip erodes our trust in our own internal knowing and intuitive insight. One client, a recovering alcoholic, says his inner critic's voice resembles the sudden urge to drink—swift, fierce, and out of the blue. In both cases the suddenness is a helpful tip-off. He acknowledges it and turns it off by saying, "Thank you for sharing."

THE HANDSHAKE FROM HELL

Sometimes the mind acts like an evil twin. The body may be screaming to get our attention and divert us from danger, and the mind dismisses it: "What danger? That doesn't make sense." During my (Kate's) first year as a consultant in 1989, Janel, the SVP of human resources (HR) for a large west coast services firm, asked me to interview an executive, and I immediately had a bad feeling about him. I left the interview and promptly headed to the restroom to wash my hands. Now that's a strong, visceral reaction!

While I recommended he not be hired, I didn't push hard with my opinion because I thought I didn't have sufficiently strong data, and in fact his experiences aligned extremely well with what this company needed. I did tell them about my bizarre urge to wash my hands after our farewell handshake. The firm essentially said thank you for sharing and brought him on board. Nine months later, after he had failed to move any project forward and alienated many coworkers, he was asked to leave. A short time later, they discovered he had embezzled about a quarter of a million dollars from the company.

After that, both Janel and I began to pay attention to my hunches. I also took a close look at why I hadn't fought harder. I push clients all the time. I'm not afraid to be confrontive. Why didn't I take a stronger stand? I realized my thinking mind had taken over and won out over my very strong bodymind signals. I also realized that I didn't yet know how to fully tap and utilize the wide array of intelligence that lived in me. I feel much more in touch with bodymind wisdom today, but I watch out for the many subtle ways I allow my mind to override its wisdom. The most powerful decision making uses logical thought and the bodymind's signals.

OTHER BARRIERS TO BODYMIND WISDOM

We cut ourselves off from bodymind intelligence most of the time by overriding our feelings. Instead of feeling, we fill the space with doing, thinking, or acting. We seem to be unaware that *feelings shift very fast, if we simply feel them for ten full, attentive seconds.* Imagine you are sitting in your cube struggling with a problem and feeling very alone. Tapping your bodymind intelligence in this situation would mean placing your attention on your feeling of loneliness and noticing how you experience it in your body.

We seldom do this, though. We take a walk and get an espresso, then munch some chips from the vending machine to try to escape the loneliness with food. Two bags later, feeling stuffed but empty, we might vow to lose some weight and call a friend to find out about the best dieting Web sites, instead of facing head-on the problem that's nagging at us and stirring deep feelings of "I can't do this alone."

Reaching voicemail, we give up on oral gratification and revert to the busyness of checking our to-do lists, reading e-mail, and straightening our desk. At our team meeting we focus on details rather than go for a challenging project. We top this off with some venting and complaining about how unavailable our manager is, how unappreciated we feel, how much work we have to do—garden variety gripes and blaming statements that people make over lunch and coffee.

The day finally grinds to a close. We go home to our family and complain about our boring job. We hardly taste dinner, then plant ourselves in front of the TV to channel-surf until we zone out and sleep. We might fantasize about getting on one of the *Survivor* shows, but we've already voted ourselves out of the adventure of life by refusing to feel. We've done everything in our power to distract ourselves from the feeling of "I can't do this alone." Feeling the feeling fully for ten seconds at 9:00 in the morning would have helped it shift and send us on to a productive day. Multiply this scenario by the number of people in your organization, and you begin to get a frightening sense of how much time can be wasted when we coconspire to avoid present-moment reality and what we are all feeling.

As he was nearing retirement, Rear Admiral Ray Archer invited me (Eddie) to work with him to see if he could develop strategies for what he called his personal battle of the bulge, something many people confront. A hungry ghost seemed to overtake him at the end of his workday and on weekends, despite his rigid fitness program that included working out from 5:00 AM to 6:00 AM during the week at the gym. As we worked together he realized that what he was feeling was not so much hunger as fear and anxiety. He also noticed that these feelings came up whenever he slowed down during a time of uncertainty in his life. Although he was looking forward to retirement from the Navy, he was facing the unknown as he transitioned into an executive role in a major corporation. As he learned to feel the feelings and acknowledge the uncertainty, he was able to let go of the need to stuff himself with food. He also let go of a number of inches around his waist in the process.

We've all developed habitual ways to deflect the bodymind—and usually we feel very justified in these particular patterns. In fact, these defenses seem as natural as breathing. Everyone seems to use them. Which of the following common barriers are your favorites?

- Just Do It and Do It and Do It

- Fretting about the Future

- Know-It-All-Itis

- Control Queen (or King)

Just Do It and Do It and Do It and Do It. With this universally favorite defense we fill every moment with activity—important things that *must* get done—so there's no time to tune in to internal sensations. We obsess with staying busy and productive. We hear neither our body nor our thinking mind.

Fretting about the Future. Most people operate in a constant state of worry and fear (generally triggered by thinking about an imagined future) and that blurs the accurate perception of what is.

Know-It-All-Itis. Convinced that "I'm right, and you're wrong," many of us feel angry and indulge in blaming. This isn't true emotion, although it's what most of us think of as emotion. It's more of a smokescreen for the real feelings—in this case, probably surface anger about not getting our way. Beneath the anger often lurk disappointment and sadness that we haven't communicated our idea better or fear that a lesser idea may be pursued. Masking deep, true feelings with self-righteous, know-it-all-itis makes it much harder to listen to and act on our intuition, or to persuade others to listen and to follow their hunches.

Control Queen (or King). We can pop ourselves out of the present by not telling the whole truth about what we think and feel to protect someone else's feelings and when we allow someone to believe we agree with them when we don't. These attempts to manipulate someone else's perception of what's real differ from the healthy control practices of planning and organizing so essential to everyday living.

Which barriers do you use most? Which one are you using right now as you read this chapter? Make a cocommitment with others on your team to keep corporate sludge at bay by noticing these bodymind barriers as quickly as you can.

EMOTIONS AS GATEWAY TO BODYMIND

Our emotions act like the keys to the treasure chest of bodymind wisdom. Many of us, unfortunately, have missed out, not realizing the key ring sits right in our back pocket. We've tended to discount our emotions—operating on the mistaken assumption that unless we check our emotions at the door, we'll shut off our brains and make suboptimal decisions at work. Nothing could be further from the truth.

If we fail to recognize our basic human feelings, they don't go away. Research shows that even if we put our emotions out of our minds, they linger—sometimes for a lifetime—in our bodies. And in lingering, they distract us and take us off track. When we dam up those basic emotions, we also cut off our spirit, our enthusiasm, and our motivation. We plod along, but our hearts, literally and figuratively, aren't in it.

When we do allow ourselves to express our emotions, we feel as vulnerable and exposed as an early tulip in a spring snowstorm. Or we worry that we're "not nice," or that we'll "lose it," splattering everyone around us and having to stay late to scrub the goop off the walls. In general most people at work attempt to avoid feeling their feelings and what they see as the irrational and undependable side of human nature that feelings represent. Emotions are neither irrational nor undependable, although if they're bottled up long enough they will become that.

Many of us get so judgmental about our feelings, we don't give ourselves any room to just feel them. We notice we're feeling irritated and think we shouldn't have that feeling—it's not nice to get angry because a colleague is promoted or our project is delayed because our logical side understands the reasons. When we tell our emotions to be quiet and behave, they lodge in our body and begin to gather steam. Instead of simply being present with the sensations of anger, some people become engulfed in righteous indignation when colleagues don't keep their commitments, believing this is the correct and only response to life. Instead of simply noticing their jaws have become tight and they feel angry, they justify their feelings. Change results from willingness to feel the feeling, not from justifying and feeling self-righteous.

Because we discount the power of our emotions, they set our agenda, govern our choices, determine our goals, and direct our lives. People who resist showing their emotions on the job are basically saying that only the head belongs at work. They're therefore doing their job with only a fragment of who they are.

Here's one example of emotions at work. One beautiful August day a car full of teenagers lost control and crashed into a tree on a local country road. A 19-year-old young woman who was about to become a freshman at the University of Michigan was helicoptered to the emergency room in cardiac arrest with severe injuries. I (Eddie) immediately began a swift resuscitation with my team and attempted to surgically control the massive internal bleeding. Our efforts went on for the next hour and half to no avail. Finally, I felt our senior anesthesiologist pulling at my shoulder.

"Eddie, you can't bring her back."

I realized in that moment that I had seen her not just as a vibrant 19-year-old young woman but as my daughter, who was nearly the same age. I finally stopped and slumped onto a stool in the corner. I knew I had to go out and speak with the 30 members of her family and dragged myself out to the waiting area. I felt a huge heaviness in my throat, all the way down to my heart. I wasn't sure I could actually speak. I knew from my years of training how to couch an unacceptable message, but those phrases didn't feel right. I looked around into several sets of eyes. Some radiated fear, some showed deep sadness, some were panic-stricken, some glazed over, some incredibly angry.

I said, "She didn't make it, she didn't suffer."

And then in what seemed like a long silence I said, "I can only share my feelings with you." I spoke first of feeling incredible anger. How could this happen? Who is responsible? Why couldn't something be done? My eyes filled with tears and I actually began to cry. I shared how this young woman reminded me of my daughter as well as the difficulty of shifting gears from trying everything to revive her to realizing it was time to stop.

When I finished, there was a long silence. Suddenly, instead of being the surgeon and the bearer of bad news, I was invited for the next hour into the warmth and love and grieving of this family. As I left them, I remembered the advice of some of my professors: that we need to stay distant. I had chosen the other direction not because I had consciously intended to but because it happened in that moment. I had stepped into wholeheartedness that was truly the basis of the profession I love.

As we take responsibility for expressing and owning our feelings, life at work becomes a lot more peaceful and relaxed, and free of sludge. It takes lots of practice to be able to feel feelings and to unwind from the buried experiences stored in our bodies. We promise, it's worth it.

EMOTIONS, EVOLUTION, AND "OUT THERE" THREATS

Over millions of years, all animals have developed four major ways of defending themselves when under threat. See Figure 3.2. Some of us may do all four, but many of us have favorites we use over and over. These were wired in a long time ago when we contended with actual predators. Today we mostly deal with imaginary threats.

We've developed an arsenal of defense tactics to avoid feeling emotions, which, if fully felt, would morph us in minutes. Because our brain developed at a time when we faced prehistoric threats to life and limb every day, it predisposes us to pay attention to emotionally laden events and to the first and last moments in an event. That's why we remember our first im-

---

FIGURE 3.2   Four Common Defenses

These are the four common approaches we use to defend against threats. Check the ones that apply to you.

Fight
- ☐ Attack
- ☐ Blame
- ☐ Criticize
- ☐ Justify
- ☐ Interrupt

Faint
- ☐ Get confused or bored
- ☐ Go blank
- ☐ Get sleepy
- ☐ Get sick
- ☐ Eat or drink (stuff it)

Flight
- ☐ Get too busy
- ☐ Change the subject
- ☐ Deny there's a problem
- ☐ Dismiss issues as trivial or illogical
- ☐ Make a joke

Freeze
- ☐ Stonewall
- ☐ Get analysis-paralysis
- ☐ Focus on minute details
- ☐ Intellectualize
- ☐ Feel "above it all"

pressions of people more strongly and pay attention to crises, using them to mobilize action, rather than operate proactively. Our emotions, buried down in the limbic system and the brain stem, evolved as short-circuit organizers to help us speed up decisions that had potential survival value. Emotions override our cerebral cortex (the thinking part of our brain).

Today, most of the threats to us aren't physical, but we respond physiologically as if they were. Someone insults us, hires away a prized employee, or is using our favorite Stairmaster when we walk into the corporate fitness center. We interpret these as threats—to career, to bonuses, to self-esteem, to our value at a very personal level. We feel afraid or angry just as if we were confronting physical threats. We then immediately try to identify a reason "out there" for the emotion.

As chief of a hospital medical staff, several years ago I (Eddie) met with Kamal, a highly respected anesthesiologist, to discuss a recent episode in the emergency department. Kamal had become irate and verbally abusive to the nursing and medical staff about the availability of equipment to support an asthmatic patient. Although the outcome had been positive and the patient had suffered no ill effects, the staff continued to feel a great degree of resentment about his accusations of incompetence, lack of caring, and irresponsibility. During the past two years there had been three or four other episodes in which Kamal had "gone ballistic" in an emergency situation and now he was in danger of losing his job.

As we worked together, Kamal realized that beneath the anger was an enormous fear of not having what he needed to do a good job. He was even able to connect it with a traumatic experience as a child when he felt helpless coming to the aid of an injured neighbor. More recently, he was feeling inadequate as a parent of a troubled teen. He realized his emotional outbursts actually insulated him from his true feelings. Kamal began to notice similar situations at work and at home, and he met with staff to discuss specific past issues to discuss how to address the problems. No similar outbursts have occurred since. In fact, Kamal has now become known not only for his expertise but also his equanimity in difficult medical situations.

We reflexively attempt to make someone else the cause of our emotions. If someone doesn't come through and do what we expect, we say (or at least think), "You make me so angry!" We then either (1) attack verbally or (2) withhold expressing the feeling (we're taught to be nice) while accumulating resentment, ensuring the other person will pay later. Instead of saying, "He makes me so angry!" use this responsible alternative: "When I don't have the resources I need, I feel angry!" *No one can make you feel a particular way. Our feelings come from our interpretation of reality.* And that interpretation leads us to feel mad— or sad or glad or scared.

Many employees today believe, "I'm afraid *because* of all the changes going on in the company and in the world," which leads them to feel like a victim of circumstances. A more accurate and responsible way to describe emotions in this case might sound like: "I'm feeling afraid. Brett just lost his job, and I'm afraid that may happen to me." Keep the focus on yourself. Undeniably, we feel emotion. What we "make up" is the cause. "I feel _____ *because* _____ is a figment of my imagination."

ZEROING IN ON OUR EMOTIONS

We use lots of different words to describe our emotions, and most of these combine some variation of the basic four: anger, sadness, fear, or joy. The biggest problem for most people isn't speaking their emotions—it's recognizing them. Most of us have had so many years of training in hiding our feelings that we simply aren't aware of them until they get overwhelming. By the time we're aware of them, everyone else is too!

Anger usually means you feel someone has crossed a boundary or that something unfair is happening. Sadness comes from any kind of loss, including a career change or your view of yourself. Fear often stems from uncertainty or a feeling of lack of control. Embarrassment isn't actually a feeling, but it indicates that some feelings aren't being felt. Use it as a cue to go deeper. See Figure 3.3 for questions to ask when zeroing in on emotions.

Use the chart in Figure 3.4 to help you see how each of these feelings escalates. Where do you hang out most of the time? Which of these seem most foreign?

Most of us get our mental and our emotional processes mixed up. We say, "I feel like we should do this," or, "I feel like you haven't done an adequate job." This language introduces confusion into our conversations, because we label many of our thoughts as feelings. Keep feeling sentences simple and clean. After the words "I feel," use only one word and select it from the emotional escalation chart in Figure 3.4. Instead of saying, "I feel like you did a great job," say, "I feel happy with your per-

---

FIGURE 3.3   Exploring Emotions

1. Which emotions are you most aware of? Least aware of?

2. Which emotions do you express easily? Listen to easily?

3. Which emotions seem more difficult to express? To listen to?

4. Which emotions feel easier to experience when you're alone?

5. How did you learn to feel some emotions only when alone? From whom?

6. What are your particular challenges in emotional awareness?

FIGURE 3.4   Emotional Escalation

We only experience four basic emotions, but the intensity of each one can vary widely. Think of each emotion as a continuum ranging from 1 (barely perceivable) to 10 (very strong).

Rate the intensity to give yourself feedback on how exactly you're feeling.

Mild								**Strong**	
1	2	3	4	5	6	7	8	9	10

Irritated ⟶	Frustrated ⟶	Angry
Worried ⟶	Anxious ⟶	Afraid
Disappointed ⟶	Sad ⟶	Sorrowful
Content ⟶	Happy ⟶	Joyful

formance." Instead of saying, "It makes no sense that I would feel sad about this," say, "I feel disappointed."

THE COST OF BUCKING UP

When we say we're doing great but don't actually feel that way, it comes across in a tone of voice, posture, or lack of eye contact. People can feel the incongruity, even if they don't notice the outward body signals.

Here's an example. Vince had enjoyed a successful decade with a major software company, and he was part of the initial team that took the company public. When they decided to launch a completely new product, he went off to run that division. Despite a technology breakthrough and broad marketplace interest, the product didn't perform as expected, and Vince was blamed in visible ways. He was attacked in meetings, and the top leaders, including the CEO, talked negatively about him behind his back.

Meanwhile, Vince was stomaching the emotional pain—swallowing his hurt, fear, and sadness that he hadn't made wise decisions for this company he loved. When asked how he felt, he lied to himself and to everyone else. He would say, "It's a tough time, but I'm fine," and then go on to talk about a business challenge—not himself. He continued to perform with determination and diligence, even though, with a personal net worth of $20 million, he had long passed the point of needing to work. When the product eventually became a solid success, he quit. The CEO, devastated at the loss of this friend he thought would one day lead the company, immediately put out his back and was in bed for two weeks. He wanted to put the whole painful event "behind" him. He felt totally unprepared for his protégé to leave him and didn't understand the consequences of his own behavior. He also missed an opportunity to tell the truth. He held it in, feigned cheerfulness, and never communicated his own hurt and pain. The two men never talked honestly about their feelings. Vince never shared the loneliness he experienced during the two years he felt abandoned by the CEO, and the CEO never discussed the sense of loss he felt when Vince resigned.

Without Vince's leadership, the company struggled. When the board of directors recruited him back nearly five years later, his leadership allowed the company to triple its stock price and complete a major acquisition. Though the story has a happy ending, think of the unnecessary pain for the company and these two men—all because they felt unwilling to honestly speak their feelings.

CATCH AND RELEASE

Emotions shift very quickly—in seconds—when you pause for a moment to feel them. Gay and Kathlyn Hendricks conducted an experiment with 20 graduate students before a major exam. The students filled out an anxiety scale, then one half read about the process of feeling their emotions fully while the other group actually practiced this technique, noticing what they were feeling in their bodies, then reporting what they felt. At the start of the experiment, the whole group averaged an anxiety level of seven out of ten. See Figure 3.5. Those who read about the attention technique reduced their level to six, while the group that actually practiced it reduced their level to three.*

I (Kate) had a recent experience of the speedy shift of feelings with my granddaughter Karissa, age five. She climbed up on a fairly high dock in a huge lake, got scared, but jumped in anyway. Then she got very scared when she went down deeper than she had expected, even with her life preserver. I helped her out of the water into my canoe. She was shivering with fear and kept saying, "I'm scared." I simply agreed, "Yes, you're scared." We said the same thing back and forth two to three times. Acknowledging her fear allowed her to step through it; as soon as she felt it fully, it went away. She jumped out of the canoe into the lake and swam back to the dock, where she plunged into the lake again. This time she came up laughing and continued playing for another hour.

Heed your feelings and body sensations. Each act of attention resembles a gift left at their doorstep. When we connect with our whole selves, by feeling our feelings and body sensations, we reconnect with our magnetism and power. But when we resist our feelings, they dig in, rooting themselves more deeply in our bodies. When we get present, we drop our resistance, and our feelings change, too—sometimes in a flash. Ask yourself these two key questions:

*Hendricks, Gay and Kathlyn Hendricks. The Hendricks Institute, Carpinteria, CA

FIGURE 3.5   Test Anxiety Reduction

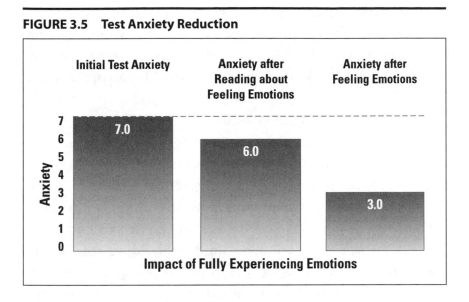

1. What specifically do I feel?

2. Where do I feel it in my body?

These questions help you focus when you feel overwhelmed by your emotions. They localize the feelings, making them seem less like King Kong and more like Curious George, and also bring us back into the present.

Most of us flee the present the way a deadbeat dodges a bill collector, because of perceived discomfort or pain. Ironically we gain the ability to make an unpleasant feeling disappear simply by staying present with it. We do have to pay up—in the form of a moment of distilled, authentic feeling—but the resulting energy and delight in life are worth it.

CUMULATIVE EMOTIONS

We're often unaware of the way our emotions accumulate during the day or how they play out in our jobs. If a colleague's missed deadline triggers some anger, but you choose not to acknowledge and communicate your frustration in the moment, that energy bubbles beneath the surface, unexpressed. That energy doesn't automatically dissipate but looks for an opportunity to be spent.

Later in the day, you may hear yourself yelling in expletives when you accidentally spill some coffee on your desk. The mishap became an outlet for your unexpressed anger over the missed deadline. You've spent your anger, but you haven't faced the real problem. Most likely you're not even aware of the connection. As you sop up the mess, you don't pause to ask yourself, "I wonder what's going on? What am I withholding or failing to face that has created this wobble in me? If I've made this mess to get my attention about something, what am I not seeing? Where am I out of integrity with myself?"

Checking inside and feeling our emotions restores our equanimity and balance. If your day began with a string of small irritations that generated a stress headache, the decisions you make from that point forward will feel poisoned by your state of mind until you find your set-point again. If you don't recover from your 8:00 AM meeting with an upset customer, and at 10:00 AM you have to lead a staff meeting, you may find yourself focused on expediency and relief at the expense of all else. The proverbial snowball is rolling down the hill, gaining momentum with each revolution.

Instead of masking, medicating, or even expressing the irritation, give it your full attention; feel it fully and let it go. Attention doesn't mean thinking about it. It means focusing your mind fully on your body sensations and then feeling the underlying emotion. Notice what you feel in your body. Itchiness or irritation under your skin? Tight shoulders or neck? Tense shoulders? First notice body sensations, then tune in to any emotions. Breathe and feel the full extent of the irritation. Describe it in detail to yourself. Don't worry about doing it "right." The fuller the detail, the more quickly the emotion will move on. "I feel a red tightness through my shoulder blades, moving up through my back and into my jaws, which seem to tingle with pulsing irritation." Breathe into the tight spots without judging them. Simply put your attention there. Notice when the feeling shifts. That's the essential action. And everyone at your 10:00 AM staff meeting will feel eternally grateful you learned to execute it.

MAPPING THE EMOTIONAL BODY

Our bodies are a great help in accurately perceiving our emotions—handy because we always have them with us. Chart an emotional map of your body to help you learn to recognize and learn your emotional body language. When you feel happy, for example, how does it register in your body? When you feel stressed, where do you feel it? When you feel fully engaged? Enraged? Some people literally draw a body map and write the physical sensations and locations of various emotions on the diagram.

I (Kate) usually feel fear in my gut, and I notice when I'm irritated about what's being said in a meeting my teeth start to ache because I've had my jaw clenched for so long. Sadness was the hardest for me to get in touch with. I experience it as a tight, sharp pain in my chest and as a lump in my throat, with slight itchiness in my moistening eyes, even though I rarely cry.

Although we all vary, people tend to feel major emotions in certain body zones, as shown in Figure 3.6.

In which parts of your body do you feel these emotions? If you have trouble registering certain emotions but recognize some of these symptoms, assume it's the emotion. You'll improve with practice. If this seems foreign to you, start with simple observations the next time you find yourself in a charged

FIGURE 3.6   Physical Manifestation of the Four Basic Emotions

Anger:	Tense shoulders and neck, clenched and tight jaw, sore teeth
Fear:	Fluttering in belly and chest, tension in face, tightness in legs
Sadness:	Tears, lump in throat, aching chest
Joy:	Bubbling or rushing sensation in chest and down arms, gooseflesh, watery eyes

situation. Make a report to yourself: "My hands feel cool. I feel a pain in my upper left shoulder. My forehead feels pressure." Even simple statements like these help us access our body's information more accurately, and our relaxed awareness eases the physical symptoms as well. More than one client has complained of an actual pain in the back—or somewhere else—then realized they also had a manager or employee who fit that description. With that realization came relief of the body pain as well as deeper understanding of the lifelong issues the coworker represented. It's as if, having gotten our attention, these sensations can quietly go about their business.

Janet was a successful senior manager for a Midwestern association management firm that had recently been acquired. As a result, Janet would be promoted and move to New York to oversee that office. She told me (Eddie), "I've noticed that during the past week or so I have been having more back pain again. Although in the past I usually chalked it off to a wrong move in my workout or gardening on the weekend, I understand the bodymind connection better now and think it's something else. It probably has to do with my move. It's happened two other times when I got a job transfer."

When I asked her if she had any other associations with it, she paused for a moment, took a breath, and said, "You know I think I might be angry that I feel afraid. I remember I felt this pain for the first time when I was about age 13. We were moving and I was about to start another school in a long succession of moves and new schools. Although I made the association with fear and anxiety, until this moment I never realized that I was actually angry and resentful, particularly toward my father for moving us from town to town. On several occasions I never even got to say goodbye to some of my friends. I really hated that."

More than 80 percent of people seek medical attention for back pain that has no definable cause from medical history and testing. Recent studies have demonstrated that acknowledging the presence of fear, and particularly anger, often makes back pain miraculously disappear.

If we don't pay attention, feelings escalate and the resulting body manifestations intensify, bound and determined to get us to notice. Realize this connection so you can use the body to access emotions that may be less perceptible to you. Use the chart in Figure 3.7 as a guide.

THE MAGNIFICATION PRINCIPLE

The magnification principal causes results as powerful as its name. Basically, once you tune into a troublesome body feeling, you make it as big as you can and experience it even more fully. The resulting shift and underlying insights often come quickly.

The management team of an East Coast food services company asked me (Kate) to facilitate a problem-solving process to address a business choice point. About an hour into the meeting I noticed I kept "absentmindedly" scratching my wrist and lower arm. I intensified the scratching, and magnified it, both in

FIGURE 3.7   Emotional Escalation and Body Awareness

The body knows! If you are experiencing any of these physical symptoms, you are experiencing the corresponding emotion in the 7 to 10 range.

When in doubt, trust your body, not your head, in assessing your emotional state.

Mild						Strong				Physical Manifestation:
1	2	3	4	5	6	7	8	9	10	

Emotion	Physical Manifestation:
Irritated → Frustrated → Angry	Tense shoulders and neck, jaw clenched
Worried → Anxious → Afraid	Fluttering in belly, tension in face
Disappointed → Sad → Sorrowful	Tears, lump in throat, aching chest
Content → Happy → Joyful	Bubbling feeling in chest, watery eyes

intensity and zone. (My hand was in my lap so this was invisible.) I realized the irritation of my skin reflected a deeper irritation that they had ignored my suggestions about keeping the discussion on course.

As I continued scratching, I swallowed very big and felt some sadness beneath the irritation. This reminded me of how I often felt at the family dinner table growing up; I could see a joyful, exciting way we could share in each other's lives, but somehow we seemed to talk around the real issues each of us was facing. I took a deep breath, experienced some sadness, then felt it pass. This awareness left me feeling much more present with the group.

When there was a pause in the conversation I said, "I noticed I was scratching my hand and when I tuned in I realized that I felt irritated that you had chosen three times not to follow my recommendation. I realize I'm feeling sad that I haven't been effective in getting us to focus on what I see as the real issue— your deeply entrenched commitment to pursue an idea you feel committed to, regardless of market data." Speaking this authentically got their attention in a new way, and the discussion shifted into focus almost immediately.

To experience how this process works, follow the directions in Figure 3.8.

The magnification principle can transform the art of managing and coaching employees by dredging up unconscious messages that repeat themselves until we break up the underlying pattern. One person, when angry, may idly stroke his moustache, while another may clench her fists. Magnification makes the pattern conscious and ends the repetition, allowing the person to discover the mother lode of underlying feelings and information and then make the important choice to speak up and take appropriate action.

FIGURE 3.8 A Magnification Experiment You Can Perform Right Now

- Think of an unpleasant feeling or thought you've been experiencing—a worry or fear or even a sense of hunger or fatigue. Feel it fully. Now magnify it.

- Make it as big as you can. Take it to an extreme. If it's a depressed feeling, make it even heavier and sadder. If it's nervousness, make it even more twitchy. Get up and act it out, if that helps.

- Notice what happens. It may go away or it may reveal some deeper truth.

THE ULTIMATE AWARENESS ACT

If you want to tap bodymind awareness in the most powerful way, love yourself and your feelings just the way they are. If you master this simple yet deep action, everything else becomes easier. Many of the ideas in this book are about unblocking the flow of energy, creativity, and great ideas. Self-criticism is one of the biggest blocks we experience, and self-love dissolves it. The more we can love ourselves, the bigger the channel for all the wonderful results that follow.

Think right now about which aspects of yourself you don't love. What's the single most difficult attribute to love about yourself? The more we stretch, the more powerful the results. If you don't feel creative, love that. If you can't reliably access your intuition, love that. If you're a natural klutz, love that.

Now put your attention on loving your body and your whole being—just as it is. Draw or imagine a stick picture of your body and circle the parts that seem least lovable. Shade in those places of your stick figure where you feel fear, anger, and sadness. Now pick other troublesome feelings: jealousy, anxiety, guilt, lust, greed—whatever's true for you. Put them on your map. Next, list your most troublesome thoughts around your head on the top of your map. You've now captured what's hard to love about yourself. Love them. And while you're at it, love your inner critic, too.

Say and feel the following for each item on your map: I commit to loving my _____.

Here are examples:

- I commit to loving my anger and frustration.

- I commit to loving my fear of speaking up at major meetings.

- I commit to loving my procrastination.

Feel love inside yourself. If you find this hard to do, think of someone you love or something you love to do, like hiking or holding your baby, then feel that feeling in your body. When we're feeling love, we're in direct contact with the wisdom of our bodymind. Your commitment and intention count as much as the feeling. Give each item on your body map your full attention, then go to the next one. Your bodymind will smile with gratitude and unleash its storehouse of energy and translate these inner changes into powerful outward results.

We realize many of the ideas in this chapter sound unbelievable. Try them in your next difficult work situation and watch what happens. The satisfaction and success we can experience in this new business era will feel equally unbelievable. Make the awareness move. Use your bodymind. Your sphere of influence will expand in proportion to your willingness and commitment.

SUMMARY

- Awareness invites us to slow down to pause, moment by moment, to tune into our whole being, including our mind, body, intuition, and feelings.

- Thinking, explaining, justifying, blaming, and complaining act like an addiction, cutting us off from our bodymind.

- Many of us have a biting inner critic that causes us to mistrust our own internal knowing and intuitive insight.

- To quickly access bodymind intelligence, pay full attention to your feelings.

- Our emotions act as keys to the treasure chest of bodymind wisdom. Emotions change very quickly—in seconds—and if you pause for a moment to feel them, they will likely shift into another feeling or an old memory will pop up to be healed.

- To process an uncomfortable situation, make it bigger. Magnify it.

- Moving the body unleashes its wisdom and clears emotions or distracting thoughts.

- If you want to tap bodymind awareness in the most powerful way, love yourself and your feelings just the way they are.

TAKE ACTION

- Recall a time when you used your whole being, both brain and bodymind, to make a decision. How did this differ from business as usual for you?

- Which of the following bodymind barriers do you use most often: explaining, being logical, rationalizing, complaining, blaming, controlling, justifying.

- How do you use thinking and doing as a way to escape feeling or the present situation?

- What can you do to soften the voice of your own inner critic? How can you encourage others to reduce the impact of the inner critic throughout your company? Can your company help tone down everyone's inner critic?

- Before your next team meeting, how can you best discharge any cumulative stress-related emotions so you can be fully present?

- Have you ignored a bodymind message about an employee? Describe the results. How could you have acted differently?

- How can you better model thinking with your whole being? What one action can you take that will help develop this ability even more, both in you and your team?

- How can you play a role in increasing the level of bodymind awareness with people you work with? How can you use your bodymind awareness to enhance resiliency when normal downturns and disappointments occur?

- Select one issue that's troubling you, bring your awareness to your body, take a few centered breaths, and apply the magnification principle. Make it larger and larger. Exaggerate it in any way you can and notice what happens.

- Draw a body map and indicate the feelings, thoughts, and body parts you find hardest to love. Then take time to love each one.

CHAPTER FOUR

AUTHENTICITY
Dropping the Roles That Bind Us

How can I become more real at work and still be successful?

How can I unlock the grip of outdated leadership habits?

How do I avoid getting hooked by the roles others play?

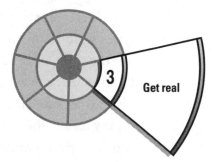

If you'll get real, you'll possess the power to dramatically reduce stress and upset at work and at home. Become authentic, and you'll joyfully thrive at whatever you do, regardless of the challenges that come your way. *In the simplest sense, this chapter is about how* not *to have your buttons pushed.*

Authenticity creates connected, productive relationships, and today business runs on relationships—with others, with your work, and with yourself. To spend more time in this land where our outsides match our insides, we must first understand the phenomenon of *personas*—"predictable patterns of mostly unconscious behaviors triggered by a few basic instincts common to all of us." Next, we need to recognize the most prevalent undesirable chain reactions our personas invariably set in motion. We call it "getting lost in The Bermuda Triangle." We'll then be better prepared to see and shift into a place of wonder—the ultimate environment for the "high-fiving" brand of teamwork that leads to radical results.

As you read this chapter, you may feel as if you're suddenly waking up in the middle of a play, where actors have played their parts for so long, their characters have lost their spark. You'll become increasingly aware of the actions we take that keep us in endless dramatic loops that ultimately become as boring and as predictable as an afternoon soap opera.

We don't know our selves very well. These "selves" go to work every day with great expectations, performance pressures, and private opinions about the shortcomings of all our coworkers. We talk about the troublemakers as if we do know them well—when what we really know, if we're a little bit honest, is how they push our buttons—and that we wish they'd just stop it. Right?

THE POWER OF ONE

A workplace that's uptight, depleted, and toxic with perpetually defended people can't make radical changes. Think about the difference between attending a high-impact meeting where teamwork really "rocks" and everyone is focused on coming up with the best solution, versus a meeting in which a few people have to prove their ideas are best by competing with and even bullying others. We all know that meeting: The Drivers get aggressive, the Complainers go into a silent sulk, the Pleasers start making nice, and productive conversation comes to a grinding halt.

Most stress and upset in every company result from the ways we get stuck in dramas and inauthentic patterns of behavior. You may feel powerless to do anything about another's behaviors and feel that working on your own behavior won't make a significant difference. We disagree. We can learn to make liberating shifts in perspective and behavior that change the work environment and empower everyone—ourselves first and foremost. One person's commitment and skills for authentic behavior can have the same effect as opening a window in a stuffy room. The fresh air wakes everyone up, and people begin to engage at a conscious level. The most stuck person at the table *can* make the shift, the energy *can* lighten, and the best decisions *can* emerge with far less brow knitting, name calling, and hand-wringing. We've seen it happen hundreds of times.

HOW RANT AND RAVE SAVED THE DAY

One of our all-time favorite moments of authenticity occurred a few years ago when an executive team at a Fortune 500 pharmaceutical company, who were familiar with leadership styles, were debating about a new acquisition. As the intensity of the discussion escalated, the team polarized. The CEO and the COO were pushing hard for the acquisition, while the more conservative members held back. The room crackled with tension. Suddenly the chief financial officer (CFO), a very large man known to be gruff and tough, commanded the room by waving his arms the way Texas Tech Coach Bobby Knight avoids a penalty with 30 seconds on the clock. He bellowed, "Mr. Rant and Rave is about to show up, and I can't stop him!"

Bursts of belly laughter instantly broke the tension. By naming his dreaded back-up style, he masterfully stepped beyond it and created a platform to review the facts with a cool head. His authenticity in that moment resulted in a persuasive argument against the acquisition. Even the CEO made a shift, dropping his Wheeler Dealer style. The COO conceded his original position and the acquisition plans were halted.

Needless to say, had the unconscious version of Mr. Rant and Rave appeared, no one would have laughed. Folks would have either gotten hooked and escalated the uproar, tuned him out, or disappeared. The meeting objectives would have dangled at the edge of the cliff. Instead, his pronouncement helped others let go of their defenses.

Authenticity—congruence between your inner state of being and your outer behaviors and actions—makes you a high-integrity player, speaking the same things to others that you say inside your head. Many of us believe we can't be this authentic at work, but every ounce of energy you spend in not being real is like a raft dragging a dead tree down the river. A lack of authenticity creates a psychic drag (i.e., sludge) on your company and on yourself, and that drag becomes more harmful as business accelerates.

Consider someone you'd describe as authentic. What are the qualities that come to mind? In our experience, they're honest, they take 100% responsibility for their choices and actions, they seem eager to learn and grow, they can laugh at themselves, they glow with self-assurance, they aren't afraid of mistakes, and they extend trust easily and wisely (as opposed to blindly). These are the folks you want on your team when difficult, exciting, and high-risk assignments come your way. Why, then, is living and working from a place of deep authenticity as rare as valet parking on the job?

HITTING THE FAMILY BULL'S-EYE

Our grumbles and complaints and the dramas they generate at the office are remnants of the family and school dynamics with which we grew up. In some cases, they are full-blown replicas of dysfunction, trauma, wounds, or our unique cultural inheritances.

More than 80 percent of the problems we (the authors) see at work occur because at some deep level people have unconsciously glued a family member's image on a coworker's face, making them a human dart board. Think a moment about someone you find it difficult to work with. Don't think about who that person physically resembles, because this isn't where the familiar pattern exists. Think instead about what's common to the way you relate to this person and the way you related to your parents or siblings. That's the bull's-eye.

Sometimes specific vivid childhood experiences shape personas. I (Kate) grew up in rural Texas where rattlesnakes were an ever-present reality. At the age of four, I saved my younger brother from being bitten. A few years later, I was thrown from a horse that was spooked by a rattler. From these two experiences, I concluded that the real dangers in life are ones you can't see, so I must become very vigilant. As a result, my intuition is uncannily reliable—a great benefit. On the flip side, I tend to be watchful for the "shadow" or problem around the corner. I don't expect or trust that life will work out well without my constant control and vigilance.

I could remain stuck in some version of a Control Freak or Chicken Little persona and spend inordinate amounts of time and energy worrying and trying to compensate for the possibility that something awful could happen at any moment. The solution is to look for a way to upgrade and expand my belief about my need for vigilance, such as: *I trust that life unfolds for the best. I rely on my inner wisdom to alert me to true danger and I learn from every problem.* I now believe that if I learn from small problems, the truly big ones occur less often. I've also realized that a welcome attitude about learning can't coexist with vigilance and a misplaced attempt to control events that in reality are beyond my control.

As in the rattlesnake example, identify some early experiences that may have shaped some of the behaviors that make you assume that's "just the way I am." Unless you are already skilled at this kind of reflection, don't necessarily expect spontaneous revelations. Do this sort of archeological dig through your memories patiently, methodically, and with a great deal of compassion. You'll know when you've unearthed something important. You may feel a physical signal like a rush of energy in your head or gut. Or you may find yourself lost in a reverie of long-forgotten memories that play out like a movie. We're all put together slightly differently in this regard, and we all have unmistakable signals.

I (Kate) recall frustrating struggles in the early 1980s with an administrative assistant I shared with my manager. She seemed to always have the time to do his work perfectly but never time to even start my work. And she was downright rude to me. We met over lunch one day to see if we could create a better working relationship. When I asked her if there was anything familiar about how she related to me, she blurted out, amazed, "I talk to you in the same disrespectful tone I use with my mother!" Suddenly our relationship changed, and from that day on Patty and I worked very well together. I graduated from being her mother to "Kate, her manager."

FOOD FOR THOUGHT

Family dynamics during childhood set the stage for personas that may not serve us in adulthood. One child may take on the role of Know-It-All if debating tensions ran high at her family table. Years later around a conference table she may find Know-It-All creates a completely different and unsatisfying set of results. Another child becomes a Peacemaker as a coping response to constant family fighting and bickering. Later in life, that same Peacemaker may undermine his own credibility with colleagues who disrespect his fairly transparent fear of rocking the boat and avoiding conflict.

During childhood, life reinforced our personas with varying degrees of applause, and this occasional adulation keeps them in place. Perhaps the sarcastic quip you learned to launch at your brother or sister is the source of a defended edge toward your colleagues when things get tense. You might have learned to work harder in an attempt to avoid criticism at home. Now at the office you frequently become the stoic Perfectionist working hard to "get it right" or the angst-ridden Procrastinator, delaying that expected criticism, because you never learned to "get it right."

Personas help us avoid pain and get recognition, and we develop several different ones to meet our various needs with various people. A child may use Accident Prone with Grandma, while Rebel works with teachers. These are mostly benign acts, but they do cover our essence and limit our full expression. *And as long as we cling to our personas, the same problems keep showing up again and again.*

EXPANDING BEYOND LIMITING PERSONAS

The first step toward authenticity is to look inside and all around you with plenty of compassion. No one emerges from childhood free of personas. By the time we enter the workforce, we have developed layer upon layer of subsets of our personalities that become who we really think we are. Stepping into a persona is something we do on autopilot. Our personas developed from our beliefs are a lot like software. They can "run us" automatically and inefficiently, if we're using old versions. They're the face we show the world, user interface software—the way things look on your computer, like the friendly look of *America Online* with all its little icons or the colorful customizable *Yahoo!* home pages. If we want to handle change more easily and deftly, we must delete our old programs and make frequent upgrades to new ones so we can adapt as quickly as our businesses to this changing world.

The childhood process of creating personas happens in a largely unconscious way. The more unconscious the persona, the earlier it probably was formed, and the more likely we'll tie our identity to it, leading us to the inevitable conclusion of "That's just the way I am." We often have to do some digging and exploring to reveal and discard the personas that block our authenticity.

You become more authentic when you realize you have the power to change and make conscious choices. *If you notice you're blaming, controlling, or seeking approval, you're probably operating in a persona.* Step into authenticity. Take a breath. Ask yourself what you're afraid of. It requires courage to break lifelong patterns. The power and self-nurturing available each time we rediscover our authentic selves make it all worth it. Here are some real-life examples of people who've done just that.

A Power Shift from Cheerleader to Ms. Harry Truman

Bob Shapiro, CEO of Monsanto, confided to me (Kate) that he planned to promote Donna Kindl to one of the top ten executive positions in the company, but he had one major concern. "Donna is just so 'rah, rah, go-team-go,'" he told me. "I like her spirit, and I know she can drive the culture change I'm looking for. But this same spirit obscures her intelligence, and I believe others are going to discount her because of it." As Donna and I began working together, she realized she'd developed one of her major success strategies in junior high school when she first made the cheerleading squad. She sustained her popularity in high school, becoming the Head Cheerleader and Homecoming Queen, continually reinforced and recognized for her personality rather than her smarts.

Bob was on target with the symptom. Now that Donna had identified the source, she was free to invite the power shift into a new persona. She literally took her cheerleading outfit down from her closet shelf and, with appropriate ritual and gratitude, packed it away in a beautiful box for storage. She acknowledged that this persona had been of enormous value to her throughout her life and that she was also ready to shift that persona into something with more meaning and impact.

Out of her admiration for Harry Truman, she invented Ms. Harry Truman and a new, the-buck-stops-here identity of influence and leadership. She went on to become enormously successful as a SVP, played a major role with the board of directors, and fielded continual requests to give keynote speeches to Fortune 100 companies across the country.

From Resource Broker to Wise Woman Executive

Linda Furiga is the CFO of the Defense Logistics Agency. The agency is the size of a Fortune 500 company and oversees a wide array of distribution and logistics businesses. She worked her way up through the ranks and managed to find the time to get a Ph.D. in Adult Education. She never imagined she'd reach this level of success, but whenever an opportunity presented itself, she would apply and compete for it. Because of her quiet demeanor, people often didn't hear what she said, and that sometimes meant more forceful executives got credit for her ideas. I (Eddie) helped her identify two personas at work. One she called The Truth Broker and the other was Peacemaker. As a child, Linda often stepped in to defend children in the neighborhood whose families were at a lower socioeconomic level and had fewer privileges than other kids. She also acted as a go-between messenger between her two parents, a role with little reward or appreciation.

She could see that these two roles had come to play in her work as comptroller in a large organization dealing with literally hundreds of millions of dollars in revenue and budget. It was her job to be sure that everyone got the information they needed so that nobody took advantage of anybody else. She also recognized that she felt resentment toward those who tried to take advantage of the system and subtly sought ways to control and undermine others.

We videoed her giving a presentation as the Truth Broker and the Peacemaker so she could see the full impact of these personas and how they subtly stifled her energy and impact. Then she created a new, healthier persona, Dr. Straight Talk, to allow her to step fully into her own authentic identity as a highly competent, seasoned, and wise executive who communicates directly and forcefully. When she gave the presentation in that persona, the difference was dramatic: Her volume went up, she spoke forcefully throughout, and she maintained a powerful presence.

She brought these skills into a very major presentation to a high-level government official two weeks later. The immediate and subsequent feedback was that this presentation was highly effective, inspiring, and clearly the best she'd ever delivered. She later heard that she touched people in a new way, as she became the inspiring leader people want to follow.

PERSONAS AS PROJECTORS

Our insides determine how we view the outside and ultimately how we portray ourselves. *We both see and are seen by the world through our personas that act as distorted lenses and color the world according to our needs.* A Driver persona sees the world as needing supervision and discipline. A Rebel sees the world as full of people to be acted against. A Jock sees people either as winners or losers. Our projections intertwine with and complement the projections of others, so authentic connection and communication become nearly impossible. *Our projections actually* demand *that other people push our buttons.*

The technical genius with a Little Professor persona hires the one person—a shoot-from-the-hip marketing guru—who pushes his buttons down the line. Why? Because ultimately what our authentic selves want is to call up these lifelong issues for healing. The more the Shooter tries to get the Little Professor to stop his endless conceptualizing and come to a decision, the more irritated they'll feel and the greater their personas will manifest. The Shooter fears that in the time it takes to analyze the market in such detail, it will pass them by. The Little Professor fears the same result if they jump in without enough research.

Both of them may have built these personas as a result of a critical or demanding parent. Each has an unconscious requirement that the other activate his survival instincts. The Shooter learned that quick decisions and moving fast kept him out of trouble growing up. He is action waiting to happen. Little Professor got attention from being the idea guy, whether at a frat party or on the job. He's learned that he's seen as valuable as long as he comes up with great ideas, but it's risky when people start acting on his ideas because then problems become apparent, he's suddenly not seen as quite so smart, and he even gets criticized. *These persona-crossed partners have a choice: engage in a power struggle or learn.*

A conscious person might think, "Out of my fear of making a mistake and choosing the wrong idea, I have chosen a business partner who's intensely focused on execution and action. What a terrific opportunity to challenge my persona and discover the real me." Most of us are more likely to say something like, "Marketing people are all alike. They just want to make the sale and don't really care about the whole truth. This isn't going to work." But, as our friend Gay Hendricks is fond of saying, "There's no cheese down that rat hole." Hang in there. Excavate. See beyond the projection.

An attorney named Greg believed that most people lie. He found it hard to imagine this was his persona's view of the world, but he was willing to check it out (perhaps to determine if the person who shared this idea about him was a liar). Almost instantly Greg remembered a time when his father had lied to him. He even realized he became an attorney because he wanted to prosecute liars. In fact, he assumed most people were liars until they were proven innocent. His courage in looking deeper and feeling those original feelings of hurt and pain helped him unhook from the persona and enjoy a world in which most people actually tell the truth.

The unconsciousness of these persona views makes them hard to change. They seem very real—another reason to let go of being right. You must assume that any strong reactions you have to others are persona projections. *When we don't like or understand something, we tend to resist seeing it in ourselves, and we project it on others, converting it, in the process, into a powerful, compelling irritant.* When we project, we don't see the big wart at the end of our own nose, and that makes us far more likely to criticize someone else's freckles.

The fastest way to identify your projections is to look at your complaints. We both certainly had a hard time accepting this truth at first, but over time we learned to apply the Rule of Three: If you find yourself complaining about the same issue three times, it looks, sounds, and smells like a projection.

Consider projection the ultimate "out there" delusion. One executive tells of her frustration with staff that didn't seem loyal. They left for other opportunities and disagreed with her decisions but only shared their objections after they left. One even lied about his whereabouts on a personal day off. More than a year later, the executive herself told a consultant her heart hadn't been in her job for some time! When she made a career change herself—when she acted in a way authentic to herself and her needs—she no longer encountered disloyal staff.

Tools you can use to become more conscious about projections are found in Figure 4.1.

There's almost always some reality to a projection, but the personas projecting on one another tend to feel their view of the other is 100 percent right and accurate. And few things in life come in black and white.

PEELING THE PERSONA ONION

Over years of working with our clients in workshops, team-building programs, and one-to-one coaching sessions, we've met scores of inventive, comical, and powerful personas. See if you recognize any old friends in the chart in Figure 4.2, particularly "familiar friends," who cause problems for you at certain times.

PERSONA WATCHING 101

The companies we work with are full of Control Freaks, Bulldozers, Worry Warts, and other popular personas. The noble intention many of these personas share is that they want to make sure nothing goes wrong in getting the job done. But in persona mode, creative problem solving, levity, and team-work don't stand much of a chance. The atmosphere is too thick with conflict or a kind of indefinable muckiness. Personas deplete joy by adding layers of tension, delays, hurt feelings, mistakes, and extra work. They obscure exciting, real-world creative challenges by generating ungratifying, unnecessary, and difficult human drama.

FIGURE 4.1   Clearing Up Projections

To become more conscious about persona projections, learn to connect them to the actions they produce. Complete the following sentences and notice what emerges.

If I am feeling _____, I'll see my manager as _____.

Examples: If I'm feeling inadequate, I'll see my manager as making me wrong.

If I'm feeling scared, I'll see my manager as hostile.

If I act _____, my manager looks _____.

Examples: If I act like a victim, my manager looks like my oppressor.

If I act like a loner, my manager looks intrusive.

If I act super-competent and need to be right, my manager looks incompetent.

If I am _____, my manager looks _____.

Examples: If I'm a rebel, my manager looks like a policewoman.

If I'm highly independent, my manager looks over-controlling.

If _____ really looks likes it's my manager's fault, I must be seeing _____.

Examples: If this failed project really looks like my manager's fault, I must be seeing this project as only his responsibility.

If this conflict really looks like my manager's fault, I must be seeing that I'm right and he's wrong.

You may decide to complete some of these statements more than once as you uncover additional projections. Once you have finished filling these in for your manager, complete them again for coworkers, vendors, and anyone else on whom you regularly project.

FIGURE 4.2   Indentifying Your Personas

Here are some common personas. Check off any that sound familiar.

☐ Accommodator	☐ Harried Harry/Harriet
☐ Action Jackson	☐ Have No Opinion
☐ Armed and Dangerous	☐ Head Honcho
☐ Blamer	☐ Hermit
☐ Boss	☐ Hip Shooter
☐ Bulldog	☐ Hunker Down
☐ Bulldozer	☐ I'll Do It My Way
☐ Chameleon	☐ I'm Outta Here
☐ Chess Master	☐ Jack Hammer
☐ Complainer	☐ Joker
☐ Conflict Avoider	☐ Juggler
☐ Contrarian	☐ Just Do It
☐ Control Freak	☐ Know-It-All
☐ Cowboy	☐ Land Mine
☐ Crab	☐ Last Minute-itis
☐ Credit Seeker	☐ Late Late White Rabbit
☐ Critic	☐ Little Professor
☐ Cynic	☐ Little Red Hen
☐ Do-It-All	☐ Lone Ranger
☐ Drama Queen/King	☐ Martyr
☐ Dr. Efficiency	☐ Me Too
☐ Dreamer	☐ Micro Manager
☐ Drill Down	☐ Milk Toast
☐ Eager Beaver	☐ Misunderstood Genius
☐ Energizer Bunny	☐ Mole
☐ Glory Seeker	☐ Name Dropper
☐ Goodie Two Shoes	☐ Observer
☐ Grudge Holder	☐ Overwhelmed
☐ Hammer	☐ Peacemaker

☐ Perfectionist

☐ Politician

☐ Pollyanna Good News

☐ Poor Me

☐ Procrastinator

☐ Prophet of Doom

☐ Quiet One

☐ Rant and Rave

☐ Rebel

☐ Resistor

☐ Rescuer

☐ Resigned to Whatever

☐ Responsibility Avoider

☐ Savior

☐ Scorekeeper

☐ Screamer

☐ Shredder

☐ Sly Cat

☐ Smart Ass

☐ Space Case

☐ Stressed Out

☐ Stealth Bomber

☐ Suicide Bomber

☐ Trickster

☐ Tyrant

☐ Uninvited Fixer

☐ Wait and Pounce

☐ Warrior

☐ Watch Dog

☐ Wire Brush

☐ Wheeler Dealer

☐ Worrier

Getting Conscious about Your Personas

Circle your three personas in the previous chart that are most troublesome at work and answer the following questions:

- What do you do when you're operating from each of these personas?

- How do these troublesome personas get activated?

- How would you describe people or situations where you "get hooked" and move into a troublesome persona?

- Can you identify the positive underlying intention of each persona?

- Can you find a better way to achieve that intention?

How can you tell when you are in a persona? See Figure 4.3.

To help you begin to see some of your personas and those of your coworkers, what follows are some of the most popular personas, along with short descriptions of how they operate in the workplace. Keep in mind that the goal is not necessarily to get rid of personas, nor to judge them as good or bad. Your target is to halt the automatic behavior, to escape their grip, to deploy them consciously, to be free to choose, and to quite literally play with them.

The ultimate usefulness of persona watching is to learn to recognize them when they show up and to easily and lightly shift into more productive and successful behavior. Their appearance is a major clue

---

FIGURE 4.3   Knowing When You're in a Persona

To find out if you're in a persona, ask yourself the following questions:

- Do I feel angry, fearful, sad? Suspicious? Anxious?

- Is my body tense?

- Has this happened to me before? Does this feel familiar?

- Do I feel overwhelmed by what's going on?

- Do I need to have things turn out my way?

When you're caught in a persona, you might notice things like the following:

- You feel impatient.

- You hang on to grudges and slights.

- You formulate and rehearse your opinions rather than listen.

- You take care of people without really caring for them.

that someone (could it possibly be you?) is stuck in a point of view that's blocking bigger, more creative alternatives.

Let's begin in Figure 4.4 with a persona nearly all of us will recognize in ourselves from time to time.

The Control Freak, like so many personas, is someone who's trying to get the most optimal outcome but doesn't know how to create accountability. Interestingly, Control Freaks usually swing between overempowering and overdelegating. When someone inevitably doesn't come through, they use this to justify their controlling behavior. Because many Control Freaks communicate poorly about what they really want, they end up disappointed with the results. And poor results only further reinforce their need to manage every detail. Control Freaks sometimes lose sight of the distinction between telling people what to do, which is their job, and telling them how to do it, which should be the decision of the people doing the work, following the agreed-upon processes. The remedy is a filtering system or a

---

FIGURE 4.4   Control Freak

Noble Intention:	To get it done right. The devil is in the details!
Observable Behavior:	Micromanaging with checklists, showing an obvious lack of trust in a direct report's abilities.
Risk:	Work backs up waiting for approval; bigger-picture, high-priority work doesn't get done as all the details are meticulously handled.
Power Shift:	**Accountability Coach** Create ownership and commitment that allows others to deliver superb results.

logical way of sorting people so you know whom to trust with which kinds of tasks and assignments.

This next persona, in Figure 4.5, also helps keep things stirred up.

Picture the Tasmanian devil, and you've tuned into Action Jackson, whose noble intention is to instigate results ASAP. The difficulty is that Action Jackson doesn't realize that quality and an enduring, unique approach may be sacrificed for speed. Action Jackson acts before he thinks. His sometimes-compulsive need for quick closure stimulates lots of activity and often creates a cycle of temporary, incomplete, wrong, or unsatisfying moves. Learning the discipline of a few deep breaths is the first skill in this power shift. Placing a higher value on the *best* way instead of the *fastest* way also avoids this persona.

Next, in Figure 4.6, comes someone who also wants results, but takes a far different approach.

FIGURE 4.5   Action Jackson

Noble Intention:	To get a lot done quickly.
Observable Behavior:	A sense of urgency; chooses speed over reflection.
Risk:	The urgency to make a decision and to stimulate action results in poorer decisions that later have to be revised or remade, costing more time.
Power Shift:	**Our True R2 Leader** Maintain a balance between **R**eflection and **R**esults. Allow things to settle a bit for the best solution to float up, instead of using action to mask anxiety about ambiguity.

FIGURE 4.6   Bulldozer

Noble Intention:	To make things happen.
Observable Behavior:	Pushes people hard and sometimes runs over them to get things done.
Risk:	People feel too afraid to be frank about their opinions, leading to second-rate decisions and venting behind the Bulldozer's back.
Power Shift:	**Inspiring Leader** Align people around a common direction and inspire prompt action rather than mandate it.

Bulldozers want the right thing done quickly, and they plow over people to make it happen. Their insensitivity results in enormous damage and hurt. People withhold creative ideas because it's "just not worth it" to take the Bulldozer on. Bulldozers generate a number of personas who are Victims, and who complain and vent about being bulldozed. Rarely do they actually save time with their tactics, but they do provide soap opera dramas for the rumor mill. The power shift comes by respectfully listening to others' ideas, even when they aren't right or best. Listening doesn't require agreement, but it does provide the opportunity to create alignment. In contrast, intimidation on the front end generates compliance and accommodation rather than full-out energetic support.

Intimidation also invites the persona seen in Figure 4.7.

Complainers are astute problem-spotters who lack self-confidence. Without the courage to address problems directly with the people involved, they rarely confront those in authority and take a real stand for their own position or ideas. While

FIGURE 4.7   The Complainer

Noble Intention:	To identify and point out problems not being addressed.
Observable Behavior:	Talking about decisions they don't agree with and problems that aren't being resolved.
Risk:	Conversations when the people who could make a difference aren't around devolve into venting and gossip that drain energy without identifying solutions.
Power Shift:	**Wise Influencer** Inspire action by sharing useful solutions.

their perceptions and concerns are often directionally correct, they're reluctant to address the issues with the people who could resolve them.

Complaining is a very close cousin to gossiping because usually there is someone else involved—either mentioned by name or by implication, and that someone is almost never in the room. The power shift begins the moment you realize you're complaining. It continues when you explore solutions and take action rather than simply vent. If you'll beef up your skills for providing clearer input at the front end, you'll avoid detailed input about what's wrong on the back end.

Another persona who can use some better up-front skills is found in Figure 4.8.

Worry Warts live in the future, where they attempt to anticipate all the things that can go wrong. They can also infect morale with their worrying, which sounds a lot like complaining. Unlike Complainers, who are focused mostly on the past, Worry Warts target the future. Like the proverbial deer in the

FIGURE 4.8   Worry Wart

Noble Intention:	To avoid or mitigate problems by anticipating them.
Observable Behavior:	Worrying out loud, often about problems they have little or no control over.
Risk:	Problems get worried about but not fixed, resulting in wasted time and energy.
Power Shift:	**The Troubleshooter** Shift from worrying about problems you can't control to taking action on the areas you can control or influence.

headlights, Worry Warts can't see solutions because they're immobilized by fear. The power shift: Commit to making a difference by looking for real-time solutions. They'll then worry less, sleep better, solve more problems, and enjoy greater influence.

The persona in Figure 4.9 points out problems but omits an important ingredient, a solution.

Critics are masterful at pointing out what's not working or the shortcomings of an idea. Sure, every project needs skillful trouble-shooting, but the Critic threatens enthusiasm, morale, trust, and even the self-esteem of others with his sharpshooting. It doesn't take long before brainstorming and creative initiatives become uninspired, measured, or withheld.

The power shift happens if the Critic will become proactive about providing input, focusing on solutions instead of problems, and facilitating other people's creative process. The Critic often reacts to problems too late in the process. Instead, the Critic should anticipate them, ask questions that stimulate others to come up with creative solutions, and provide clear and useful input up front.

FIGURE 4.9   Critic

Noble Intention:	To make things the best they can be.
Observable Behavior:	Pointing out problems without offering solutions.
Risk:	Sharp comments alienate others, dampen their enthusiasm, and damage their self-esteem.
Power Shift:	**Idea Coach** Invite creative reflection and problem-solving.

Fewer Critics will evoke fewer of the next persona found in Figure 4.10.

The Accommodator, a pleasant, peaceful soul, wants to create harmony and efficiency and still have the best ideas persist. They often show up in meetings where the agenda has been packed too full. Rather than participate in a lively and compelling discussion, Accommodators appear to agree, assuming this is helping to move both the project and the meeting forward. Afterwards, they complain in the hallways, drumming up some truly negative energy around the project. The original decision is often remade. In the interim, a valuable month has been lost to untold hours of distracting hand-wringing and divisive strategizing. In the first meeting, if the Accommodator were to persist a little longer, be more convincing, or more prepared with some advance work, something much better could have happened.

People who accommodate typically have a single tool they use to influence the flow of meeting conversation. They speak up once, if at all, and then withdraw. The shift comes by beefing up your ability to articulate and inspire a group by the logic and use-

FIGURE 4.10   The Accommodator

Noble Intention:	To avoid being criticized, to avoid irritating person in charge, to create a harmonious way to work.
Observable Behavior:	Flat energy, compliance, passivity, falsely agreeable.
Risk:	Initiates hallway gossip, which results in lost time and escalating negative energy.
Power Shift:	**Captain Courageous** Stop pleasing people and commit to making a difference in the moment by tactfully taking a courageous stand.

fulness of your own ideas and learning to handle defensive responses to your ideas. You'll then move from a place of depleted power and influence to one of energizing flow and rewarding participation. Don't just make nice. Make things happen.

THE PERSONA INTERVIEW

Use the interview process anytime you, or a coworker, catch you venting, complaining, or feeling stuck. *Learn to catch yourself the moment you start to feel a familiar murky, mucky, flattening of energy you can't quite name.*

Every time you can only see two options—the one you're strongly attached to and the other one that looks like a bad mistake from your point of view—you are in a persona. For instance, let's imagine someone points out that you're overreacting and you respond with, "Well, what do you want me to do? Let this project go down the drain, and the company right along with it?" Your extreme response is a dead giveaway to you and to anyone listening that you've been hooked by one of your personas.

The Persona Interview will practically guarantee a break-through, and the more fun you have with it, the more truth will bubble to the surface. Walk through the questions found in Figure 4.11 with a coworker or alone. Because being in a persona means being stuck in a particular point of view, we find it extremely helpful to do the moves physically. Get out of your chair. Step into the persona as if your Oscar depends on it, and then conduct the interview.*

Select a situation or a behavior that's causing problems at work that you want to change. Pick something that will really make a difference. Then follow the steps in Figure 4.11 and apply them to your problem, so you're working with a real issue as you read. For best results, ask these questions in the order listed and remember to have fun!

Naming the new persona can sometimes feel like a challenge. You can use a symbol or object to represent the new persona or perhaps take on a new posture or tone of voice—anything that will make this new aspect more real for you. *You'll know you sincerely want to change because you will.* If the process seems to reinforce your stuckness, take this as a sign you're so attached to your point of view and to being stuck that even this focused attention isn't budging you. Accept that the problem lives in you, and resist the temptation to make the situation the source of your discomfort. Continue to ask yourself, "What is my unconscious intention? What significant learning am I resisting?"

------

*The interview process resulted from extensive field-testing by Kathlyn Hendricks, Ph.D., who developed the tool and later taught me to apply it in corporate settings.

FIGURE 4.11   Persona Interview Questions

Step 1   Name

What's the name of this persona?

Step 2   Character

When you're ready, please step fully into this persona, as if you're putting on a suit of clothes. Act out the persona. Ham it up. Be dramatic. Assume all the body postures and mannerisms this persona takes on. Use props if you wish.

Step 3   Interview

1. *(Persona Name)*, When did this persona first make an appearance in your life?

   (If the answer is "at work," think of a related persona you had in childhood, one that this work persona grew from.)

2. *(Persona Name)*, From whom did you learn this persona?

   (In particular, think about people who played central roles and had a great influence in your early life.)

3. *(Persona Name)*, What are you most proud of?

   (Answer from the perspective of this persona.)

4. *(Persona Name)*, What are you most anxious about?

5. *(Persona Name)*, What do you do today that feeds this fear? Which of your behaviors or choices trigger this fear?

6. *(Persona Name)*, How do you create difficulties at work?

7. *(Persona Name)*, What do you most want today?

   (Ask this question three times; each time, answer from the perspective of this persona.)

8. *(Persona Name)*, Are you willing to find new ways to honor the success or value this persona brought you in the past?

   (If your answer is "yes," take a step or two away from where you were standing when you answered and create a new space to stand in. If your answer is "no," either you aren't committed to change, or it's not really a problem. Reexamine the intention to change, or cycle back and summarize how the persona is creating a problem, and explore your willingness to modify the persona.)

9. *(Persona Name)*, From this new place of expanded awareness and confidence, what do you want to create? What actions are you willing to take in the next month or two to create this new you? What name will you give this new, happier, krypton-powered persona?

THE BERMUDA TRIANGLE

Personas resemble individual software applications, like MS Word, while The Bermuda Triangle is like Office Pro, involving several different personas that interact with one another. A real pro, however, learns how to step out of scenarios like this one: Jim pushes too hard on Donna. Donna feels powerless; and Bob, seeing Donna's situation, steps in to "help," reinforcing Jim as the Villain, Donna as the Victim, and Bob as the Hero. They can shift roles easily, where Bob suddenly feels victimized by always having to rescue Donna, or Jim feels like Bob is persecuting him by interrupting what he was attempting to accomplish with Donna, perhaps hoping to heroically rescue her from a lower-level position by pushing to develop her skills.

When life gets complicated, we want to understand the interpersonal dynamics in order to find a solution, so we oversimplify by placing blame. While we are all stuck in the blame game, glued to the drama with self-righteous anger, it feels very real to each of us. Meanwhile, valuable time passes. Emotions flare. Others get involved. Clear heads do not prevail. But as soon as one person shifts his or her behavior, so does the entire reality. The Triangle formed by the interaction of three roles is just as real as the single-headed personas we have already discussed. You can learn to alter your behavior and change the reality by locating yourself in Figure 4.12.

We seldom step into The Bermuda Triangle alone. When one person digs in her heels, others follow suit. As a combo Bulldozer-Martyr (Villain) remarks, "I can't believe you blew the deadline. Do I have to be responsible for every little thing around here?" The Excuse Maker (Victim) responds with, "What did you want me to do, send out the sales report full of holes and errors? You just don't understand. It isn't my fault everyone was late turning in their figures. And besides that, the server was down for five hours today. Is that my fault, too?" The Fixer (Hero) tries to soothe the ruffled feathers with, "Hey guys, the deadline isn't actually blown. I'll work late tonight. I don't really mind. I don't have to see my son play ball this evening. He'll understand. Give me what you've got, and I'll get the reports whipped into shape in time for tomorrow's meeting."

On the surface, this seems like a simple, familiar exchange. Beneath the surface lurks the Loch Ness Monster of complications. All three have the same basic noble intention—to get the sales reports ready for the meeting. But the undercurrent of emotions in their exchange is what's going to keep them "personified" and defending their role positions, perpetuating The Bermuda Triangle. If everyone walks away at this point, The Triangle is guaranteed to stay in place. The Bulldozer-Martyr feels justified and in control. The Excuse Maker feels humili-

FIGURE 4.12   The Bermuda Triangle

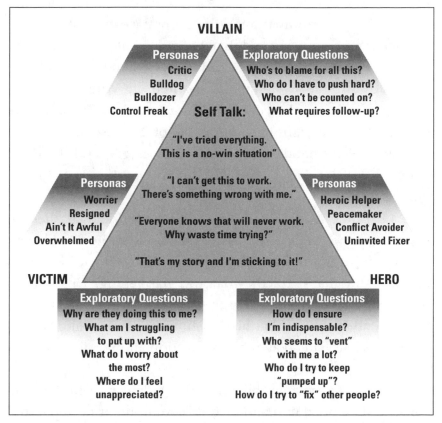

ated and hurt (and equally justified). The Fixer feels sympathetic, heroic, and yes, you got it, fully justified! And they all feel lousy. Because misery loves company, the chances are excellent they'll each recruit other people in the office who will share and even feed their individual points of view. And the beat goes on. And on. And on. . . .

THE DOCTOR HEALS HIMSELF

Chandler was a physician executive who was an effective leader but was overly blunt and impatient with his employees

(Villain). Howard, his mentor, was president and CEO, and had acted as his sounding board, advocate, and buffer (Hero, according to the other physicians) for several years. Howard announced he was retiring and that a search would be undertaken for his replacement. Chandler had always assumed he was being groomed for this position and wanted it. When he asked Howard (Villain) about this, Howard said he wasn't sure Chandler was the right person for the job because of his heavy-handed style. Chandler felt incredibly angry and betrayed (Victim). He decided to "Just bail out and let the whole institution go to hell!"

As I (Eddie) worked with Chandler, he suddenly flashed on his fear that when he took his current position he would work very hard but not receive recognition and credit for his contribution. And that's exactly what was happening. Chandler, a hard-charging macho type of guy, softened up, got some tears in his eyes, and realized that his "pushing hard" dynamic laid on top of this fear had created his exhaustion and possibly even his high blood pressure.

He took full responsibility for the Villain role he had unconsciously slipped into and made a commitment to step out of The Triangle. He shared with the CEO how he had come to see that he placed others in the Victim role when he was bullying and commanding. He also had some moving and very honest conversations with the staff he had pushed around for years. He subsequently moved into his mentor's position, and the clinic continues to thrive in an environment where successful multi-specialty clinics are relatively rare. His staff says they now see "the Real Chandler," whom they like and respect.

Chandler listened to the coaching from Howard and from me. But when someone you're coaching doesn't respond positively, where do you move in The Triangle? Persecute by hammering them to make sure they fully understand the total consequences of a failure to improve? Then rescue by overencouraging the person and saying things that aren't precisely true in an effort for them to think it's not all that bad? After the coaching session, do you complain like a Victim about the other person to your manager or a peer? Notice that your Hero and Villain behaviors ensure that the person will stay locked in their Victim spot, and Victims rarely make substantive changes.

LOOK AND UNHOOK

No one looks in the mirror every day and says, "Mr. Villain, today is your day!" Or, "My, what a lovely looking Victim I see." Or, "Gee, I sure hope I can find someone to play Hero with today." These are not roles we consciously wish to identify with. Yet in our experience we are all 100 percent capable of stepping into those behaviors that are triggered by two things in tandem: first, the right set of circumstances, and second, assumptions that may or may not be true about ourselves, others, and the circumstances.

Many of your habits and beliefs about "being right" have been programmed through a long succession of events in your life that colored your perception of what's real and what it takes to survive. You are likely addicted to certain behaviors and pay-offs. Villains get power, Heros get applause, and Victims get sympathy. If you no longer want to feel downtrodden like a Victim, exhausted by your endless heroic work, or lonely and angry because of the Villain role that you choose again and again, take heart. Help is on the way!

But first let's get more familiar with the key players. See Figure 4.13. Each holds a particular attitude toward the world, which they express through specific personas and tone of voice. They each also display certain "smokescreen" feelings (not to be confused with the genuine feelings we discussed in Chapter 3)

FIGURE 4.13   Key Roles in The Bermuda Triangle

Use these detailed descriptions to help you recognize when you slip out of authenticity and into a Bermuda Triangle role.

Villain

Attitude:	To heck with you		
Individual Personas:	▪ Driver ▪ Bulldozer	▪ Bulldog ▪ Petty Tyrant	▪ Critic ▪ Perfectionist
Tone:	▪ Blaming	▪ Impatient	▪ Judgmental
Smokescreen Feelings:	▪ Vigilance	▪ Indignation	▪ Righteousness
Basic Stance:	▪ Judges, dominates, and controls others to get desired outcome. ▪ Genuinely believes it's the other person's fault.		

Hero

Attitude:	Poor you		
Individual Personas:	▪ Pleaser ▪ Pacifier	▪ Caretaker ▪ Rescuer	▪ Uninvited Advisor ▪ Conflict Avoider
Tone:	▪ Smothering	▪ Very nice	▪ Gushes helpfulness
Smokescreen Feelings:	▪ Apologetic	▪ Sympathy	▪ Feeling sorry
Basic Stance:	▪ Assumes other person is in trouble, incapable, or needs help. ▪ Protects others from the consequences of their actions.		

Victim

Attitude:	Poor me		
Individual Personas:	▪ Worrier ▪ Rebel	▪ Excuser ▪ Space Case	▪ Ain't It Awful ▪ Procrastinator
Tone:	▪ Whining	▪ Complaining	▪ Self-Pity
Smokescreen Feelings:	▪ Confusion	▪ Embarrassment	▪ Hurt
Basic Stance:	▪ Sees life as "being done to them"; feels "swept away by circumstances." ▪ Blames others for their problems.		

that mask the basic emotion driving this role. Smokescreen feelings are part of the glue that keeps The Bermuda Triangle in place. They show up when a person is attached to a particular role in The Triangle and allow a person to justify their stance, ensuring a lock-in on a limited way of working and being.

Villains

The underlying intention of Villains is to place blame "out there." They feel the yoke of responsibility to find the causes of a problem and their modus operandi is fingerpointing. Usually the Villain's noble intention is about getting work done efficiently and thoroughly, but she doesn't trust others to do it without exercising inappropriate amounts of overt and covert control.

Subtle blaming escalates into not-so-subtle attacks. Generally, the consequences of a Villain on the loose are blurs in the hallway—people diving for cover. Villains do not often take responsibility for *their role* in creating the problem. Perhaps the Villain delegated the project to a person she knows is a mediocre employee and failed to follow up properly. Or perhaps she allowed work on a lower priority project first, while knowing a deadline was fast approaching on the project that has mushroomed into a crisis.

Victims

A Victim's noble intention is also to get the job done, but a blind spot or two locks into a belief they are working at someone else's mercy, virtually powerless to alter the situation. They are often self-righteous and judgmental, casting aspersions on managers and coworkers who, through their eyes, take horrible advantage of others. Victimhood is not about hierarchy but about an underlying need to have a bad guy in order to support their good guy identity. Victims show up in boardrooms and executive planes just as surely as in support positions.

For Victims, life just doesn't work unless they, too, can point a finger—in any direction as long as it is away from themselves. Failure to take responsibility for their own choices and an inability to stop believing in the illusion of good guy/bad guy keep the Victim down, which, ironically, tends to be within their comfort zone.

When someone points out problems about a Victim's work, the Victim hears criticism instead of feedback and the chance to learn. His response is invariably a litany of reasons and justifications. To feel misunderstood and unappreciated requires a Villain. Victims rarely, if ever, see their own contribution to the plight in which they find themselves and are strongly attached to seeing the problems as belonging to someone else.

Heroes

Without effective Heroes, many Victims and Villains would be fired or quit. In fact, this often happens. Heroes inadvertently throw a body block in front of problems, delaying or preventing breakthroughs and solutions. They save the day by running interference, explaining what the Villain or Victim *really* meant, softening the impact of the Villain's harsh language, or by lightening up the Victim's mood by allowing him or her to vent. The Hero's noble intention is to protect and take care of people in trouble. Buried in the intention are a rash of huge problems that operate as the glue that keeps The Triangle dance going perpetually. Heroes need problems and upset people to allow them to habitually save the day whether they are asked to or not.

HOW TO POP OUT OF THE TRIANGLE

Nearly all of our individual personas can be defined as having strong flavors of Villain, Victim, or Hero. In entering The Bermuda Triangle, most of us favor one or two of the positions. My (Kate's) own Villain-Hero two-step in our office meant that first I delegated more work to people than they thought they were capable of. Then I'd sense their being overwhelmed and want to alleviate their stress with some coaching. And that pretty much kept the game going. My behavior reinforced feeling overwhelmed and also reinforced some Victim personas, where people felt like they were overworked and then complained about me.

Shifting out of The Triangle means *paying attention* instead of responding automatically. See Figure 4.14. When we look for familiar patterns, we surface the Bermuda Triangle predicament. Ask, "I wonder what I did to create this situation where people don't deliver what I expect? Do I fail to provide infor-

---

FIGURE 4.14   Stepping out of the Triangle

- Take full responsibility for whatever is upsetting or troubling you.

- Wonder about how you created or fueled the situation.

- Explore the underlying familiar pattern in whatever is occurring.

- Express your feelings without blame.

- Shift into curiosity about what you need to do to create more joy and ease.

- Brainstorm solutions.

- Take action and keep your commitments to the solutions.

mation, fail to follow up, what? Or make the wonder question more generic: "How did I help create this?" See Figure 4.15 for more role and persona questions.

Operating from a place of wonder helps us take a conscious step out of the familiar drama of The Triangle into the unknown—where big wonder questions are valued over great

---

FIGURE 4.15   Shifting out of the Bermuda Triangle

The set of questions below will help you discover more about your personas, the positions in The Triangle, and yourself. The next time you find yourself panting with pent-up emotion, check yourself out by reviewing these.

Villain:

- Who's to blame for all this?
- What irritates me the most?
- Who do I have to push to make things happen?
- Who isn't dependable or competent enough for me?
- What wouldn't happen if I weren't so vigilant?

Victim:

- Who's doing what to me?
- What am I struggling to put up with?
- What do I worry about the most?
- Where do I feel unappreciated?
- What or who do I wish would "just go away?"

Hero:

- How do I keep myself and others "pumped up?"
- Who needs my help and how do I try to help them?
- What abilities do others lack that I make up for?
- How do I try to fix things?
- Who am I trying to protect?

answers. "I wonder what my learning is here? I wonder how this is a familiar pattern in my life? How long has this been going on? Let me see if I can do a little tracking and excavation here. What can I open up to?" A place of wonder means newer, better, more profitable possibilities. We know we're interested in learning if we step beyond the typical place we get stuck. This intention, above all others, will eventually guide you safely beyond The Bermuda Triangle and back to your authentic self.

THE AUTHENTICITY HALL OF FAME

Steve Price, director of HR for the Public Business and America International (PAI) segment at Dell Computer, had spent his life as a star. He was an A student, a college football hero, and a free-agent selection for the Denver Broncos. He quickly rose through the ranks at Johnson Wax, where he worked 13 years. Steve joined Dell in 1997 during a major hiring surge. The company grew over 50 percent and the employee head count went from 18,000 to 27,000 in his first year; his business segment grew even more aggressively, which stressed all HR systems.

One Friday afternoon he met with his manager, Executive VP Ro Parra, to review a presentation he was to deliver the following Monday to the executive management team. He thought it was some of his best work. Ro quickly reviewed the document and then politely set it aside, saying, "Look Steve, this looks really good but we'll never have time to do all of this at Dell. We move too fast. What I really need is for you to tell us what we need to do in the next 30 days. You need to rework this presentation over the weekend or I am going to take you off of the agenda."

Steve's confidence was shaken and he went home that day with a deep-rooted disbelief in his abilities. He wondered if the move to Dell had been a mistake and if Ro regretted hiring him.

Should he resign? Around 2:00 AM he got up and went into the bathroom. He stood there, staring in the mirror. His wife, Stacey, came to see what was wrong and Steve said grimly, "I think we are going to have to put a For Sale sign in the front yard tomorrow."

Stacey listened to him as he explored his fears and doubts. Steve expected sympathy, but what he got was valuable coaching that challenged him to face the situation head-on and to rise above these circumstances. Stacey said that if he left Dell feeling the way he did, like a victim, he would carry it with him the rest of his career. Steve needed to get back on top of his game, into his authentic center, and then if he still felt Dell was not the right place, he could leave knowing that he had faced his wall of fears and had conquered them.

The sunlight of Saturday morning and the tough words of a loving wife brought new perspective. He realized his self-worth depended on how he chose to see this situation and how he would respond. He reflected on Ro's words: "This is good work but we'll never have time to do all of it." Then it hit him: If they both thought it was good, then the only issue was the timing. So, he broke the HR plan into a series of 30-day priorities that would have high impact on the business and that the organization could appropriately execute.

As it turned out, Ro was experiencing his own share of self-doubt. I (Kate) had just shared his first 360° in which he received intensely positive feedback about his business leadership but remarkably critical feedback about his people leadership skills, especially his ability to lead a team and coach people. He was beyond tough, and people were afraid of him. He'd confessed that he'd always had what he referred to as "The Wall," which he used to keep people out and which kept him from being the emotionally connected leader he longed to be.

Remarkably, Ro had shared a similar emotional conversation with his wife, Cheryl, in the early morning hours. The extraordinary business success he'd experienced felt like a shallow victory. With Cheryl's support and prodding, Ro found the courage to face this issue. He talked openly with Steve about his Wall persona and began to take responsibility for Steve's success, coaching instead of criticizing. Within a year Steve succeeded in creating a hiring process and a first year development and orientation process that brought extraordinary levels of new talent into Dell. It also supported the new hires in rapidly growing and learning to handle the massive onslaught of change created by Dell's growth.

When they became authentic, the unit shifted from a bunch of driven individual executives to a team with incredible cadence and rhythm. Steve became "The Glue." The executive team, which included some remote international leaders, also magically jelled. Michael Dell acknowledged Ro and the unit, which had gained visibility, as the feeder pool for a large number of talent transfers to other groups.

Steve enjoyed the astounding turnaround and also developed a warm relationship with Ro, who had never allowed anyone to get this close to him before. Ro experienced the power of bringing down "The Wall" and discovered that it didn't create the vulnerability he had feared.

When Steve left the unit to head up human resources for Dell Europe, his replacement, Mike Vescuzo, became Ro's coach. Because Ro had learned to release The Wall, the organization never missed a beat. People in general became less intimidated as he became more approachable. Several confided in him about very personal issues that were affecting their performance. In his 15-year career, he had never experienced that level of trust from his employees.

Steve had the privilege of helping Ro drop his persona and become one of Dell's most respected leaders of people. Ro asked me to redo his 360° on a regular basis. In 1999 and later in 2000 and 2002, he got unbelievably positive feedback about his ability to lead people, as well as lead a business.

Operating from a place of wonder helps us take a conscious step out of the familiar drama of The Triangle into the unknown—where big Wonder Questions are valued over great answers. "I wonder what my learning is here? I wonder how this is a familiar pattern in my life? How long has this been going on? Let me see if I can do a little tracking and excavation here. What can I open up to?" A place of wonder means newer, better, more profitable possibilities. We know we're interested in learning if we step beyond the typical place we get stuck. This intention, above all others, will eventually guide you safely beyond The Bermuda Triangle and back to your authentic self.

SUMMARY

- Authenticity means congruence between our inner state of being and our outer behaviors and actions. One person's commitment and skills for authentic behavior empowers everyone else to shift.

- Our grumbles and complaints and the dramas they generate at the office are remnants of our childhood dynamics, resulting in personas or predictable patterns of mostly unconscious behaviors triggered by a few basic instincts common to all of us.

- To catch yourself in a persona, notice if you feel overly controlling, impatient, irritable, or tense. Make the power shift by exploring how you learned this persona and its underlying intention. Then find a more effective way to achieve that intention.

- The big three Bermuda Triangle behaviors are blaming, complaining, and sacrificing.

- The Bermuda Triangle of Victims, Villains, and Heros feeds on itself and continues to expand, with people switching roles, until someone steps out of a role.

- As we step into a place of wonder, we know we're interested in learning if we move beyond the typical places we get stuck.

TAKE ACTION

- Which personas live in your department and your company? Eager Beaver, Overworker, Martyr, Wheeler Dealer, Analytic, Micro Manager, Bulldozer, Nice Guy?

- Which of these personas best match your style? Which ones do you work best with? How does that impact your desire to change yourself?

- Which personas are too extreme and require offsetting balance from other people? For example, too much attention given to the big picture, Visionary personas can create many great ideas with poor follow through and execution, where there's too little completed and shipped out the door.

- Which personas (Micro Manager, Bulldozer, Bulldog, etc.) create problems in your work culture? In what specific ways do these personas need to change to retain their essential value but drop their energy-depleting traits?

Look first for the value of each of these personas. For example, Micro Manager ensures that people pay attention to details and that work happens.

- Which of these personas are difficult for you to work with? What personas do they trigger in you? For example, if Bulldozer or Micro Manager is part of your culture, and you like to complain about these people, then you must be willing to step out of your Victim addiction in order to create a change in your work group and in your company.

- What specific changes do you intend to make as a result of reading this chapter? Once you've changed, how can you support others in changing? How can you become a more effective coach to your peers and even your manager?

CHAPTER FIVE

ACCOUNTABILITY
Stepping Up and Taking Responsibility

How can I become more accountable?

How can I hold others accountable when they don't report to me?

How can I create accountability without blaming people when they fall short?

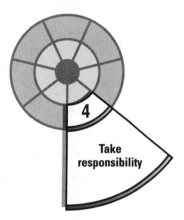

4

Take responsibility

Here's some simple math to transform your life and your work:

100% Responsibility + Solid Agreements = Accountability

In most companies—especially those with a management philosophy based on fear—*accountability* means to "account for" what I have done in the past, instead of defining what I will do now and in the future. The latter is proactive accountability and has far more power. Accountability enables individuals and organizations to influence events and outcomes *before* they happen, rather than create a defense after the situation cannot be altered.

When things are sailing along smoothly, we rarely rush in to ask, "Who's accountable for this?" Only when progress falters and problems emerge do we start searching for the responsible party. We think of accountability as an after-the-fact reckoning when something goes wrong or when we're trying to determine cause and pinpoint blame. We are called to be accountable for our lapses and failures, creating the perception that being accountable is something that happens to us, rather than something we initiate and monitor ourselves.

Somewhere along the line, society, schools, and businesses have caused people to feel more responsible for explaining *their results than for* achieving *them.* Many people seem to think an adequate explanation can excuse a poor result. No wonder we spend so much time explaining and justifying poor results with tired lines like, "That's the way we've always done it. It's not my job. I didn't know you needed it right away. They wouldn't listen to me."

The brand of accountability many of us encountered early in our careers arose out of an authoritarian childhood model, when our parents and teachers definitely knew more than we did and had the upper hand. By the time we reach the workforce we have too often learned to operate our lives by the maxim: *Every problem has a scapegoat; convincingly point a finger and you're off the hook.* U.S. President Harry Truman probably didn't intend to become a national icon for accountability when he declared, "The buck stops here." Yet, in a culture of trust, where radical results become the most valuable perk of all, employees approach their jobs as Harry did, making action and results the ultimate accountability yardstick.

In today's intertwined, matrixed organizations, we are rarely *given* responsibility for 100 percent of anything. Rather, we must *take* 100% responsibility for the piece of the picture that's ours alone. Ironically, the very organizational structures that make it so tempting to go into blaming and finger-pointing also provide the most exquisite opportunity to positively affect others with our shift into responsibility. When we act with the deep conviction that our actions generate endless ripple effects, we help create an environment of trust. Without trust, we hesitate to tell the truth, question the status quo, and take risks. Life feels flat and dull. Accountability is the reality thermostat for corporate culture and company morale.

Our eagerness as a nation to play victim feeds a lot of lawyers, and our increasingly litigious society spawns a lot of victims. The McDonald's customer who put a hot cup of coffee between her legs, burning them when it spilled, won $2.9 million. Who placed the coffee there?

The unanchored day-to-day shifting of what's reliable, real, and true can feel devastating to people and destructive to momentum. Fudging on deadlines, spinning the sales report at the monthly executive powwow, passively nodding yes or no in meetings, gossiping at the water cooler, and venting behind closed doors all indicate accountability lapses. Whether you're the CEO, a middle manager, or an intern in the mailroom, you have the capacity to affect the culture (and stock prices, profits, and bonuses) for better or worse, up or down, expanding or contracting, by your capacity for full and complete accountability.

CALLING ALL MISSING INFLUENCE SKILLS

Have you ever noticed how the people who complain about office politics are the same ones who haven't yet developed accountability skills? Knowing how to persuade someone to change her mind, support an alternative idea, or see a situation from another perspective only looks political to the person who doesn't know how to do it. As long as they call it political, they are destined *not* to change and advance.

Brett faced this issue, as a physician and VP for Development and Integrative Medicine Programs at a major healthcare system. He was looking for ways to add alternative modalities to their program and felt significant interference from Dr. Williams, Chairman of the Community Health Board, who had become a one-person crusade to keep these new approaches out of their health system. I (Eddie) suggested to Brett that he was attached to Dr. Williams' defensiveness and politics. For a moment he looked as if I were from another planet. "What do you mean?" he said, "How could I be committed to such a thing? I want exactly the opposite!"

I suggested that Brett step into full accountability by claiming his role in the situation. After a few moments Brett said, "I get it! What you're saying is that I've been using Dr. Williams to speak my own hesitation about committing to this program and the dollars and resources it would require. I have to admit I've had my own moments of indecision which I've never faced, and therefore I've skipped past some potential risks."

In the next couple of weeks Brett clarified his view and expressed his own concerns to Dr. Williams and other members of the board. The result was astonishing. Others shared similar concerns, and most surprisingly, Dr. Williams transformed from the greatest obstacle to a strong proponent for going forward to respond to this community request. Because no one else had been willing to communicate their concerns, Dr. Williams had automatically taken on that role. As everyone articulated their concerns, the issues could be openly addressed instead of resisted as one person's contrarian view. We make a radical change when we choose to take personal responsibility for the outcomes and results we see around us rather than blaming organizational politics, insurance companies, or demanding patients and customers.

Taking 100% responsibility does work in strange, synergistic ways. When I (Kate) joined KLA-Tencor as VP of human resources, I learned that half my performance bonus, which was 30 percent of my annual compensation, was dependent on holding the turnover rate at a mere 5 percent a year for the company's top quartile performers. This was Silicon Valley in the early 1980s when turnover averaged 30 percent, and I loudly protested the unfairness of this arrangement. Ken Levy, our CEO, responded, "You'll figure out how to meet it because you've got so much riding on it."

And he was right. I took on the challenge. I put so many "love your buddy" programs in place that, in my five years in the company, we lost fewer than five top technical people a year, and they were all out-of-state spousal transfers (who certainly did love their buddies). This is the alchemy of accountability, when you take 100% responsibility for areas over which you, on the surface, have no control.

Want tangible proof of the subtle and not-so-subtle patterns of self-sabotage we each have? Look at the gap between what we say we want and what we actually create, the commitments we make and what we actually deliver. Because our organizations have become complex webs of relationships, just a few glitches can create significant problems—generating wobbles throughout the company. By shining the light of accountability on our actions, we make the invisible visible—like launching paint balls or throwing powder on the Invisible Man, we see what is and become more powerful.

Accountability lapses—not showing up, shirking responsibility, giving less than our best all the time—signal glitches and unintended patterns that keep us stuck at a suboptimal level. They also catalyze corporate sludge. To unleash your individual and collective potential, you must combine some art, a handful of science, a little faith, and a generous daily dollop of courage. Much of our work for the past 20 years has involved sensing underlying behavior patterns—obstacles begging for release.

To us, the somewhat abstract notion of human potential means energy and talents are present but unexpressed. When we name the glitches and work them out, flow happens. Potential frees up. Problems merge into solutions. We've seen it happen thousands of times. The difference in the "before" and "after" is nearly always the same release point: *Individuals must decide to become accountable for their experience and their results.* This can feel daunting. Yet it's fundamental to health, purpose, genius, and joy. To be a better manager, a stronger leader, a rising star, a valuable team player, or a fulfilled human being, we hope you'll commit to becoming accountable. You'll then be able to create a culture of trust where radical change is as easy and obvious as a hole-in-one at a Par 3 on a perfect morning in May . . . when everyone is committed to 100% responsibility for every shot they make.

THE ACCOUNTABILITY HALL OF FAME

I (Kate) witnessed a dazzling example of accountability in action at the beginning of 2000, when Dell reported its worst quarterly performance in many years. Anyone could have pointed the finger of blame at the business unit VPs. All had agreed to certain financial targets tied to Y2K sales projections, and all had failed to meet them. In their quarterly meeting with top executives and in a later meeting with all 300 of Dell's VPs, however, Michael Dell and Kevin Rollins, Dell's president and COO, did something highly unusual. They confessed to having given poor Y2K direction. They also acknowledged that some of the senior VPs warned them about less-than-expected sales, but neither Michael nor Kevin wanted to see that; therefore, they'd sent the VPs back out with higher targets than the VPs believed they could meet. As I sat in the room with several hundred VPs, I viscerally experienced their sighs of relief, amazement, and respect for the two guys at the front of the room.

I've seen many other situations, and you have, too, where the postmortem consists of blame and finger pointing: The CEO blames people below him for not meeting targets, and they blame the people who report to them, and blame keeps rolling downhill until someone goes home and yells at poor, blameless Rover.

Michael and Kevin, however, publicly took full responsibility for their own mistakes, setting something magical into motion: No one wasted time hurling accusations or echoing the blame. Instead, the VPs focused on why they hadn't pushed harder for the targets they believed in. Everyone connected into a deeper level of responsibility and experienced new juice and enthusiasm. As a result, the Dell company focused, energized, and mobilized rapidly. By April, the stock—which predictably dropped at the earlier news—was back up 35 percent and the company grabbed another chunk of the PC market from its competitors.

READY, WILLING, AND ACCOUNTABLE

Most of us don't receive training in *how* to make solid agreements and take responsibility for our experience. Our instruction tends to begin and end with the directive to *be* responsible, and we are left to our own devices to figure out what that means—usually through trial and error. The confusion persists as we progress in fits and starts. Why are we under deadline pressure so often? Why all the complaining, passive resistance, and stressed faces? Why do we fall short of our targets when our strategies seem so airtight, our team so success-ready? Why is someone from HR always trying to improve us?!

When you take responsibility for the results in your life, it practically guarantees you'll never be left on the bench when what you want most is to play. While the gifted and talented may lead a team in scoring, those who log the most game time overall, especially when the stakes are high, are the people who are 100 percent committed, 100 percent of the time. The most challenging and stimulating explorations of our lives, and the ones with the greatest payoffs, have been learning what it means—and what it doesn't mean—to commit to full accountability in every situation.

Accountable people are steadier in a crisis, reliable on tight deadlines, focused thinkers, and full participators. They communicate frequently with updates, clarifications, and assists of all kinds. They rarely drop the ball, nor do they manipulate reality to stand solo in the spotlight. They masterfully transform resistance into service. They also tend to have fewer mental and emotional burdens. As a result, they manage to enjoy extra reservoirs of strength and energy.

Sound like people you'd feel eager to work with? Us, too! Is such behavior learnable? Absolutely. What do these folks do that you don't? *They look inside themselves a lot, wondering about their contribution to problems, inquiring how the situation could be different.* Their slogan is "Claim, don't Blame." When things go awry, they ask themselves: "How did I participate in this disappointing outcome?" When things go well, they ask the same question: "How did I participate in this positive outcome?" And when correcting the course, they ask: "What changes in my own assumptions and behaviors do I need to make?"

See Figure 5.1 for more accountability questions.

THREE STRIKES, YOU'RE RESPONSIBLE—THE RULE OF THREE

We've found one guideline particularly useful when monitoring our commitment to responsibility—the Rule of Three. For example, if someone in the group interrupts and talks over me once, I'm not responsible. But if the same person does it three times or if three different people interrupt me, then it's wise to wonder what I can do to change that behavior. (The alert

---

FIGURE 5.1   Questions That Invite Accountability

- What is it about my attitude or behavior that keeps this going?

- Do I have a hidden, unexamined personal agenda?

- Is there anything I'd like to communicate but haven't?

- Have I broken or missed any agreements?

- What about this situation feels familiar? How do I continue to create this problem?

- What can I learn from this situation?

person's sensors are activated when something happens twice.) If someone gets irritated with you once, it's their problem. Avoid going into The Bermuda Triangle by taking it personally. By the third time, *you* are also responsible for taking corrective action.

Likewise, if someone doesn't keep a commitment with you, they're 100% responsible the first time. If someone in the group discards or discounts your intuition once, they're 100% responsible for that. By the third time, they're 100% responsible and so are you—for consistently producing that result in your life.

THE "OUT THERE" DELUSION

Unless we routinely use the Rule of Three or have done some other inner work, most of us constantly delude ourselves, believing all problems come from "out there." This attitude guarantees that problems don't get corrected. *So long as you don't address your part of an issue, the situation or problem will return again and again, as faithfully as the crabgrass in the spring.* "Out there" thinking permeates our culture, not only in the tabloid headlines that scream at us in the grocery store, but on TV, talk radio, literature, and music. It permeates our corporations as well—unless they're conscious companies that know the most powerful focus lies within.

"Out there" thinking derives from our prehistoric response to threats. In fundamental ways, the evolutionary processes that shaped our minds haven't kept up with the rapid transformation of modern times. Evolution gave us fear to get our attention so we face threats squarely—whether it's a tiger, losing our job, or closing our company—and take action. Our ancestors who reacted quickly lived longer and had more offspring; the more reflective had fewer because they often became food. Selectivity gave us brains aimed at quick reactions when we're under stress, not the contemplative thinking and carefully planned action that complement the intuitive leaps we need in today's companies. We continue to use "out there" situations to mobilize action, rather than take proactive steps or deeply consider our own contribution to situations. Use the wonder questions in Figure 5.2 to help you sort out the causes and conditions of results you want to own when you don't yet see how to make the shift into accountability.

BEWARE THE WORK POLICE

If "work police" is another name for the managers in your office, an "out there" standard of enforcing workflow is required to compensate for the shortage of "in here" ownership. Defensiveness, compliance, or complaints tend to trigger the work police, who show up and write a ticket in an attempt to force some level of accountability and problem solving.

Accountability can be taught and learned best by demonstrating what it looks like and sounds like. It's contagious! If you're a manager, be the first one to say out loud, "How have I

FIGURE 5.2   Shifting into Accountability

If you find yourself . . .	*Then shift by asking . . .*
Feeling angry, sad, or fearful	How can I choose ease and confidence instead?
Repeatedly having your buttons pushed	How do I keep making choices that sustain this pattern?
Feeling bottled up, stressed, with flat energy	What emotions haven't I let myself feel?
Repeatedly having bad luck or negative results you don't want	Do I have an unconscious intention for things to turn out this way?
Avoiding certain people, being distant, or aloof	What agreements have I broken? What unspoken communications do I have?

contributed to our predicament?" Your employees may feel eager to have that conversation with you—after they've picked themselves up off the floor from the initial shock.

Let's say you give high-level direction for a project and then unleash the team to make it happen. Days later, at the agreed-upon checkpoint, the team is beaming with the pride of accomplishment, while you're grimacing at the result that's miles off the mark you expected. How do you each avoid the gridlock of criticizing, blaming . . . and the traffic jam at the community aspirin bottle?

First, as nonjudgmentally as possible, describe the gap between your expectations and what was produced. Then invite each person to ask the question, "What did I do to create this situation?" It sounds so obvious, but in our (the authors') experience 95 percent of us look first and most intently at what the *other* person didn't do or should have done. This guarantees gridlock, which also takes time and energy to clean up and the highly likely probability that the pattern will repeat itself until a majority of people are awake at the wheel. Meanwhile, let your team know that you're also inquiring into your accountability for the problem by asking yourself, "How could I have communicated my expectations more clearly? How was the assignment not completely understood and owned?" Beneath these issues lies the most revealing one of all: Are you committed to working and learning with ease and speed, or to the notion that disappointment and missed expectations are an unavoidable element of your work life?

OFFICER KATE JOINS THE 3% CLUB AND HANGS UP HER BADGE

Based on our observations of thousands of people, we (the authors) estimate that only 3 percent of all people consistently keep their agreements. Can you imagine how you'll stand out at work if you join the 3% Club? A few years ago I (Kate) realized I was spending too much time organizing and policing everyone else's work in my own office. I also began to sense that my employees were complaining about me. I didn't have to be psychic to know my own irritability about what I saw as their lack of performance was perceived by them as blame. I began to wonder what would happen if I stopped doing this, declaring a moratorium on all follow-up reminders and my resulting irritation. This would change the game, which I wanted to do, but I felt afraid that not following up would create huge performance shortfalls and dropped projects.

In a staff meeting I owned up to micromanaging, which I had previously justified because of people's erratic follow-up, and I invited everyone to imagine our office as a virtual caldron of responsible and empowered people doing work they truly loved. Interestingly, two people stepped up and made dramatic changes, while the others just couldn't seem to manage the shift, regardless of how much coaching and effort I invested. So I took my responsibility to the next level. In the last quarter of 1997, I fired four of my six employees.

I hired four new people, then recreated a similar pattern of micromanaging, where people felt blamed when details were dropped. Finally, accountability master teacher, Katie Hendricks, helped each of us make the inner shifts that allowed us all to join the 3% Club. Our office was never the same.

Erin Miller took specific steps to ensure the changes took root by creating a unique system for managing deadlines and workflow. Within three months, her plan eliminated 60 percent to 80 percent of overwork. My role as her manager was merely to remain open to her genius. Trust flowed, and so did the work. With my policing days behind me, we moved to a whole new level of fun and profitability.

ACCOUNTABILITY IN ACTION

When you have a recurring situation that absolutely looks like an "out there" problem, take 100% responsibility by identifying your part and by staying open to organic solutions. Joel is a physician executive of a large multispecialty medical organization in the South. In an environment of declining resources, increasing technical costs, and expanding patient demands, the contracts with physicians often require renegotiation to address complaints and demands. After listening for a long time about the unmanageable neurosurgeons and their demands and stubbornness, I (Eddie) asked Joel what his primary complaint was.

He said, "They are unwilling to take ER calls, and they only want more money. I do everything I can to make them happy, but it's never enough."

When I asked if he were willing to take responsibility for these results, he rolled his eyes but agreed to explore this because he truly wanted to solve the problem. In fact, his family had nicknamed him "Old Yeller"—a play on the title of a favorite childhood film—because of the ongoing shouting matches with his father over equitable compensation for his chores as a kid. I asked Joel how he kept the problem going. He thought for a minute then said, "Well, I use the same process over and over to try to deal with it, and it never works any better. Just like with my dad, I always used the same but louder logic with the same result. I guess that's what my discussions with my neurosurgical colleagues look like as well."

Joel took responsibility. He asked the physicians to make clear requests, stated his own feelings with appreciation and curiosity, and established an agreement with himself and his colleagues to solve issues with respect. Some time later, I asked him how the problem was. He smiled wryly and said, "What problem? I keep letting go of my problem and seem to create new solutions! Joel had identified where the problem had lived in the past and how he was keeping it going. And then he physically "stepped out" without knowing how, only to find new ways and solutions. Figure 5.3 outlines a step-by-step method to do this.

SAYING YES TO WHAT IS

You'll find accountability potholes everywhere. If your supervisor would take last place in a Mr. or Ms. Congeniality contest, you can feel justified about the perpetual tension in the air, or you can take 100% responsibility in order to transform resist-

FIGURE 5.3   Taking 100% Responsibility

To break free of old patterns, take each of these steps in order listed below. Do not feel discouraged if you feel challenged by Step 3. Often just after it seems as if there's nothing else to add, a breakthrough happens.

1. Identify a complaint. State the complaint in "unenlightened" terms. Be dramatic and ham it up.

2. Physically step into 100% responsibility. Find a place in the room that represents your internal shift to being 100% responsible.

3. Prime the pump by inquiring into your position. Do this by filling in these blanks, repeating several times until you have what feels like a breakthrough.

    a. From the past, this situation remids me of

    _____.

    b. I keep this situation going by _____

    _____.

    c. The life-long pattern I'm noticing is _____

    _____.

    d. I can demonstrate 100% responsibility concerning this issue by _____

    _____.

4. If, during Step 3, you do not see a satisfactory solution, go back to Step 1 and repeat the process.

ance into solutions. If tight deadlines make it impossible to maintain high quality in your department, you can belt out the ain't-it-awful blues that help keep morale flat and uninspired, or you can become the visionary team member who looks for a better way—the one who sees the connection between morale and profits and does something about it.

I (Kate) had a personal opportunity to become accountable early in my career, when I wondered why the all-male team I worked with didn't seem to take me seriously. In meetings, even when I spoke up with conviction, expertise, and passion, I felt ineffective and somewhat invisible. Initially I felt tempted to blame it on the fact that I was a woman—my ego's defensive way of justifying my ineffectiveness. To my surprise, as soon as I looked for an explanation linked to something other than my gender, which I couldn't change, I discovered new creativity and initiative around my dilemma. My breakthrough started with *my willingness to own the problem* and look at what *I* could do differently, instead of wishing things were different.

As soon as I made this important step, I immediately got the idea of observing an unusually skillful male peer who successfully influenced our CEO and his peers, as well as his own organization. I learned a successful style in this new work culture by observing and listening to him, and by being willing to modify my approach and my communications to be more like the people who were the acknowledged fast trackers. I soon began to reap the rewards, making progress and receiving positive affirmation for my commitment to learning.

Be careful about buying into the prevailing injustices and prejudices of the culture that hypnotically keep us in the role of victim. Reinforcing what's wrong and unfair by venting and giving it energy won't make things right. Instead, work with the reality at hand and leverage your learning, upgrade your skills, ask questions, pursue your worthy intentions. Positive change will occur.

If you don't believe you have the authority to take responsibility for these kinds of issues, begin with a less threatening question. "I wonder what I would do about _____ if I *did* have the authority." Give it a few moments of your full attention and step into the possibilities that present themselves in your imagination. This exercise works, we promise. There are plenty of "legitimate" beefs we can conjure up, confront, blame, and complain about. The question to ask ourselves, however, is why on earth would we want to complain when more rewarding outcomes are waiting just off stage?

Blame is the killer problem because it destroys relationships. Blame creates adrenalin and drama, while responsibility creates a different biochemistry that is less stimulating on the surface. What's remarkable is that many people consistently choose to blame someone rather than develop the skills they need to build a strong relationship built on mutual respect and effective communications where they get the support and trust they need to be successful. Shift from blaming to claiming to make a visible shift in your impact.

The most powerful step in taking responsibility is to assume that whatever gets created "out there" is the direct result of something I have done or failed to do and is not somebody else's fault. In fact, "out there" has been set up to teach me an important lesson—and if I don't get the lesson now, then I can count on an escalation path that's designed to get my attention.

As we write this chapter, I (Kate) am in the process of coaching a CEO on this very issue. He wants so desperately to be liked within the company, and this seriously compromises his leadership. Specifically, he has huge resistance to the difficult task of terminating people, long after it's obvious to everyone that they aren't the right fit for the job. In delaying, he believes he is helping them out. In reality, he's not helping anyone. The backwash of this behavior has polarized the office, and people complain and gossip behind his back about his ineffective leadership.

I often see this problem that is created by admirable but misdirected intentions. This CEO thinks people will like him more because he's giving them the benefit of the doubt. However, because they're failing, they aren't really taking responsibility for their own success. If they were, they'd either correct their problems or go into another job. Instead, they invest their energy in making him wrong, pointing out to everyone who will listen that he won't tell them what they need to do, that he avoids talking with them, that he's never available for coaching, etc.

So while he's trying to accumulate heavenly merits by being a nice guy, he in fact is incurring massive ill will on the part of the people he thinks he's helping. Meanwhile, people all over the company feel resentful picking up the work of the nonperformers and make up their own stories about the CEO's unwillingness to confront people. This man will miss out on some important learning about his urge to please so long as he continues to avoid facing his issue regarding terminating people.

Now that you have a sense of taking 100% responsibility for your experiences, let's take that skill into the second half of the accountability equation.

MAKING SOLID AGREEMENTS

Solid agreements create the foundation for trust. If you can't count on someone to keep their agreements, then you've got a low trust relationship that tends to make people vigilant, watchful, and uneasy. The roots of the word *solid* mean "whole or safe." The details of solid agreements are whole and complete, and the agreements feel safe because they're clear. They build a foundation of trust among everyone involved. When we don't keep our agreements, we create chaos.

Art is the founder and medical director of a unique wellness and preventive medicine center at a high-profile golf resort and spa. He asked me (Eddie) to help with a continuing problem of employee dissatisfaction, conflict, and turnover that hampered effectiveness and growth and created an unhappy workplace.

What I found was that Art routinely didn't do what he said he'd do. Then he made endless excuses and justified his lack of completion. The staff complained that he didn't follow through on his promises to complete medical records and return calls to patients. Patients often had to wait for appointments, so Art could finish a report. The staff sought endless and creative ways around his behavior, including "dummy" time slots and manipulating his schedule to account for his consistent late arrival or prolonged patient consultations. Staff meetings never started on time, were often interrupted by multiple phone calls, or even abruptly ended by calls from friends or marketing people.

I set an appointment for the feedback session with Art three times, only to have it postponed. On another occasion there were so many interruptions that I called it off. Art blamed the patients, the staff, and everyone but himself. He had a little-boy way of apologizing that was more charming than genuine. When we finally met, Art said, "Well, can you see what I've got to contend with? Who should I fire? Why can't doctors get the help they need to take care of the patients?"

I said, "Art, you don't keep your agreements!" He said, "What do you mean I don't keep agreements? Nobody in this office keeps his or her agreements with me!" I said, "Art, it starts with you. You haven't kept your agreements with me, and I've observed numerous agreement glitches while I've been here."

Art continued to explain how difficult it was when patients called unexpectedly, wanted too much of his time, and generally irritated him. He went on about the staff and how they shirked responsibility and actively sought to irritate him. As we worked together, Art slowly and reluctantly began to get it. He went on to tell me about the many agreements that were not kept in his family and how angry and disappointed he felt. We came up with some strategies about time agreements and consciously making and breaking agreements. That simple shift to conscious agreement also created a shift in the harmony and success for the clinic that began to prosper at an entirely new level.

FIGURE 5.4   Making Solid Agreements in Four Lessons

Lesson 1:	Only make agreements you feel completely aligned with and committed to.
Lesson 2:	When you feel you have no choice about an agreement, remind yourself that honesty and directness are *always* choices. Share your feelings and speak candidly about your own internal experience without blaming or complaining.
Lesson 3:	Keep your agreements.
Lesson 4:	The moment you see the need for a change, let those who will be affected know and renegotiate the agreement.

In my last phone call with Art, I said we'd talk soon and he humorously asked as we parted, "Is that an agreement?"

Figure 5.4 teaches four lessons about making solid agreements.

Solid agreements have three facets: making clear requests, making new agreements, and handling broken agreements. Each is an art unto itself.

Making Clear Requests

At first glance the art of making straightforward requests doesn't appear to be all that complex. You ask someone to do something, and they say "yes" or "no." You must, however, clear several internal and external hurdles. Unspoken feelings and unconscious intentions can cloud the clarity of seemingly simple requests and contaminate how we hear the other person's response.

Perhaps we choose the indirect route because we've encountered people who feel offended by another person's directness in asking for something. A lot of people feel this way, including my (Kate's) very own family! They act as if I've put them on the spot by being clear about what I want. Another hurdle is that if people have asked for something directly, and the other person said "no," the requestor felt rejected or put off, then decided their feelings were "caused" by the negative response. Sometimes we hold cultural values and beliefs that say it's not okay to ask. Do everyone a favor. *Ask.*

Most of us hesitate to ask directly for what we want, and asking in a clear way is powerful! The two most common ways people make indirect requests are through complaints and hints. Neither works as well as asking clearly and directly.

Complaints. Think of a complaint as a request in camouflage. Usually the complainer hasn't summoned the courage to ask directly for what he wants, so he does it obliquely and indirectly. When pinned down, the complainer sometimes doesn't actually know what he or she wants. And the intention and tone behind complaints usually guarantee his or her desire won't be fulfilled.

How does it feel to hear a complaint like this: "Why don't you ever talk with me before turning in your reports to our manager?" Would you feel inclined to cooperate with the embedded request? Would you even hear it? How would you feel? Now try on this version that articulates the hidden request: "I want us to share our reports and discuss them before turning them into Mike."

When you receive a complaint, do your best to translate the hidden request: "So, you want me to talk with you before giving Mike my report, and I imagine you want to get together before we turn in our reports and pool our data and share ideas. Is that so?" Make a radical change: Use "I" statements to keep the focus on yourself and your responsibility, rather than telling the other person what she should be doing.

Hints. If you hope other people will sense what you want if you drop a few key words, then feel upset because your wish hasn't been fulfilled, it's time to get real. By hinting, you're failing to take 100% responsibility for creating what you want. People generally can't read your mind, and it's not their responsibility to figure out what you need. It's yours. They're all thinking about what they want, focused on their own goals and needs. Sometimes we don't show our feelings, so people have no idea if we feel happy with things or not. Sometimes we don't know. Don't invest energy wishing, hoping, and dreaming. Ask. You're actually giving a gift when you let others know clearly what you want. Often they don't have a clue. And they often say yes. Sales professionals, fundraisers, and public relations (PR) people know this. Most of the rest of us don't.

To learn more about making clear requests, study Figure 5.5.

Asking Clearly

When you ask, be as specific as you can. Describe the vision of your request and how the other person plays a part in this.

FIGURE 5.5   Making Clear Requests

- Clearly state what you want the person to do.

- Clearly communicate criteria for fulfilling the request.

- Clearly communicate the time frame for completion.

- Listen for a clear response with one of four alternatives:

  1. **Accept:** "I'll be glad to do it for you."

  2. **Decline:** "Sorry, but I can't do it for you."

  3. **Present a counteroffer:** "I can complete this new project if I reschedule a customer visit."

  4. **Negotiate delivery date:** "I can't by the 5th. How about the 9th?"

Details infuse it with reality and make the request more power-ful. Mention the benefit the other person gains by granting your request. Following are excellent examples of the many simple requests linked to benefits all around us:

- "For your safety, please fasten your seat belt."

- "So that we may serve you better, this telephone conversa-tion is being recorded."

- "So that we can complete our proposal by Friday at noon, please e-mail your part of it to me by end of day Thursday."

Most of us have a particular pattern for making a request, and it's useful to know your own. For example, you may make a request about things you feel entitled to, in which case you're likely to feel miffed if you get a "no." Or you may feel like you have to exchange something to get your request filled, like, I'll review your proposal if you'll review mine. One of my (Kate's) friends promises to do something in the future if I'll do what he's requesting now. Another feels uncomfortable "owing" any favors and continues to ask how and when she can repay some-thing I've done for her until the "debt" is settled. Another asks for what he wants and assumes I'll do the same, and if it feels too out of kilter, one of us will speak up. This is my particular pref-erence and the way I attempt to get all my friendships and work-ing relationships to work. What's your pattern?

Making New Agreements

Agreements range from the profound (the merger of two behemoth companies) to the mundane (putting the trash out by the curb on Wednesdays before leaving for work). How do you make new agreements with others? Are you specific? Do you write them down?

Before you make any agreement, think carefully and only make agreements with which you feel a strong alignment. Write down all major agreements and all controversial ones and scrupulously keep the agreements you make. Recognize it when agreements aren't working and renegotiate them before they "default."

Making an agreement you don't want to make and therefore aren't likely to keep gives you an express ticket to The Bermuda Triangle. Are you a Victim, making agreements you don't really want to make; a Hero, who doesn't require others to keep their agreements; or a Villain, striking bargains with people who never come through and then blaming them?

Handling Broken Agreements

Broken or fuzzy agreements are nearly always a significant contributor to any conflict. Whether you or someone else breaks an agreement, face it head-on, fully acknowledging what has occurred. Take responsibility and let go of excuses and judgments. Ask yourself, "In what ways am I responsible for what occurred?" Then share this with the other person. Communicate any emotions you have about the problem. Ask about the other person's emotions about the situation, then listen. Finally, address the source of breakdown, so the pattern isn't repeated. People frequently go first to the fact that they have too much to do, got overcommitted, said they would do something they didn't have the time or resources to do. But usually there's more significant learning that lives behind this. People most often don't keep agreements because they agreed to do something they really didn't want to do just to get the person off their backs. They made the agreement unconsciously.

PANNING FOR GOLD

The heartbeat of accountability is, of course, *commitment—* literally, an "agreement to do something in the future." To do it, even if we're having a bad day, or circumstances change, or the world appears to be falling apart, or an agreement is handed to us we wouldn't purposefully choose. Think of looking for the hidden value in these commitments as panning for gold.

We've all been handed drudge assignments that strike us as dumb and boring, and I've certainly had my share of them. Very early in my career, I (Kate) was assigned the task of providing a daylong training for all salaried employees on our company's compensation system that included salary grades, job descriptions, benefits, and bonus guidelines. *Bor-ing!* I considered it a total waste of everyone's time. To prove my point, I even spent a weekend calculating the "real cost" of the program in terms of people's lost work time. I proved myself right, but being right didn't get me anything but the emptiness of feeling justified and impotent. I had to do the program just the same. Luckily for everyone, I looked for *hidden value.*

Hidden value almost always emerges when we can take something that seems deadly dull or apparently irrelevant and look for the human face on it. In this case, I thought about all of the lost time, tension, and ruffled feathers that result from disappointments over salary increases (or the lack of them!). Instead of leading a training on a compensation system, we spent the day exploring this system as a tool to help people move out of complaining and feeling victimized about money, and into a space where they were actively creating what they wanted in their paycheck. At the end of the program, three people came up to me and said, "Today's program has changed my life." For an HR leader, it doesn't get any better than that. These radical results permanently changed my attitude about drudge assignments.

See Figure 5.6 to learn how you can transform drudge assignments too.

If you say you'll do it, then commit your heart and soul! With such alignment between your task and your values, you may just be the one to discover the mother lode, reservations and all. If you've wholeheartedly owned the project and the results you'll create, you'll uncover some remarkable learning or a new way for your creativity to shine forth. The best way to stop this new growth is to blame other people, focus on what others should or shouldn't do, or wish life were in any way different.

MEETING IN THE MIDDLE: SOME THOUGHTS ABOUT MEETINGS

To quickly create a culture of accountability, toss out everything you know about meetings. Typically, companies start monthly or quarterly business review presentations with highlights—all the great stuff they've accomplished. The noble intention—to celebrate people's accomplishments—creates problematic results because little, if any, discussion ensues about what learning has occurred.

FIGURE 5.6   Transforming Drudge Assignments into Valuable Contributions

- Look for the gold—some hidden gift or benefit. Assume there's a learning for you in the situation or a special way to use your talents.

- Stay vigilant and keep out of The Bermuda Triangle. Refuse to blame, complain, or sacrifice.

- Express your reservations while setting an intention to find a creative solution.

An accountable culture opens meetings with what they've learned. Next, they share unsolved problems. Because learning typically occurs in the midst of some big hairy situation, 90 percent of the discussion or presentation focuses on how to understand and resolve problems. They wrap up by talking about what they've accomplished and their highlights for that month or quarter.

In most presentations when someone shares an idea about an approach to a problem, the most common responses address why the idea won't work, that it's been tried, or thought about and discarded. In an accountable culture, when people offer ideas in meetings, the automatic stance sounds something like, "Hmmmm, I wonder if I could apply that idea here or there." Change your meetings, change your lives.

Radically Responsible Meetings

Energizing and efficient meetings would alter work more than any other single element. The definition of *meeting* is "to come upon or encounter, come face to face with or into the presence of." Sounds a bit like the romantic language of love, doesn't it? Wouldn't it be a terrific world if our business meetings consistently inspired the same intensity of attention and heart-felt quality of consciousness? Given the possibilities, why are so many meetings the one thing we would gladly trade for a root canal?

Seriously, there you are in an exciting job doing important, stimulating work with some of the most brilliant people in your field. You're getting paid for all that fun. And you don't look forward to most opportunities to sit around a table together and talk about all of that?! Instead, we space out, write our to-do lists, pick up our e-mail, or pass notes back and forth like we're in eighth-grade study hall. Is it the routine? Is it poor meeting plans? The view out the window? The unimaginative selection of herbal teas? What is it about meetings, exactly, that makes us lapse into a passive or complaining mode?

Instead of taking responsibility for the quality of the meeting before it starts, we assume the person calling the meeting is fully responsible for making it a success. Our only obligation is to show up to discuss a project, or prepare our presentation, deliver it, and await people's input. The sludge starts building. On the other hand, we've all experienced the thrill of a radical meeting where ideas and passions flow, debate is lively, and creative breakthroughs generate a raucous round of "high fiving." What fun they are!

The difference between traditional meetings and radically responsible meetings is the number of people taking 100% responsibility for the quality of the experience. If you find yourself feeling critical or bored during a meeting, ask yourself, "What can I do right now to raise my energy and productivity, for myself and for the whole group?" We call this *radical responsibility,* where we trust that everything—obstacles as well as opportunities—contain the unfolding of higher order learning and expansion. Let's take a look at the factors that determine the energy levels in meetings.

Give Up the Need to Be Right. We all know people who seem to love being right more than they love making a genuine contribution. When someone is locked into being right, idea generation becomes a combat zone, where there's little chance for ideas to be tossed around and improved upon. We rarely see ourselves as needing to be right, but believe that if the other person would only listen to reason, then everything would move forward so much faster. When you find yourself caught in this eddy, stop the churn and listen consciously (Chapter 6).

Put Truth on the Table. One of the big reasons meetings become a drain on time and a drag on energy is that we tend to hold back our real truth. We usually have justifiable reasons for not speaking up when we disagree. Intimidation. Introversion. Shyness. Dominating personalities. Deference to the hierarchy. Grumpy mood. Lack of adequate expertise on the topic at hand. Time crunches. Maybe experience has repeatedly proven that nothing but tacit approval is expected in meetings unless they are specifically labeled as brainstorming sessions. But if we dare to adopt as our personal mantra some version of results, not reasons, the radically responsible meeting becomes reality more often than not.

Several years ago the executive leading Motorola's semiconductor business asked me (Kate) to work with him and his team to raise the quality and effectiveness of their meetings. We agreed I would attend their four-day off-site working session, observe and mingle for the first two days, offer my feedback on the third day, and on the fourth day help them institute recommended changes. I could smell a breakthrough opportunity, but I wasn't sure how it would come about.

I explained to everyone on the morning of the third day that I would be overly dramatic in offering my diagnosis. Although my feedback for them was somewhat strong, I had a close relationship with this group and had imagined them laughing at themselves as I rehearsed my presentation the night before. So in a fairly lighthearted, Inspector Poirot manner, I played back their meeting behaviors for them. "First of all, significant topics generate limited discussion in the meeting," I reported, "but plenty of discussion in the hallways. Most of you have the tendency to withhold your truths in meetings. I don't know what *you* call that, but here's what I call it. At best it's compliance, and at worst, it's the same as lying."

No one chuckled. Instead, the room got dead quiet. My stomach lurched, and I continued: "You think you have the well being of the group in mind by not speaking up—saving time by keeping your disagreements to yourselves as if you were helpless victims instead of the executive decision makers you are . . .

"The hallway and lunch table conversations may feel productive and necessary to you as you talk about decisions and actions your peers and your president are taking that you don't support and agree with, but they pave the way for the inevitable—complaining once you're back at the office about decisions over which you apparently have no control. You'll criticize, vent, blame, grumble, and make the best of it. But in my book, when you talk about someone in a critical way who isn't present, you're gossiping."

As I continued, the stillness was deafening. I finished my monologue to no thunderous applause or good-hearted chortling—just a long pregnant silence. I felt surprised and scared. This was so different from what I'd expected. And I also knew I had spoken the truth. I opted to let the uncomfortable quiet continue to fill the space. It lasted for about three of the longest minutes in recorded meeting history.

That's how it is with accountability—you observe what seems to be true, act on it, and stay with it in full integrity until the breakthrough moment is ready to pop. It takes a bit of nerve at first. Sometimes the immediate result looks like an uproar, giving you the titillating and not always welcome experience of living on the razor's edge. Experience teaches you to trust this decision, and the results are nothing short of exhilarating. The skills to cultivate include listening and clarifying, listening and clarifying some more, until the breakthrough is ready to happen, realizing that massive disagreements (or deafening silence) are often a signal that things are going well, and not falling apart.

Finally, Mario Rivas, a dynamic leader, broke the silence and took a radical action. "I'm choking on the words, but I have to say I'm a gossip." He then proceeded to confess to their faces what he had said about these same people behind their backs. As he owned his behavior and committed to speaking up more in meetings, he created the opening for many other people to do likewise. An hour and a half later, everyone around the table was in full integrity, deeply committed to better meetings by ending compliance, gossip, and boredom. It was a radically responsible meeting with breakthroughs none of us will ever forget. I recently heard from Mario, who's now an EVP of Royal Philips Electronics, and he credits much of his ensuing success to that pivotal moment of accountability.

I developed the Meetings Engagement Scale, shown in Figure 5.7, as a learning tool to help create radical meetings. A number of our clients have adopted it as part of their "meeting culture" and, based on their results, we urge you to consider doing the same. The rules are simple. Merely ask everyone to be mindful of their engagement and to agree that every 30 minutes a designated driver who's free of "meeting goop" will prompt everyone to check in with their own energy and rate it, using the Meetings Engagement Scale.

The Meetings Engagement Scale can instantly pop meetings onto another level. On one memorable occasion, Arnold Donald, then SVP at Monsanto and now CEO at Equal Sweetener, became so engaged in truth-telling that a couple of large tears rolled down his cheek, triggering the CFO to announce, "My engagement level just dropped from a 7 to a 3. Emotions have no place in a business meeting." If you'd been in that meeting, what would your reaction have been at that moment? How would you have ranked your engagement, following the CFO's comment? Would your level have slid to a 4, withdrawing after

FIGURE 5.7   Radical Meetings Engagement Scale

Select the number that best describes your level of energy. To increase your level of engagement, select and practice a behavior with a higher number on the scale.

0   Committing to do something you don't have the time or re-sources to do

1   Complying, pretending to agree when you don't

2   Blaming people who aren't in the room

3   Aggressively grilling the presenter, judging and criticizing people

4   Accommodating, while mentally judging and criticizing people

5   Polite disinterest, vacillating between engagement and zoning out

6   Turning complaints and criticism into requests about what you want

7   Expressing genuine curiosity about the issue and how you can contribute

8   Communicating your full truth in a self-disclosing way without blame

9   Actively and enthusiastically exploring problems and making decisions

10 Bringing issues to closure at the right time; creating a follow-up plan

hearing this remark, or flashed to a 9 at the prospect of exploring problems and making decisions?

We have the tendency to speak our truth when we believe it will be shared or supported. It's a lot harder and riskier when you're a lone voice, and the rewards are often in proportion to the risk. All of a sudden we had a real cliffhanger. What happened next? Just the richest, most meaningful, authentic discussion imaginable about the value of emotions at work and the importance of honoring our individual uniqueness. The conversation evolved into a profound dialogue about compassion, friendship, and bonding in the workplace. The punch line may surprise you. The CFO who first registered his protest about emotions in the workplace, a man who by nature resisted the "soft stuff," adopted an entirely different view after the fact. Yet it was his act of courage and authenticity that took the group into an incredibly important discussion that ultimately helped move him and everyone else forward.

Find the courage to become 100% responsible for the results in your life. Time and space will move in service to the accountable person.

SUMMARY

- Accountability lapses—not fulfilling our agreements, not giving our best effort all of the time—are symptoms of glitches and patterns of unintended behaviors that keep us stuck.

- In most companies—especially those with a management philosophy based on fear—*accountability* means to "account for" what I have done in the past, instead of defining what I will do now and in the future. The latter is *proactive* accountability that stresses what I can do now to get better results.

- Accountable people make solid agreements and take 100% responsibility for their experiences and commitments. They communicate frequently with updates, they're reliable on tight deadlines, they rarely drop the ball or manipulate reality to stand solo in the spotlight.

- The distinction between traditional meetings and radically responsible meetings is the number of people around the table taking 100% responsibility for the quality of the experience.

- Change your meetings to focus on sharing your learnings and asking for support.

- Only make agreements you feel completely aligned with and committed to. Keep your agreements. The moment you see the need for a change, let those who will be affected know, and renegotiate the agreement.

INTO ACTION

- When have you modeled a lack of accountability to your team? What one step can you take today to increase your level of accountability?

- Are there agreements that you chronically make and don't keep? What changes can you make to break this pattern?

- Get into the habit of asking yourself wonder questions that invite accountability: What issues, clues, or information did you ignore or pretend not to know? What is it about your attitude or response that keeps this pattern going?

- Consider each of your team members. Are there specific ways you can support each one in becoming more accountable?

- Is there one area in your company that would particularly benefit from a greater level of accountability? What specific steps can you take to help achieve this?

- How can your organization tie accountability to perform-ance reviews?

- What policies and procedures can be put into place to in-vite greater accountability in all departments and at all lev-els of your organization? How can the language of your company—in public documents, forms, and Web site re-flect greater accountability? How can you help your or-ganization to move in that direction?

- When you lead meetings, how can you change the tone and supportively encourage participants to drop their defenses?

- As a participant, what active role can you play in meetings to set the stage for learning and dropping defensive behavior?

CHAPTER SIX

CANDOR
Telling the Truth and Turning the Tide

How can I overcome people's tendencies to "shade" the truth?

What's the best way to resolve long-standing problems with others and clear the air?

How can I create a corporate culture based on the truth?

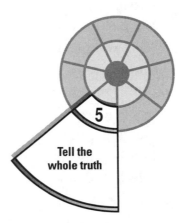

5

Tell the whole truth

The ability to navigate constant change is directly related to the level of truth telling. If you want your organization and your career to move at warp speed, tell the truth 24/7. Avoiding the truth—not speaking it or not being open to hearing it—creates a culture of indecisiveness that markedly increases bureaucracy and politics and slows your organization to a crawl. Truth instantly gets all the information out on the table, so we quickly make the right decisions with the benefit of 360° of detail and opinion. Truth clears the way for everything to speed up: effective teamwork, the flow of information, needed changes, and high-quality work. *True power and enormous speed result when people deal directly with the truth and with one another.*

We've never met anyone who thinks of himself as a liar. Yet, what are the odds of finding an adult on the planet who *hasn't* experienced life in the *false* lane—that uneasy, foreboding journey that sends us on unintended detours before we find our way onto the main road again? From little white lies to major whoppers, from those we hand off to others and especially the lies we tell ourselves, the odds of finding someone who's never detoured via a lie are probably something approaching six billion to one. We seem to have a commitment to conceal, not reveal.

Venting and complaining about people who aren't around isn't being candid, frank, or truthful, and neglecting to disclose the whole truth is the equivalent of a *silent lie.* If we witness a lie and don't correct it, we're liars as well. Withholding details, concealing information, spinning stories, and massaging data are all forms of lying, because they all involve an *intention to deceive,* whether the deception is on the personal level or the corporate level, inside the company culture or out there in the marketplace.

Even though everyone lies, we don't call everyone a liar. It's easy to use that term if it's someone we don't like, but hard if it's someone we like and admire. We call their lies "spinning," "shading the truth," and "massaging data." From what we've observed, lies occur at epidemic levels in companies. Many people live much of their work time in the zones of conning or being conned, both of which imply basic mistrust and disrespect.

WHITE LIES, BLACK LIES, AND EVERY SHADE OF GRAY

Fortunately, we're hardwired for truth. Though not infallible, human radar is reasonably reliable and highly tuned. People who lie don't broadcast it the way Pinocchio did. (Can you imagine how often we'd poke and be poked in a single day if our noses indicated our current level of truthfulness? Most of us would be downright dangerous!) But we perceive lies fairly easily with the data that comes in through our five senses—in a fleeting gesture, nervous eye contact, an altered tone of voice, a conveniently misplaced fact, an agreement that doesn't ring quite right. Some of us have developed our intuition, an inner sixth sense that tunes in to lies. And all of us feel a lie in our hearts when we recognize one in the making, whether we are on the giving or the receiving end—the duper or the duped. Some unnamed part of us suffers a low-level, pervasive anxiety, even a dulling sadness when what we know to be true is represented otherwise, especially when it involves people we want and need to trust.

The FBI's chief lie detector operator has given more than 3,000 tests and has had several hundred confessions in the middle of the test, when the person broke down and told the truth. Every year during the holidays he's showered with cards from prisoners who are so grateful they confessed. This tells you something about the power of telling the truth, if a person will write you a fan letter because you were there when he or she confessed—even if that confession resulted in prison.

With such huge capacity for truth in our bodyminds, the problems and challenges we encounter with truth are in the software—in the realm of our beliefs, values, and habitual behaviors. We invite you to read this chapter as if it were offering you a free *truth software upgrade* taking you to expanded levels of discovery, clarity, capacity, and productivity. This candor upgrade enables you to tell the truth in ways that create trust and openness, allowing higher order solutions to emerge, based on what's real. Best of all, you can continue to upgrade for the rest of your life at no additional charge. You'll benefit and your company will, too.

WHY WE LIE

Our childhood lessons about truth are filled with paradox, and many of us have learned or concluded over the course of our lives that telling the truth often makes things worse. As children, how many times did we hear the following:

- "If you can't say something nice, don't say anything at all."

- "Tell the truth or you'll get it" (which often led to being punished anyway).

- "Tattletale!"

- "Don't tell. You'll get into trouble."

- "Don't you say that to your _____ (mother/teacher/minister). Show some respect!"

It turns out that much of our childhood truth training may actually have been a primer in how to tell a whopper. If you internalized any of these messages as a child, they may have stunted your inner growth in the area of truth telling.

Most of us have emerged from childhood believing the truth hurts and that we must lie to survive. After working with more than 1,000 executives and experiencing my (Kate's) own array of close-up lessons on this topic, I've come to a different conclusion: *The truth heals and lies hurt.* Hiding feelings or deeds destroys relationships and companies. Speaking the truth, with no blame, restores connection. I have found no exceptions.

We lie to ourselves and to others when we don't value truth enough to trust it without editing or embellishing. We lie to avoid hurting someone's feelings because we mistakenly believe we can control how others feel. We lie because we don't trust our teammates. We lie to manipulate outcomes—to avoid penalties or receive kudos. We lie to get ahead. We lie because it's our corporate culture. We lie because everyone else does, and our lies don't always seem like lies. Where do we find the courage to break ranks with the silently sanctioned culture of "nice lies" and move into the zone of uncompromising self-assured participation with the truth? When we're ready for the adventure of our lives.

I feel endlessly fascinated by the spectrum of human behavior that causes us to look the other way. I was once paid $30,000 to essentially tell someone he shouldn't talk with his mouth full. Another time, I received $20,000 to help an executive eliminate the four letter words in an opening speech she was giving to over 1,000 members of a very conservative industry association. Yet another memorable assignment involved coaching a COO who was perceived by many of her peers to have "big problems" within the company. After many hours of interviewing ten of these peers, one brave soul told the truth: The "big" problem was that the COO picked her nose in public! (I know. The glamour in my job is boundless. Who wouldn't leap out of bed each and every morning with these fascinating knots to unravel?)

Why didn't people, who genuinely cared about their colleagues, tell them the truth? It's the old "spinach in the teeth" challenge. We dismiss someone's ideas about a project to his or her face, but evaporate at the prospect of giving personal feedback. Ironically, we act as if we have the right to complain widely behind someone's back about hygiene or table manners but could never, ever, mention the issue directly for fear of embarrassing them. An enormous amount of "withholds" (and wasted time and energy) occur in this personal zone.

Without a doubt, fear—the *other "F" word*—is the most prevalent motive for not telling the truth. What's the source of the fear? Modern versions of executing the messenger, expressed in the form of blame ("You should have come out with this months ago!"), downgrading ("Maybe you can't handle the responsibility you've been given here."), or even the big bust ("You're fired!").

Our worst fears about telling the truth happened to me very early in my (Kate's) career when I was a staff member working for the director of a mental health organization. One day I told her I was certain she was losing the confidence of the board and also gave her much unsolicited but very well-intended advice about what to do differently. A month later, just as soon as I'd completed a huge project (which the board loved), she fired me. I can see in hindsight that my lack of skills in *how to tell the truth* generated a power struggle between us—one I wasn't even aware of until it was too late.

In contrast, Michael Dell brought in Mort Topfer in 1994 as vice chairman, knowing he needed a wise advisor. It's not unusual in the high-tech world to bring in a "gray hair" to learn from; what's remarkable is that Michael actually listened! He also gave Mort, who had a successful international track record in the emerging consumer electronics markets, the room to bring his gifts to Dell. Within a year, Mort was functioning more as COO than vice chairman, with Michael's support and blessings. Michael faced the reality of his own limitations and was eager to rely on someone else's genius to the benefit of everyone involved with Dell.

TRUTH AS TONIC

Chronically withholding or manipulating the truth is like damming a river: There are consequences. Problems begin to mount both inside and outside. We cut our spirit, our enthusiasm, and our motivation. We plod along, but our hearts, literally and figuratively, aren't in it. When you withhold the truth, you stop your energy and your ability to be *for* that person. You ultimately compromise your integrity because you've been willing to put on an act. When you withhold, you halt not only the relationship's expansiveness but your own. When you step up to the truth, you turn contracted, protective, fear energy into expansive, intuitive, visionary energy. In the end, you do it for yourself and your own full potential, which spills over into the potential of the relationship as well.

Imagine that your personal integrity is like a passbook savings account. Each act of deception—withholding, concealing, or falsifying—is the equivalent of a withdrawal. That storehouse of energy inside of you is real! It takes a hit every time you lie, and it expands every time you see and step up to the truth. The more genuinely difficult the truth navigated, the greater the deposit, and the richer you are for it. With practice, your interest in the truth will accrue at ever-increasing rates.

Truth acts like an energy source. Feeling dragged down? Instead of munching a high carb bar or sipping a protein drink, ask yourself if some truth needs to be told. Just as food nourishes the body, truth is sustenance for our spirits. We hear lots more laughter in companies where truth is a way of life. If we can learn to give and receive truth just as we give and receive respect, love, affection, and friendship, we enter into a dynamic partnership with its teaching and healing qualities.

The Truth Does Set You Free

In my (Kate's) corporate career days, Bob Riopel, who knew nothing about HR, became my new manager. I felt so upset that I actually considered leaving the company. I liked him well enough; I just didn't respect him as a potential manager. Yet I liked the company, and I loved my work. I dragged around for about a week, trying to figure out what to do.

Finally, I told him, as *clearly* and as *kindly* as I knew how, that, in my opinion, he didn't know anything about HR. I explained that I was only willing to work for him if he stayed completely out of my area. If he did, then he could count on me 100 percent to keep him completely informed about what I was doing. If he had concerns about anything, I would listen to them, but if I didn't agree, I wasn't going to act on them. In other words, I was going to treat him like a peer, not a manager.

To my amazement, he said he was eager to learn from me. That meeting was the beginning of a close, successful, productive relationship. In fact, he encouraged me to write my first business book that helped launch my consulting business, and I put him high on the acknowledgments page of the book.

Truth, the Best Remedy

I (Eddie) worked with a pharmaceutical company to help resolve a conflict between the marketing and research departments. The directors who headed these groups both hotly stated that they always felt as if they were getting different stories from Dimitri, VP of their business unit. They had begun to distrust his motives, create assumptions, interpretations, and agendas, and they had become progressively more vigilant and hesitant in their relationship and communications with him.

I met with the CEO, the directors, and Dimitri, who immediately launched into his own story about how he felt misunderstood. He had simply been trying to communicate what was essential for each of the different groups and this often means different information. He felt unjustly accused because his choice of words was being interpreted as spinning and untrustworthy. Dimitri looked genuinely puzzled and said he'd had no intention of being inconsistent or less than truthful.

He could not see that there was anything for *him* to learn. The whole situation seemed to be about other people not hearing him correctly, coming to incorrect conclusions, or just plain misunderstanding his intentions. We seemed to be at an impasse until I asked him at a break about his family and early school experiences growing up. He said that, as a first-generation Russian in a very middle-class neighborhood in a small town in Nebraska, he felt different. To survive, he developed a successful strategy to be liked by everyone. "There were many cliques in the school, and I was a member of every one of them," he said with a grin. He suddenly saw that being able to speak an acceptable language to often diametrically opposed groups had meant survival for him as a child. He immediately connected this experience to his work challenges. We then explored new behaviors within the team. The directors agreed to let Dimitri know when they felt they were being spun, and Dimitri agreed to get clarity by having the others repeat what he said. A new sense of camaraderie was palpable as we ended our meeting.

Focusing in on the Truth

Another truth telling challenge looks like this: We want to get our way, and we don't believe our managers or our peers understand the issues. In an attempt to exercise influence, we go a bit too far. We feel tempted to massage the data and spin the truth, twisting the facts or focusing on our perspective, while minimizing other valid points of view.

More than 15 years ago, when I (Kate) was HR VP of KLA-Tencor, I caught myself not telling the truth in the middle of a conversation with our CEO about a compensation program for our brilliant technologists. I wasn't lying, but I certainly wasn't disclosing all that I knew. I told myself this was more data than he needed. But when I looked inside, I realized that I wasn't disclosing everything because it might make it harder to get what I wanted.

This was one of those moments when the world simply stopped. Everything turned into slow motion. I realized if I wanted impeccable integrity in my life (which I did), I would have to give up everything I knew about getting my way. In the past I had been, frankly, manipulative. I had ethics about "massaging the facts" *too* much, but I was more invested in getting my way than getting to the best answer. My behavior would have a defining influence on how our CEO would relate to me, so I chose to tell the whole truth. My proposal was not adopted, but my decision to tell the truth so strengthened my relationship with the CEO that he gave me the latitude to implement a bonus program that later won recognition from several professional organizations for its trend-setting impact.

THE COST OF NOT TELLING THE TRUTH

The price we pay for withholding the truth is measured in human terms as well as cash. Withholding some perceived truth, even just a kernel of insight, puts us out of integrity with ourselves. Once we lose that sense of inner alignment, we have handicapped our capacity to think clearly and act with confidence. Nothing happens in isolation, and we can even begin to manifest physical symptoms such as headaches, ulcers, back problems, indigestion, and colitis.

I (Eddie) knew a very bright, midlevel university administrator who had an endless succession of surgeries (gallbladder, thyroid, stomach, colon). These led to further complications, and she became dependent on painkillers. Her colleagues thought it was "bad luck" that she seemed to get one disease after another. This whole time, though, she was out of integrity in her marriage, there were endless secrets in her family, and she and her daughter were estranged. The people she worked with were out of integrity, too. Her manager was having a long-standing affair, and she covered for him with his wife.

Evidence strongly suggests our emotional bodies are not only guidance systems for truth, but are also linked directly to our immune systems. The truth, therefore, can be viewed as an important factor in maintaining physical health!*

---

*If you've never been directly exposed to these ideas, you might want to explore titles by one of these best-selling, pioneering authors who have written for the mainstream: Herbert Benson, MD, Larry Dossey, MD, Candace Pert, Ph.D., Joan Borysenko, MD, and Andrew Weil, MD.

Just one withheld truth has the same effect on your nervous system as one wheel out of alignment on the car. This is not a problem if you're driving 5 to 10 MPH, but if you're going at the warp speed most companies want, anything causing a rattle now will become a fatal vibration as you pick up speed. Choosing to remain in a lie is like turning up the radio really loud so we don't notice the wheel is out of alignment. It throws our bodies and our committees off, and nothing gets done until we restore harmony.

LET GO OF THE UNCONTROLLABLE

About 95 percent of the time we lie because we don't want to upset someone, then have to deal with consequences. When we think we withhold the truth because we do not want to hurt their feelings, we're actually lying to ourselves because we cannot control someone's reaction or their emotions. *The happiest and most efficient people on earth direct their energy toward things they can control.* Everything in life fits in one of two files: (1) things you can control and (2) things you can't. Stress shows up when we make a filing mistake, confusing one for the other.

When we neglect to deliver critical feedback to an employee because we don't want to upset him or her, bypass an intuitive hunch that keeps popping up because our coworkers don't like the direction of a project, or set an unrealistic product launch date to make our manager happy, we're living in fantasyland, not in reality. You'll find it much more rewarding in the long run to notice and soberly accept what is than to focus so much attention on what you hope will occur or how you wish people will behave or how you want people to feel about you.

Here's a list in Figure 6.1 to help make some of these distinctions clearer.

FIGURE 6.1   The Control Files

Things I Can't Control:	Things I Can Control:
Whether it rains	Choosing to carry an umbrella
Whether a new product ships on time	How I communicate to the customer that the product will ship later than expected
What happened in the past	My behavior in the present
What will happen in the future	My attitude about the future
Whether someone respects me	Whether I deliver on my agreements
How someone feels about me	How I behave and communicate with people
Emotions I feel in the moment	How I act on my emotions
Other people's emotions	How I react to other people's emotions
How well an employee in my group performs	How much feedback, encouragement, and coaching I give the employee
Whether someone responds defensively to my feedback	How I deliver my feedback
Whether I'm promoted	How well I do my job, how committed I am to getting needed information and building relationships I need to succeed

We waste enormous time and energy trying to control the uncontrollable. Susan Campbell, author of *Getting Real,*[*] conducted a three-year study of 500 people focusing on the new human capacities we need in our tumultuous world of change and information overload. *She found that 80 percent of people spend a significant amount of their workday focused on the uncontrollable.* Imagine the energy and the opportunity we'd release if we focused on what we can control.

Let's say you are given a hot new project to manage at work, and you feel thrilled by the opportunity. Accepting it, however, means you'll be working long hours over the coming few weekends, when your family, partner, or friends were counting on your availability. A controlling, martyred truth would sound something like, "I'm sorry guys, but my boss needs me on a major project. If I don't do it, I might get passed up for promotion, and you know, we really do need the money. I can't afford to say no."

A more radical and impeccable version of the truth might sound like this: "Honey, I have great news! The project I wanted to manage has finally landed on my desk. Accepting it means I'll have to work this weekend, next weekend, and perhaps a few long nights. I really want to do it. Would you please support me in this? I know it will take away from our family time, and I'll miss our hiking trip. Even so, I really want this project, and I hope you'll be okay with the extra time I need to give it."

Telling the truth doesn't guarantee that people around you will immediately say yes or offer their support. It does, however, ensure that you stay in integrity, which ultimately means that problems get resolved instead of feeding the sludge of withholds and spun truths.

---

*Campbell, Susan. *Getting Real.* Novato, CA: New World Library, 2001.

SIX FUNDAMENTAL TRUTH TOOLS

Even if you don't feel very handy around the house, you probably own a few basic tools like a hammer, screwdriver, tape measure, and pliers, and you know how to use them. To maintain truth in your life, your basic tool set, seen in Figure 6.2, should include the tools that help you deal with the truth both on your own and when interacting with others.

If you master the crucial skills in Figure 6.2, you can use them in a wide array of truth work (because truth works), repairing the past and creating a stronger future.

Recognize Your Own Truth Slips

Getting beneath our habitual emotional responses to an immediate, ongoing connection with our integrity requires meticulous observation and ongoing reflection. Feeling tired and don't know why? Finding yourself argumentative or on edge?

Turn inward and wonder what's going on. Scan for something withheld, spun, or fabricated. The few seconds you take to wonder about this will restore you to a higher level of clarity and self-assurance. The master key to unlock the truth is to ask, "Is this a

---

FIGURE 6.2   Basic Truth Tool Set

- Recognize your own truth slips.

- Face the truth.

- Separate story from fact.

- Speak responsibly from your own perspective.

- Listen consciously.

FIGURE 6.3   Uncovering Truth Slips

1. Notice when you feel physically or emotionally "off."

2. Ask yourself what's going on.

3. Identify familiar patterns.

4. Wonder how you sustain these patterns.

pattern?" When the answer is "yes," the next step is to wonder, "How do I feed and manifest this pattern in my life?" Uncovering truth slips involves the four steps listed in Figure 6.3.

Once you've realized you've had a truth slip, you can employ the next tool.

Face the Truth

Our biggest cons, in our experience, are self-inflicted because we won't face the truth. Many of us, for example, keep underperforming employees far beyond the time they should be released to find a job that matches their particular skills.

Everything in our lives starts with the choice to face something or to avoid it. Facing things squarely renews our hearts, souls, and bodies. Avoiding reality destroys us both personally and professionally. If you don't feel happy at home or if you don't feel creative in your work, you're not facing something. We may not be facing that we have a drinking problem, or we need to take better care of our body, or we don't like our job, or a thousand other things. *At the bottom of all problems is always something we are afraid to face, and we slowly destroy our lives if we continue to avoid facing it.* Whatever it is—turn and face it squarely.

This is the secret of life. To keep it simple, look first in three places, as listed in Figure 6.4.

FIGURE 6.4   Three Quick Ways to Face the Truth

1. What *feeling* am I not facing?

2. What *experience* am I not communicating?

3. What *agreements* am I not keeping?

The majority of unhappiness in our lives comes from the three places seen in Figure 6.4. As soon as you face them, you'll fast forward into far greater ease and speed. Perhaps you've done something you feel guilty about and you haven't come clean with the other person. You may feel angry with someone or hurt about something that someone has said, and you haven't told the person directly. If you don't communicate the truth directly, you won't feel good, and your inner self will keep reminding you with random flashes and thoughts.

Perhaps you didn't follow through on a commitment. Or you did something you said you wouldn't. These little moments of slipped integrity—even agreements as small as saying we'll take out the garbage and then we don't—tend to drag our energy down and create an unsettled rattle in us. All we have to do to get back into integrity is handle the broken agreement—again, through some kind of direct communication.

So ask yourself, "What do I most need to face right now in my life?" Stop right now and do this. Take a few minutes in silence to see what emerges. This is how we break out of life-long self-limiting habits and move on more rapidly. The final step in this important and life-changing process is to commit to doing something about it. Is there someone with whom you need to communicate? Is there something that you need to do? What will actually heal and resolve this particular issue? Each time we're willing to move through this process we become happier, lighter, faster.

Separate Story from Fact

As human beings it's our job to make sense of the world around us by using our knowledge and experiences to help us interpret and explain events. Often, however, we have incomplete information, and we must make assumptions or guess at the meaning of things. In other words, we make up a story that explains the situation. A critical comment from our manager about a detail in the project (fact) might be interpreted as, "My manager doesn't like the work I do" (story).

There's nothing wrong with interpreting information and creating stories—it's what the human mind does so well. *The problem occurs when we don't check out our stories, and we act as if our interpretations are facts, blaming others and taking things personally.*

We sometimes "get lost in our story" because we enjoy the effects on our listeners of our whining, complaining, and blaming. If you're feeling some emotional charge about the story or it's taking a long time to tell, you're probably lost in the story.

Here's how several people stepped out of their stories into the facts and a happy resolution.

A hospital patient and his family requested that the chief surgical resident be taken off his case. They said he was arrogant, dishonest, uncaring, and condescending. I (Eddie) approved the request and also asked that during the postoperative and recovery period we all meet to discuss this situation. The meeting occurred two weeks later in our office. The patient, his wife, son, and daughter filed into the conference room, and when the surgical resident arrived, the air was charged with tension and discomfort.

The patient's son said one day he passed the resident and his entourage as they left his father's room and asked how his father was doing because the night before his father had called several times complaining of pain and feeling frightened that he was going to die. The resident had replied quickly, saying his father was doing fine, then rushed off with his team. When the son entered his father's room he saw bloody bandages still lying on the bed, a very pained look on his father's face, a dirty patient gown, and an untouched cold breakfast.

The resident explained that he and the surgical team had rushed off to a young patient in intensive care, who had suddenly had a cardiac arrest. He acknowledged that he had been brusque and that he had felt terrified about the impending disaster. There was some softening in the room, and the patient spoke next. He said, "You know, I liked you, Dr. McIntosh, and up until that particular morning you were my favorite doctor. I enjoyed your sense of humor and your humanness; you joked around with me and you seemed to understand what it was like to be a farmer. Now that I'm out of the hospital I'm not mad anymore. I think I was just scared." The son said, "I guess everybody in this room is both real and human. Thank you for taking the time to meet. I realize now that my dad was in the best possible place for his care."

I believe honest and self-disclosing conversations like this would dramatically reduce malpractice lawsuits, which are invariably based on a bunch of stories that lead someone to feel not well cared for.

So, how do we begin to pull apart the facts from the stories? It requires seeing the rigorous distinction between the simple description of events and the story you created to make sense of it. Then you have to be equally rigorous in rewriting or giving up your story if it's not accurate. See Figure 6.5.

The most growth-oriented people we know have learned to question their assumptions with inspiring skill, tenacity, and flexibility. They are also masters at spotting the familiar patterns that masquerade as reality and replacing them with new insights and more empowering behaviors.

The other practice that wreaks havoc every day is assuming your interpretation is reality. Study Figure 6.6 to see how assuming your interpretation is reality usually plays out.

FIGURE 6.5   Separating Story from Fact

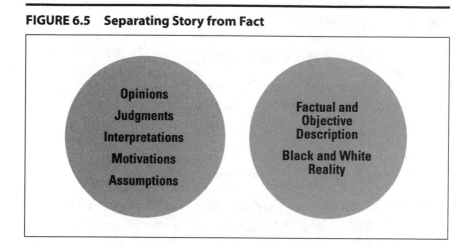

As a result of assuming your interpretation is reality, the problem isn't resolved, and your distrust escalates. When we believe our unsubstantiated stories, we can make our lives needlessly miserable.

Speak Responsibly from Your Own Perspective

I (Eddie) worked with Jerry, a CFO, a few years ago who's known for telling the truth to your face. He has courage. He's direct, straightforward, and blunt. So the good news is you get the truth from Jerry and can learn. The bad news is that the way Jerry packages his truth sometimes requires some recovery time because he expresses his opinions as facts. And sometimes it's hard for people to hear the nuggets of truth, because it's delivered in a package that's somewhat irritating. The net result: Most people don't get a chance to see how caring and heartful Jerry is. They just hear his "truth delivery system" and make up all sorts of opinions based on that. What happens, in Jerry's case and for many of us, is that he expresses his opinions as facts. He mixes up his interpretations with reality, and then people who

FIGURE 6.6   Assuming Your Interpretation Is Reality

1. Someone does something that surprises you or that you don't like.

2. You interpret the person's actions (e.g., you make up a story to explain to yourself what happened).

3. You act as if your interpretation is reality and fail to check out your "story" directly with the person.

4. Or you check out your interpretation with the person, don't like what they say, and end up believing they aren't being straight with you.

work with him do exactly the same. They hear his gruff, confronting voice and assume that he doesn't value their input.

When we speak from our own experience or interpretations, we're saying this is simply our experience and leaving the door open to others to have their own beliefs and interpretations. "I" statements help us tell the truth about our own point of view (fact) without making someone else wrong (story). Any time we can stay out of blaming and take responsibility for our experiences, we are giving the other person a way to listen to our point of view, while minimizing the likelihood of defensiveness. See Figure 6.7.

Become a Conscious Listener

We've felt amazed at the impact of attentive listening and equally dismayed at the havoc wrought by poor listening. We've seen great listening resolve conflicts—even long-standing ones— when nothing else seemed to work. Conscious listening requires

FIGURE 6.7   Blaming versus Radically Responsible Communications

"You" Statements:	"I" Statements:
You're not listening to me.	I'm not communicating in a way that inspires listening or learning.
You don't "get it."	I'm not communicating what I'm saying effectively.
Why don't you stop micro-managing and let me do my job?	How can I build my credibility with you?
You don't do what you say you're going to do.	I want to find out how we can keep our agreements with each other.

that you patiently put aside your agenda, your assumptions, and your need to be right long enough to actually hear the other person's facts or point of view. Then you must listen with the goal of understanding their ideas, their feelings at that moment, and their noblest, highest aims.

Conscious listening does not mean being quiet while you mentally prepare and rehearse what you're going to say as soon as there's a pause. It's also not about parroting what the person is saying or handing out unsolicited advice or telling about a similar problem you've dealt with in the past. Look at the other person the way you would a work of art. Instead of feeling frustrated that they don't communicate as quickly and directly as you'd like, listen closely to discover their uniqueness, the interesting and different way their mind works. What's remarkable is that if you listen like this, you create the space in which the other person often resolves the issue or thinks about it in a more creative or useful way.

You'll also find the person more open to coaching afterwards about how to adjust their communications to fit your own preferences. But if you've been hurrying them along, interrupting, and attempting to control and direct the conversation to meet your needs, any direct attempts by you to change their communication style will feel like criticism, because it is. And they will likely respond with some sort of defensiveness that makes it less likely they will make the change that you'd like, unless you've got power and a big stick on your side.

In Figure 6.8 are the main components of Conscious Listening.

Which of your work situations or relationships would benefit most from better listening? The next time you notice yourself slipping into a defensive mode, take a breath and simply be present as the other speaks. You should then be able to capture the content, the emotions, and the noble intention of the person who stands before you.

HOME AND WORK IMPROVEMENT PROJECTS

You've now got the basic truth skills, and you're ready to embark upon some major home and work improvement projects. We'll start with some basic repair work, learning how to

---

FIGURE 6.8   Conscious Listening

Content:	Summarize the key points of the message.
Emotions:	Highlight the mood and feelings of the speaker.
Noble Intention:	Point out the speaker's unstated, underlying noble intentions and commitment.

clean up a lie, then move on to the major cleanup of sharing withheld truths and clearing the air. Finally, we'll master the maintenance actions of resolving differences and giving honest feedback on a daily basis. You'll then be equipped with the tools and skills to bring truth into all parts of life and your company.

Cleaning Up a Lie

To enjoy a lifetime of the increasingly rich rewards described in this chapter, here's your fundamental candor action: *If you mislead someone, address it immediately.* The more thoroughly and quickly you do, the greater the rewards. One of the ways we perpetuate problems is to hold back until the "right time" and then the right time never comes. In fact, what's more likely is that, in a meeting with other people, something comes up about the information we withheld and it's much harder to come clean. So the first moment you catch yourself putting a spin on reality, call the person involved and let them know there's something you need to share with them. Handle it on the phone or in person—this isn't something for e-mail. Use the steps found in Figure 6.9.

Avoid slipping into defensiveness and justifying and explaining away what you did. Be direct and frank. I did such and such, I don't feel good about it, I made a judgment error, and I want to clean it up. Then listen—and listen well. The person may attack and blame you and display significant anger. They may stonewall and withdraw. They may feel victimized by your withheld information. Or they may feel relieved and grateful to finally be getting the real truth. Instead of sounding the alarm and raising your defensive walls, listen and reflect back their content, their emotions, and their underlying intention. Learn.

FIGURE 6.9   How to Clean Up a Lie

The Lie:	I misled you by saying _____ _____.
The Truth:	The real situation is _____ _____.
Your Feelings:	I feel disappointed in myself because I didn't tell you about this when I first had the opportunity.
Your Story about Their Feelings:	I'm worried you'll be angry or disappointed or _____ (whatever emotion is true for you at that moment) with me.
Next Steps:	I'd like to do whatever I can to clear this up with you.

Even if the person "chews you out," their underlying intention is probably to make sure you never do this again, which supports your success and your happiness. Acknowledge this.

If the other person minimizes the situation or says it wasn't so bad, take responsibility and appreciate their willingness to be so supportive, but say to them that you believe you set off an unfortunate or suboptimal situation, and you want to clear it up and ensure it doesn't happen in the future.

Express gratitude, but only if you feel it. Many times after a truth-telling session, you feel grateful the other person was willing to allow you to clean up what you did. Even if they feel angry with you, they gave you the chance to come clean, and you're bound to feel better.

Giving Feedback

We have a nearly daily opportunity to tell the truth when it comes to giving feedback. We rationalize that it's not our job, or that the person doesn't want to hear the feedback.

I (Kate) once had the pleasure of facilitating the four-person executive team of a major consumer products company as they helped one another change their styles. One SVP would periodically burst into rage when a team hadn't addressed a chronic problem or hadn't kept an agreement. One of the others was a perfectionist who always needed to be right. The third executive wanted to learn to give positive feedback, to show others what he was feeling, and to share more of his thinking and ideas with his team, instead of hoarding information. The fourth executive wanted to work on the opposite ability. He felt he had a difficult time giving critical feedback to people he liked, and his unrealistic hopes for improvement overcame his better judgment at times.

All four of them felt nervous about the process. Who wouldn't be? Yet, these four people didn't let the fear of looking bad get in the way of making this radical change. Fear of being embarrassed and fear of looking stupid prevent millions of us every day from making useful contributions that can help our companies. Their fearlessness is the reason they sit near the top of the company and are worth what they're worth. I believe that to some degree we define our worth—both at heart-level and wallet-level, by how open we are to feedback.

In the year after they opened themselves to learning, each doubled his personal net worth. The company's stock went up 70 percent, profits increased 50 percent, and employee morale soared as well—now that's a radical result! They wanted to speed up the change process within their company, and they made the extremely smart move of doing it on themselves first.

When people don't invest in creating authentic, fully open relationships, they don't build the trust that lets people know that someone is truly "for" them. Figure 6.10 lists the way I recommend you do give feedback.

After moving through the previous exercises, the feedback steps in Figure 6.10 may seem like a cakewalk. If so, congratulations! You're feeling more and more at home with the truth.

HOLDING BACK VERSUS STEPPING UP

Here's a common cycle that keeps us from telling the truth: We hold back and don't say anything, hoping the situation will improve, the person will go away, someone else will intervene, or an act of God will occur. We hint too long or we coast on hope. We talk to other people and vent about our dilemma, but we don't take our feedback directly to the person involved because we don't want to hurt their feelings. We're willing to gossip but not to speak candidly to the object of our objection. Not surprisingly the change we want doesn't occur.

Meanwhile, our emotions build up, and when we finally come clean—when the last straw occurs—we tell the whole truth about our opinions about this situation or individual. By then we've collected dozens of justifications for our opinions, feel self-righteous and indignant, and we're also feeling irritated, anxious, disappointed, or some combination of all three.

As a result, we approach the subject in a heavy-handed way that triggers defensiveness and not much listening in the other person, who understandably overreacts. Their upset tends to trigger us to overreact, and we can easily derail from listening to the truth. We may think the other person's truth is *making* us feel sad, angry, afraid. Or we may wish it were different, that the person didn't have these feelings or that point of view.

FIGURE 6.10   Giving Feedback

1. **Willingness**
   - Ask if the other person is willing to hear your feedback.
   - Look for openness, not compliance.

2. **Facts**
   - State the bare facts about what happened.
   - Avoid even subtle hints of judgment or blame.

3. **"I" Statements**
   - Focus on *your* own experience.
   - Separate your assumptions from the observed facts.
   - Point out any unarguable negative consequences that have occurred.

4. **Listen Consciously**
   - Listen carefully to the other person's reactions.
   - Avoid the tendency to rehearse your retort instead of listening.
   - Do not try to sell your point of view.

5. **Noble Intention**
   - Look for and acknowledge the other person's underlying positive intention.
   - Speak to the value he or she had hoped to provide.

6. **Request**
   - Make a specific request of the other person.
   - Clearly state what you'd like in the future.

7. **Agreements**
   - Translate your input and insights into action.
   - Agree on changes.
   - Write them down.

Sometimes we get stuck on getting the other person to change instead of looking at what we can do.

We spend many unpleasant ensuing hours in cleanup mode, making sure the other person knows she is valued and doesn't quit. We both go home feeling bruised and battered, and feel reinforced in our belief that speaking the truth is not such a good idea. We then draw the conclusion that it's not worth it to stir up stuff that's been put to bed. So we hold onto our thoughts and feelings, continue to feel resentment and distrust that tend to build momentum.

If we withhold our thoughts and feelings long enough we usually end up with a strained relationship, and eventually these turn into conflicts. There's a specific progression to keeping the lines of communication open: (1) sharing withheld thoughts and feelings as you notice them, (2) clearing the air when things have accumulated and there's a subtle undercurrent of tension, and (3) resolving conflicts that have become overt and are visible to others.

Sharing Withheld Truths

We withhold telling each other the full truth much of the time for what seem to be very valid reasons. There is, however, usually a price to pay. *Withholding the truth stops your own ability to be* for *the other person.* You stop seeing others as possibility. Instead, you judge. You end up being inauthentic, and that ultimately compromises your integrity with yourself for your willingness to put on an act. When you withhold, you stop not only the relationship's expansiveness, but your own expansiveness as well. You stop yourself.

With the business pressures you've been under—plus just being human—we would feel shocked if you haven't withheld thoughts or emotions many times, possibly out of the fear of throwing a wrench in the gears when time and energy seemed so precious. Our own (the authors') commitment is to share our thoughts and feelings as promptly as possible, in an authentic and caring way, anytime we want a strong relationship—whether it's at work or in our personal lives. When we do this, two things happen: It (1) frees us to be at our best and (2) allows our relationships and collaborations to be at their best.

Withheld truths create distrust that lays the groundwork for conflict. Figure 6.11 illustrates three ways to create distrust.

FIGURE 6.11   Three Easy Ways to Create Distrust

1. **Withhold your opinion.**
   - You disagree with what someone says.
   - You don't tell them.
   - You build up resentments and stories.
   - You share these with other people.

2. **Fail to negotiate through differences.**
   - You withhold your input in the meeting, and go to the person in private.
   - The person has a long-winded explanation.
   - You give up.
   - You then work around the person and bypass them.

3. **Refuse to disagree with someone in power.**
   - You hear about a plan you don't support.
   - Someone in power asks for input in a meeting.
   - You (and others) withhold your frank opinion.
   - You blame the person who developed the plan for not getting your buy-in in advance.
   - You label the person as "untrustworthy" or uninterested in your POV.

Here's one of our favorite examples of sharing a withheld truth. Due to its growth, the Dell company often brings in more experienced people to lead businesses. This happened to Gabe in 1998, who headed up a business unit that had grown 50 percent a year for several years.

While he saw it as a sensible and logical approach, Gabe felt hurt about being moved out of his role and having a new manager from outside the industry replace him on the executive committee. He also harbored secret suspicions that Michael Dell didn't respect his judgment and that this influenced Dell's decision. He felt afraid this would make future advancement impossible; he's independently wealthy due to the rise in the company's stock price and was not sure if he should remain with the company. He decided to share these very personal concerns with Michael.

Michael matched his openness and talked frankly about Gabe's need to get several years more experience before he will be ready to take this rapidly growing organization to the next level in its growth. He also helped Gabe understand that his lack of assertiveness and directness in the past caused problems to linger.

Gabe felt delighted about his conversation with Michael. Imagine how differently this could have been for Gabe and the company if he'd withheld his thoughts and emotions about the situation. Or what if Michael had attempted to control the un-controllable—someone else's feelings—by withholding information? Gabe would likely have felt suspicious because he would have sensed he wasn't getting the straight scoop. If Michael or anyone else had withheld their full truth, Gabe probably would have felt demotivated, deenergized, and angry. His productivity and contribution would have lessened. He might even have left the company.

Withheld truths often create a strong undercurrent of fear. Because people tend to avoid fear, the tension shows up as anger, irritation, and distrust. In general, we withhold four types of truths: facts, emotions, agreements, or reactions to avoid disturbing a relationship. In the example above Gabe had withheld his feelings and his reactions. The chart in Figure 6.12 addresses each of these.

Clearing the Air

If you're human, you've probably got a few—or maybe quite a few—strained relationships with some of the people you work with. This happens both with people who are new to us and with people with whom we've worked for decades. The speed of

---

FIGURE 6.12   Sharing Withheld Truths

> **FACTS: What truth is not being spoken?**
>
> - "I told John _____, and I didn't talk directly with you about this."
>
> **EMOTIONS: What feelings are not being expressed?**
>
> - "I'm dependent on your capabilities, and I'm afraid I won't be successful."
>
> **AGREEMENTS: What agreements have been broken or misunderstood?**
>
> - "Last month I told you I would do _____, and I never did it and didn't get back to you."
>
> **REACTIONS: What are you reacting to based on your interpretation of what is going on?**
>
> - "I've made up a story that you don't feel comfortable working with me after what we went through three years ago."

change and the wear and tear of work in the old, sludgy style will do this.

Other kinds of "withholds" that need to be cleared up are fuzzy or broken agreements or a thought, emotion, opinion, or interpretation you haven't shared that has lingered in your mind and resulted in conversations in your own head or with other people.

You'll know you have something to communicate if a past conversation with this person had "subtitles" in your mind. So that all the time you're saying something to a person, there's another thought rolling around in your mind that only you know about. You might say, "That idea has some merit," and the subtitle in your mind says, "That's an awful idea but I don't want to hurt his feelings!" You might say, "Good luck in implementing this idea," and the subtitle says, "I doubt that you can pull this off." Or you listen silently to someone's idea, all the time thinking, "You always want it your way!"

I (Eddie) once worked closely with Dr. West, a competent and highly trained surgeon. Our styles of patient care couldn't have been more different. I focused on people and the big picture; West focused on data and details. Over time we both experienced a progressive sense of discomfort and conflict regarding the management of patients. We both lost energy by fussing and fuming as well as by being consumed by opinions, assumptions, and interpretations. It became apparent to both of us that our conflict was obvious to not only our patients but to our colleagues and to our office and nursing staffs. We chose to approach this directly and cleared the air. Although our personalities and our way of doing things probably did not dramatically change, discussing our differences of style as well as our similar commitment to high quality care for our patients radically improved the entire environment in the operating room, in intensive care, on the clinical wards, and in our office. Our open direct communication seemed to lead to quicker patient recoveries and fewer unexpected complications. The nursing staff overheard our conversation about this conflict and immediately began clearing the air for better intensive care in their daily work.

When you clear the air, you turn contracted, protective, fear energy into expansive, intuitive, visionary energy. In the end, clearing the air is designed just as much to free up your own full potential as it is to free up the relationship's potential. Energetically, it's a lot like the before and after photos in weight-loss programs. Losing the burden of all that's unsaid often shows up in your face, which looks more vibrant and relaxed, and in the way you hold your body, which feels lighter and more awake. The clear-the-air process is summed up in Figure 6.13.

You may notice yourself resisting the invitation to clear the air. After we conduct a clear-the-air exercise with teams at off-site meetings, they feel fired up (as opposed to pants on fire, as in liar, liar). But when they first hear they are to share truths they have withheld, we repeatedly hear concerns like the following:

- "Why say things that you know will cause conflict, hurt feelings, etc.?"

- "Maybe I don't want meaningful relationships at work."

- "There's a real danger of doing irreversible damage to a relationship."

- "This is way too touchy-feely for me."

We heard the same comments while working with the Defense Logistics Agency (DLA), a Department of Defense organization the size of a Fortune 500 company. Agency leadership, however, knew that open communications mean greater speed and bottom-line results. Because of that, the DLA direc-

---

FIGURE 6.13   Clearing the Air

Objectives:	To acknowledge what happened, to eliminate old baggage, and to claim your part of the issue.
The Past Situation:	_____ happened.
Your Contribution:	I didn't do (or I did) _____.
Your Feelings:	I felt _____.
Your Story about Their Reaction:	I'm concerned that you felt or thought _____.
Next Steps:	I'd like to clear this up with you.

tor encouraged his managers to take an open approach, including talking directly with him about issues they had with his leadership style. The director's own openness to hearing the truth set the stage for a penetrating two-day program that laid the foundation for a completely different level of trust.

We asked the top agency executives to list their irritations and concerns about their teammates who were all present in the room. The list included pet peeves, private nicknames, and old history they were hanging onto, as some of these people had worked together in various roles for 15 or more years. Over the course of two days, they shared their feedback with one another, first by talking candidly about issues that impacted how others fulfilled their responsibilities. Later, the executives mingled for an hour and a half, selecting the various people they wanted to clear the air with and sharing what was on their mind. Then they went on to the next person.

In a few hours of highly charged conversations, they sorted through all the places where they had never discussed their version of the truth. They communicated for the first time about their own failures to keep agreements or the blame they still put on others for breaking an agreement with them. We invited each person to take full responsibility for each event. In other words, we worked toward eliminating blame and truth-hiding during the course of an entire afternoon.

Two months later this organization launched the first wave of a three-year systems transformation project. They did not slip into blame about places where the implementation was rocky. Instead, they supported each other and openly shared glitches with an eye toward a solid fix. They didn't have to hold two-dimensional conversations—the one in their hearts and the one coming out of their mouths. They jumped straight to the cheese—an increasingly important skill, when the target keeps moving.

Here's the bottom line: Clearing the air allowed change to happen with more ease and speed, less friction and resistance. Coming clean allows organizations to move at the speed of today's business with less wear and tear on the human moving parts. Everyone moves more quickly and easily through the day-to-day wear-and-tear of challenges when integrity is impeccable and the whole truth is discussed.

THE CANDOR HALL OF FAME

We want this story to be *yours*. As we look over this chapter, most of the stories are about the consequences of *not* telling the truth that we think reflects our experience and the general state of affairs out there. As individuals, businesses, and nations, we have some distance to go. We invite you to create the next success story in expanding your capacity for truth. Then send it to us at <www.worthethic.com>, and we'll share it with the world.

Our commitment should be, as Gandhi once declared, "to truth, not to consistency." Speak the truth and enjoy a world that is continually new and perpetually interesting as it unfolds.

SUMMARY

- Lies occur at epidemic levels in companies. Avoiding the truth—not speaking it or being open to hearing it—creates a culture of indecisiveness that markedly increases bureaucracy and politics and slows your organization to a crawl.

- Truth instantly gets all the information out on the table, so we quickly make the right decisions with the benefit of all details and opinions.

- Many of us believe telling the truth often makes things worse. Fear is the main reason we lie.

- Neglecting to disclose the whole truth is the equivalent of a "silent lie." Withholding information, concealing information, spinning information, and falsifying information are all forms of lying because they all involve an intention to deceive. If we witness a lie and don't correct it, we are liars as well.

- When we wait to tell the truth, emotions build up. As a result, we approach the subject in a heavy-handed way that may trigger defensiveness and not much listening in the other person.

- Here are words to use in cleaning up a lie: "I misled you by saying _____." "The real situation is _____." "I'm feeling _____ because I didn't tell you about this when I first had the opportunity (or whatever emotion is true for you at that moment)." "I'm worried you'll be angry or disappointed or _____ with me. I'd like to do whatever I can to clean this up with you."

- To clear the air, say, "Here's my story about what I did in the past. I don't know if it irritated you or not, but this is what I imagine you think about me, based on these past interactions. I want to air this so we can do anything we need to do to move our relationship forward and ensure there's no lingering resentment."

TAKE ACTION

- What do you habitually mislead others about? Your capabilities? Your past experiences? How you feel? Where are you likely to omit or massage the truth?

- What's your own particular pattern of lying? How do you go about convincing someone you really are telling the full truth and can be completely trusted? How do you spin the facts? For what purpose?

- Do you sugarcoat performance feedback, in an effort to ensure someone stays motivated or doesn't get angry with you?

- Do you support team members in deceiving themselves when they commit to deadlines they cannot keep or when they habitually overwork? How can you change this lying miniculture within your department?

- What sort of lying occurs automatically in your company's culture? What happens in your company with new product releases? Are customers misled about the quality or the delivery date of the product? Do you live up to your PR? All research shows that companies with long-term success records display honesty and take responsibility for misses with their customers. What will it take to drive this value into the company?

- If this situation is only too familiar to you, why is that?

- With whom do you most need to clear the air? What one step will you take today to start the candor process?

CHAPTER SEVEN

GENIUS
Awakening the Sleeping Giant

How can I discover my genius?

How can I bring my genius to work?

How can I mesh my life purpose with the company's mission?

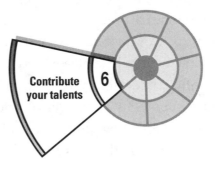

Contribute
your talents **6**

When individuals and corporations awaken their genius, working in their areas of greatest strength, each new twist and turn in business becomes an exhilarating adventure. When people are actively engaged in making their highest contribution, they work well, they work hard, and they like it so much that they stay. We do not leave the place that brings us joy and satisfaction. This is the new way of work, filled with the intrinsic excitement of fulfilling your innate potential rather than the extrinsic fear-and-reward system we've all known until now.

We must awaken the genius in everyone who wants to participate in the life-changing culture of radical results. Imagine a life in which you spend most of your time in your genius zone, doing what you do better and faster than nearly anyone else. Imagine all your employees coming to work each day with delight as they think about the work they so love doing. Think of them returning to their homes each evening feeling renewed by their jobs, instead of exhausted and stressed. That's the power of helping every person in your company identify and work from their area of genius.

This possibility probably seems like a fantasy to most of us. Our puritan work ethic runs deep, and it almost seems illegal to get paid to do what we love or to compensate employees for doing their favorite type of work. We have a heritage of hard work and sacrifice that causes most organizations to focus on improving our incompetencies. Organizations invest their time and energy on correcting employees' weaknesses and making them competent in most things, rather than capitalizing on their talents and strengths.

Competent means "suitable or adequate." We're essentially telling employees to spend their time and energy becoming adequate—to suit up and shut up the genie within that wants to give us way more than three wishes. Companies (and our school systems) seem to want everyone to be solid B students in everything, instead of an A+ student in a few areas and a C student in most others. That is why they remain "B" companies and "C" school systems. This approach—we call it "incompetent competence for all"—keeps us from finding true happiness in our work and keeps our companies from getting the very best from people. It also sets up many of the time drains at work.

Who wouldn't procrastinate and drag their feet if faced with tasks that don't fuel their passion? Who wouldn't complain about work, if only 10 percent of their time is spent in areas where they truly add unique value?

Genius can be developed from already excellent talent, but it can't be taught. *For maximum return, truly successful people get "good enough" at basic skills, then optimize their natural gifts, their areas of genius. Your mantra needs to be: "Develop your gifts; delimit your shortcomings."* In most companies, however, the worse you are in a given area, like strategic thinking or presentation skills or problem solving, the more likely it is that you'll be sent to a training program in that area. If you're already quite competent at something, you're rarely given someone to learn from whose instruction and wisdom can take you to the next level.

Consider how Tiger Woods developed his gifts and delimited his shortcomings when he worked with coach Butch Harmon reinventing Tiger's greatest asset—his swing. They could have focused on his greatest weakness—sand shots (he was ranked 61st in this particular competency)—but they didn't. They didn't spend an hour or a minute on sand shots. They focused instead on expanding his genius. When Tiger Woods won the British Open the following year, his swing was so superb, he was the only player who didn't have to contend with a single sand trap during the four-day tournament at St. Andrews—a course known for its treacherous pot hole bunkers.

The difference between masters like Tiger Woods and most companies is that companies focus on sand shots. You can focus on improving weaknesses or you can focus on expanding strengths. And when you multiply this decision by 100 or 1,000 or 10,000 times for all your employees, you end up with either a company of Tiger Woods or a company of B and C players.

Genius originally meant "an attendant spirit," and in fairy tales rubbing a magic lantern awakened the genie. In corporations and individuals, genius is awakened by noticing and naming those moments when *we're* magic, then spending as much time as we can in that zone. *Our genius is the unique combination of skills and endowments we each have. Our purpose, resting at the core of our being, is the particular way our genius contributes to the world.* Focusing on our vision and our impact on the world is far more energizing and motivating than correcting weaknesses. The latter is like showing employees how to become expert magic lantern collectors instead of unleashing the resources of the lantern each one already owns if only it were dusted off. When people feel purposeful, contributing to the world by doing what they do best, they energize everyone around them and catalyze their companies. Projects are assigned to the people best able to create a runaway success, and turf wars become extinct because each team member helps the whole by contributing her special genius. The entire organization flashes ahead.

We always feel profoundly moved by the look on people's faces after they've identified their genius. We see energy, light, hope, and focus radiating from them, with their feet also firmly planted on the ground. The people and companies who move most comfortably with change leverage those areas of noticeable gifts and develop excellent skills so they blossom into genius. This is how to make the most of our brain trusts and compete effectively.

IGNORE "REALITY"

Noticing your penchants and following your passion often require that you ignore the advice the rest of the world offers up, requested or not. When I (Kate) left engineering with a new Bachelor of Science (BS) in hand and made the radical change to pursue psychology, my parents felt horrified. Fifteen years later when I gave up my role as VP HR of a prestigious Silicon Valley company to start my own consulting firm, my friends thought I was crazy to leave all those precious stock options on the table after investing five years of my heart and soul in the company.

In 1988 my consulting buddies thought I was even crazier when, as a single parent with a child in college, I invested $10,000 to create a software product to help me give executives performance-based 360° feedback and individualized coaching before these techniques were even considered useful in the workplace. No one used the term "360°" back then, and the approach was considered radical and way too threatening to executives. Early innovators began using 360° feedback four years later in 1992, and it became mainstream by 1996.

At each juncture I held fast to my vision of my career and my life. I'd spent 1987 noticing the areas of my work that inspired and excited me. There were two: (1) when I worked individually with executives on some deeply entrenched habit that sabotaged their success, and (2) when I worked with two executives who were embroiled in a duel to the death.

Both situations kept me literally on the edge of my chair. I felt focused, fully contributing, and 100 percent present. How much of your work engages *you* this way? This was the work I wanted to do—and I knew I brought unique skills and talents to these areas. During this year of noticing, I realized I'd exhibited these unique talents early on. In elementary school I frequently brought warring factions together, inviting different sets of kids who weren't getting along to my home. Sometimes their dislike was so great, they wouldn't speak to each other. Dodging the dirty looks between them, I'd orchestrate activities that required us to play together, and within an hour we'd be having so much fun together the barriers would dissolve.

Another skill showed itself around that time as well. I remember dealing with Josh, a bully who was threatening the other kids on the playground. I zeroed in and sank my teeth into him, biting his wrist and not letting go until he promised to lay off the other kids. Thirty years later I realized that this act of demented oral aggression on a kid twice my size was an early expression of my genius. I have made a career out of standing up to bullies in the corporate world. (My present-day techniques— potential clients will be relieved to know—are much more subtle than the one I used on the playground.)

I decided I wanted to build my whole career around these areas. My vision was to spend nearly all my professional time doing work that was so much fun it felt like play. I'd noticed many of the people I worked with talked about loving their jobs, but they felt wiped out at the end of the day. I adopted a clear measurement for fun: that I'd feel as energized at the end of the day as I felt when I woke up.

I didn't care about making money, and I ended up making more than I ever dreamed possible back then. My goal was simply to do work I loved, and I loved it so much and had so much fun I found I no longer procrastinated about certain tasks. I made every minute count, happily and joyously, because the work felt so satisfying. This is radical change at its best—moving easily and rapidly around obstacles and over hurdles with a smile on my face. It was a surprisingly nice benefit to discover I was grossing well over a million dollars a year five years after launching my company—only because I was so very good at what I did. Think of the multiples for your company if everyone worked in their zone of genius.

PLAYING PEEKABOO WITH OUR GREATNESS

Gay Hendricks once told us about giving a talk to a roomful of extraordinarily talented people in the Young President's Organization (YPO). To get into the room every one of them had to run a business with at least $5 million annual revenue. Yet even with this incredibly talented group of people, it only took the following two simple questions to immediately throw them into a confrontation with their limitations:

1. "What is your personal genius?"

2. "What is the genius of your company?"

The reason for these questions is to bring to light the magic that occurs when you match the genius of your company to the genius of your employees. The most successful entrepreneurs create companies where their life purposes and essential qualities of their employees contribute to the essential purpose of the company. You must match these essence elements to reap maximum benefit from your employees' talents and gifts. The reaction of the YPO group to these questions shows us the challenges we face in tapping people's genius.

First, the silence was deafening.

Then resistance erupted. Just about everybody in the room mounted a vigorous argument against claiming his or her personal genius (the reaction these questions typically trigger).

Surprising, isn't it? You might think that extraordinarily bright people would be able to define and accept their genius at the drop of a hat. Instead, the exact opposite happens. The more talented people are, the more difficultly they seem to have defining their genius. When they finally do, however, they experience profound shifts in performance and job satisfaction. Once this acceptance takes place, whether a workplace is made up of 5 employees or 5,000, you can feel the atmosphere shift to one of hope, excitement, and passion for playing at your best.

Until people reach that acceptance, however, they often feel uncomfortable identifying the various aspects of their genius. Perhaps they think it's arrogant: "Who am I to stand up and claim my genius?" Or perhaps they fear no one will agree. Or maybe they believe the special facet of themselves might evaporate if fully claimed in the light.

Often the resistance rears its head because the genius aspects of ourselves emerged when we were very young, before we had the language or the consciousness to understand them fully. Sometimes, too, the genius in us is squelched when we're very young, so it has to be lured out much later in life, if we want to love what we do. Our culture considers genius strange, weird, alien . . . even vaguely dangerous. To accept our genius is to accept the chaotic, unpredictable, and unknown aspects of *the self* that might not "fit" into the corporate world as we know it.

CALLING FORTH YOUR GENIUS

These reasons for resistance are all speculation, but certainly one barrier to claiming our genius is the lack of familiarity with the question itself. Most of us have never stopped and wondered for ten seconds about our specific genius. If we haven't asked ourselves this question, we're like a primitive culture that's asked which of 200 channels they want to subscribe to on cable TV— unlikely to have even a vague answer.

Lacking knowledge of our true genius handicaps us for a very simple reason: If we don't know our genius, we're likely to waste our time on projects that don't tap our finest talents. We end up doing miscellaneous tasks others could do just as well, instead of living on purpose by making our unique contribution to the organization and to the world. Because we have not identified greatness and put it to use, we often spin our wheels slogging around in the mundane.

Genius and *genuine* have the same Latin root, which means, "to beget." We become genuine when we tap our genius and sire our full identities. When all employees in a company can unleash the power of their genii, think how the company can unleash its own. The chart in Figure 7.1 is a handy way to identify and rank your many talents, differentiating between the various gradations of passion and skill.

Embracing our genius-level abilities can only happen through frank self-analysis and spin-free communication on the part of both company and employee. Treat yourself to some time

FIGURE 7.1   Genius Continuum

Identify which of your skills and abilities belong in each zone.

Excellent

- What do you consistently get positive feedback about in your work?

- What do you do better than just about anyone else?

Genius

- What work do you so love doing that it doesn't seem like work?

- Which aspects of your work generate the highest ratio of positive results compared to time spent?

Mediocre

- What do you consistently get negative feedback about in your work?

- What work do you do that just about everyone can do better?

Competent

- What work do you do that others can do just as well or better?

- What work do you do well but doesn't feel totally satisfying?

---

with the chart in Figure 7.1 and prepare to meet your genius. In the Genius Zone, list those qualities, skills, and activities that make your heart sing, that you do better than nearly everyone else, that you'd do even if you weren't being paid, and that your company would have a hard time replacing.

The first quantum leap in your effectiveness comes when you move from the first two zones to the second two. The second quantum jump comes from moving from your Excellence Zone to your Genius Zone. These two acts make a profound difference. *Your productivity excels when you spend at least 70 per-*

cent of your time working in your Excellent and Genius Zones. This means saying an emphatic *No!* to those activities you're merely good at (and, of course, avoiding your areas of mediocrity completely).

Use your genius to set priorities. Most people spend a preponderance of their time on activities that lie in their Competent and Mediocre Zones and far too little time on their areas of excellence and their unique abilities that could be called genius. This happens for two reasons: First, many people (including us) have been brainwashed to think there is a character-building nobility in doing things we're not good at. We act as if suffering and hard work confirm that we're on the right path and that if we work hard enough, we'll prove we're good enough. Some of us suffer to accumulate complaints because of our attachment to victimhood and The Bermuda Triangle.

A second and possibly more surprising reason for focusing on less competent areas is, ironically, our fear of failure. If we hide our genius, we never have to risk rejection and failure in those areas we most love. We use our jobs and our companies as excuses for tying up vast amounts of our time and energy doing things we're not good at. By staying in the rut of routine, we don't have to risk those unsettling waves of fear in the belly that often accompany excursions into the unfamiliar, especially when it matters so much. And what could matter more than giving our special gifts to the world?

We're asking you to make a fundamental shift in the fundamental paradigm of your life. It's the first step toward embracing true joy. The company benefits by getting higher per capita performance from each employee, more joy and harmony within departments, better retention, and a crescendo of breakthrough ideas from all levels. It also saves significant amounts of money by getting rid of all those training classes aimed at improving your sand shots. Tiger would be proud.

When I (Kate) got clear about my genius in 1985 I resigned from all work that wasn't using my core talents and gifts. That meant handing over the responsibility for a large administrative staff and also telling our CEO very nicely (and radically) that, "No, I did not want responsibility for facilities," that I wanted my time focused on work where I could add unique value. More responsibilities don't necessarily mean more visibility, more success, and quicker promotions. This is a case where less is more. Way more. What parts of your job might you hand over to someone else that perhaps lies in *their* zone of genius?

This won't happen overnight. Prepare yourself for a slow but steady transition as you consciously shift into focusing on your areas of genius. Until I understood the value of spending as many of my waking hours as possible working in my Genius Zone, I spent too much time on things I'm okay or not-so-okay at—and even on things I'm good at. In fact, it took a whole year to find someone to take over my areas of competence, and after relocating him from another state, he didn't work out. Sometimes our first efforts at making a big change don't work. Has that happened to you?

In my own company, I made a deeper commitment to my genius and brought in Kathlyn Hendricks to help my team and me to match our genii to our work. I had to delegate some of my other activities so I could spend more time in my areas of greatest talent: giving people critical feedback and motivating them to address whatever issues emerge—no matter how uncomfortable. It took less than three months to implement the bulk of the changes in my company.

Your areas of genius may bear no relationship to the degrees you earned. Don't put any particular qualifications or limits on the categories of talents that may land in your Genius Zone. On the other hand, don't list anything that isn't absolutely in the stratosphere in terms of your gifts.

DISCARDING THE DETAILS, DOING DEALS

One of my (Kate's) favorite client examples of focusing on the Genius Zone involved the late Bill Kimpton, the brilliant entrepreneurial founder of the Kimptom Group, a billion-dollar, award-winning restaurant and hotel company. Bill himself won countless industry awards, created five of San Francisco's top twenty restaurants, and was a master dealmaker and developer.

He made no secret of the fact that he truly disliked dealing with the thousands of tiny daily details that kept a large business like his running and growing. He also didn't hide the fact that his business was somewhat stagnant 12 years ago—and that the stagnation, he believed, was in large part due to the fact that the micromanagement he did was partially "okay" and partially "good" but not "excellent" and certainly not in his Genius Zone.

Rather than stumbling along (or sliding backward), Bill hired Tom LaTour to serve as president and later as CEO to handle those thousands of details. Bill became the soul of the organization and Tom the brains. When Bill brought Tom on, he had two hotels and one restaurant. Today, under Tom's leadership, Kimpton Boutique Hotels has grown to 36 hotels and 29 restaurants. The same detail-management that Bill so disliked was in Tom's Genius Zone—and as a result, the company has experienced explosive growth because Bill stopped spending his energy outside of his Genius Zone. He took steps to make his job fun and enjoyable because of his shift into doing genius tasks.

Moving into the Genius Zone means growth and forward progress from one level of functioning and competence to another. It's also about recognizing where you *don't need to be a genius* and delegating those areas to others, divesting yourself of things that either don't play to your skills or don't make full use of your position, goals, or passions.

To leverage your genius, you must identify your areas of less skill, those areas of weakness. Perhaps this is one of the reasons so many people approach the idea much as the YPO group did, with initial suspicion and resistance. In my (Kate's) case, I'm a more than adequate writer, but when I realized that retaining control over assessment reports was slowing down my office— reducing our profits, while keeping me focused on areas of mere competence—I loosened my grip and delegated the reports to others, carefully watching for matches of genius and abilities. As a result I helped my team grow professionally, lowered our frustration, and saved my clients both time and money.

In talking with people I learned I was only an "okay" manager of *me*. Once I saw my limitations clearly, I found someone who positively shone with the specific type of management genius I needed. I worked with her to set up schedules, methods, and processes within the office.

Whether we're discussing a famous CEO or you or me, it isn't always simple to make these changes and focus on the Genius Zone. We get rooted into certain ways of working. The familiar becomes comfortable; the comfortable becomes habit. We may no longer notice the quiet havoc we can wreak with our not-so-okay actions, and the okay actions can become an accepted and expected baseline of performance.

Until we make a commitment to our genius, we haven't experienced its powerful rewards, so we may not think of this paradigm shift positively from a cost-benefit angle. The true inner and outer rewards—for both the individual and the organization—are like the perfect crème brulee: an experience you'll never forget but couldn't describe eloquently enough if your life depended on it.

In the Genius Zone there's no wasted motion. Imagine your company humming as each person does what he or she does best. Meetings become effective, politics vaporize, joy expands, and creativity hits an all-time high. We can't make a commitment to genius without affecting our surroundings. Likewise, if we're surrounded by people poised in genius, it can't help but move us closer to our own potential and purpose.

GIVING OUR GIFT TO THE WORLD

Long-term research of more than 250,000 successful men and women by the Gallup Organization and SRI concluded that each of us has a unique potential defining our destiny. Our genius is the combination of special gifts and talents we use to fulfill our life purpose, or special contribution to the world. Life purpose is the through-line that runs between and connects those "high" moments where we feel inspired, use our talents to the fullest, and contribute to the world in a way that feels deeply satisfying. A clear purpose helps us steer the optimal course in the world, moving quickly and easily over rugged terrain, and deftly turning away from the Sirens on the rocks in the form of work that doesn't best match our highest calling.

Most of us are swept along by the busy-ness of life and spend little time reflecting upon our deepest purpose. We run on "automatic." When we're running the hardest, we may find ourselves feeling the least satisfied, knowing that somehow we've lost touch with that quiet inner voice that could direct us toward greater fulfillment.

Most people fail to look beneath the veneer of their surface goals (and even their talents) to engage their deepest purpose. For example, our dear friend Gay Hendricks left college wanting to write the great American novel and ended up teaching at a boy's school in the East as a way of earning money while he wrote. Luckily for him, somewhere along the way he realized his gift to the world wasn't writing a novel but writing books that change people's lives, which actually had been the deeper purpose for his original novel. Today he's written more than 20 self-help books, and his workshops and writing have changed the lives of hundreds of thousands of his readers and students.

So, how do *you* discover your life purpose?

I (Kate) have come across many methods, and one way that works reliably in the corporate world is to use a few simple, yet extraordinarily provocative questions. Read the following example and look for the key question that, in my opinion, brought this woman's life purpose to light.

Michele Dunkerley, a Dell executive, had been working at Dell eight years and was a highly valued contributor. She was beyond working for money. In fact, she had passed the net worth mark that earns you the status of Volunteer at Dell. The company's alchemical culture inspired her to continue working about 55 hours to 60 hours a week. At one point she began to notice her energy for work was flagging. She talked with her manager, Tom Green, and said she was beginning to feel burned out.

Tom suggested she look for some new project she'd really love doing. He asked, "What sounds like so much fun that you can't wait to come to work every day?"

If you can't imagine your manager doing this, take a moment to wonder if you'd even be willing to initiate the conversation with him. Because most of us don't have such ample resources sitting in our bank accounts, would you be willing to let your manager know you were bored and burned out anyway? If this is a step you feel ready to take, think about how you can discuss this issue without any blame or whining. Your manager will more readily listen and support you when you're taking 100% responsibility for using your genius at work.

If you're a manager, reflect on what might stop you from helping employees find a niche at work that feels deeply satisfying. Do you have some sort of misguided puritan work ethic perception that work isn't supposed to be fun or meaningful? Do you believe that allowing employees to create a vision for themselves and their jobs might threaten the control you have over your staff? Are you ready to make a cocommitment to thriving on the job?

Michele developed the idea of doing a project that ordinarily would have been done by a completely different department. It also would require significant funding for consultants. Tom said he would need to get the support of the person who headed up the other department, and because it would represent a notable budget variance, Dell's vice chairmen (VC) and the CEO would have to approve it.

One of the magical things comes from knowing what your purpose is, and the clearer you are about it, the more effortlessly life seems to flow. Normally a complicated process, the new project was approved within a couple of days, and Michele took on a year-long special assignment in addition to her normal day-to-day work. The special project focused on continuing to build a workplace where Dell's Volunteers want to work, actively addressing some of their concerns to increase their organization's ability to move at the speed of change. Michele had been working in the legal department, but she realized her life purpose involved a richer connection with people. In her new role she worked with people to uncover and meet their deeper needs. After a month of doing the special project that, remember, was in addition to her usual job, she felt reengaged. Dell won. She stayed and worked with even more passion and commitment. And *she* won because her work took on new meaning.

I use a variation of the question Michele's manager posed: *What do you love to do so much that you can't wait to get to work to do it?* Another way to say this is: *What do you love to do so much that it doesn't feel like work?*

What would your answer be? Set the goal of creating your job around it. As Michele did, you can continue to work at your old job while you're moving toward your goal. This process doesn't require you to quit your job or take a leave of absence. What it does require is that you let go of the belief system that says your employer would never go for something so radical.

Think about it. You're offering to continue to do your job. At the same time, you're also offering to take on another role, a role to which you bring genius, and one that brings you joy and satisfaction. The result is likely to be one that keeps you with your company longer. What's the downside for either side?

THE LIFE PURPOSE PROCESS

Think of your life purpose as the biggest possible vision of why you're here. These steps, which we call the "Life Purpose Process," are extremely simple—and incredibly powerful. All you do is focus on the satisfaction and joy you felt before you gave in to the path of least resistance. I (Kate) have watched time and again as our clients use this process and make the changes that take them from a place of frustration and dissatisfaction to a place of joy, passion, and purpose. There was a time when you lived your purpose before you took the job that brought you the least hassles or the most approving nods or the fattest paycheck or whatever it was that made you believe that strolling the streets of Paris playing a violin wasn't in your future after all. I've heard and witnessed scores of magical stories about people who have made substantial shifts in the way they're living or invent an altogether new life, all by practicing these two amazingly easy steps.

The first step is to identify your areas of passion and life purpose by recalling memories of events and activities that brought rich feel-good experiences inside. The examples don't have to be visible things to other people. In fact, it's important that they aren't, so you break out of achieving for others and notice where you felt genuinely happy. Make a few notes about an experience that stands out every year or two, as early as you can remember.

In your life, as in mine, you'll find a whole series of examples that illuminate the main theme of your life. Usually our personal purpose shows up early in childhood antics and stories that became part of our family legacy. For example in our family, I (Eddie) was the one who could handle my parents best, especially if it involved something they might not want to hear. My siblings' refrain was, "Let Eddie handle it." Throughout my medical career, this same ability emerged, as partners in my practice deferred to me when it came to handling staff problems.

I (Kate) made sure each person got a chance to talk about their day at our dinner table. I especially wanted to draw out what made each person happy, rather than hear about complaints.

My earliest memory of having passionate feelings about people having happy lives occurred when I was four, living in a neighborhood with 20 kids in a two-block area, all four years to eight years old. There were no fences, and we often played together in a friendly horde. Then a little boy moved in across the alley and began stealing all our toys. I was the one who marched into his yard, confronted him, and said, "If you do this again, we won't let you out of your yard. In fact, we'll make you leave our neighborhood!" How does this show up today? I have always tended to be direct and confrontive—no complaining behind people's backs for me. I've never been afraid to confront people with whatever it is in their behavior that causes unhappiness—for themselves or others.

By age nine, I was committed to taking personal responsibility for issues that affected many other people as well. As I mentioned earlier, in the fourth grade I took on Josh, the schoolyard bully, matching his macho with my molars until he agreed to leave the other kids alone.

That story had a further twist. I skipped the fifth grade and lost track of Josh, because I was now a year ahead of him. Many years passed, and when I was 30 years old and home for the holidays, I ran into him at a party. He left me dumbfounded by thanking me for changing his life. He said he would have become a bully alcoholic like his dad, had I not stopped him. He also told me that he'd had a crush on me all through high school—which taught me that biting could pay off. I learned from this that I couldn't judge the impact of my actions by the initial upset. I've also learned to use my words, not my teeth, to nip at executives and get their attention.

The second step in the Life Purpose Process is to look for the themes in those experiences—the background music that's been playing all your life. You won't necessarily look for surface commonalities, but for the more subtle ones that will tell you what skills and strengths the experiences have in common—the core themes that bring you joy. You can see the glimmer, in my stories, of my own purpose that is oriented toward helping key leaders realize their fullest potential. I got early practice working with powerful people by taking on the bullies who tried to rule through physical or psychological power instead of personal power.

I heard that what Warren Buffett wanted for Christmas once was one of those things you wear on your belt and make change with. Michael Dell's genius also showed up early. He received a calculator when he was a kid and took it apart to see how it worked. When he was 16 years old, he attended a computer show and calculated the difference between the cost of the component parts and the cost of finished computers. Fascinated with efficiency and removing steps, he realized this could be a viable business if distributors and sales reps were eliminated from the chain. And the rest is history.

Once you've identified these themes, your next step is to find ways to create more of those experiences in your existing job. Much to the amazement of many people, that's often possible. A career change or even a company change often isn't required. What's needed is your own commitment to infuse your work—

and your entire life—with renewed energy, reactivated passion, and incredible purpose.

Longer lives mean people want meaningful work that enables them to continue to make a significant contribution on a part-time basis after retirement. Midlife career changes often pave the way. After practicing vascular surgery for 25 years, I (Eddie) redirected my passion for integrative medicine and a holistic approach and created a practice focused on increasing the vitality of people during their middle age and beyond. I discovered that my true genius is inspiring change in others, both one-on-one and in groups. I began to see that many midlife executives had a pattern of rising blood pressure, increasing unhealthy types of cholesterol, and other stress symptoms. Combining my love for holistic medicine, my vascular surgery and executive experience, and my job-coaching skills enables me to help executives continue to do work they love with less wear and tear on their bodies.

ADDING LYRICS TO THE MUSIC OF YOUR HEART

It's truly helpful to have your own *purpose saying* or slogan. It doesn't have to be fancy or refined. It doesn't even have to be a sentence. Phrases and words do just fine. The key is whether they resonate in your inner essence like a plucked guitar string. Take a moment now to jot down some key words that capture your own life purpose.

Following are a few examples:

- "I see beyond the boundaries and inspire others to do the same." Jean LeMoin, President, Moving Companies Ahead (MCA)

- "I am a merchant of hope." Elizabeth Jeffries, CSP, CPAE, consultant on change, leadership, and teambuilding

- "I bring energy, excitement, and passion to my relationships with others and inspire them to see what is great about themselves." Donna Kindl, SVP, Monsanto

Donna Kindl, you may recall, was the woman in Chapter 4 who put away her cheerleading outfit to create a more professional expression of her genius. Because you got to know her earlier, you can see how her higher purpose has always been a life theme for her.

Our purpose statement may evolve over time. As a child, if I (Kate) had thought about it, mine would have been: "To encourage each other's happiness and joy." Today it's: "To guide key execs in opening their hearts and bringing wisdom and compassion into our world."

Here's a great story about someone else who's been clear about his purpose.

THE GENIUS HALL OF FAME

Dan Lynch, affectionately known as the "Mother of the Internet," began his career as a programmer for the Air Force. After working in a number of companies in technical positions, he made three unsuccessful attempts to start companies of his own, feeling the pressure of one day putting his four children through college. His breakthrough moment came in 1985 when he put down the burden of being the breadwinner and looked to his passion. He decided that if his children really wanted degrees, they'd find a way. After conferring with his wife, he gave himself permission to do what he wanted: explore how to make a nifty new development—the Internet—widely available to businesses and individuals.

Dan formed a small conference named InterOp so that interested parties could get together and explore ways to use this new technology. Four years later, in 1990, InterOp had exploded to 200 exhibitors and 20,000 attendees and was acquired by Ziff-Davis Publishing for $25 million.

Dan continued to live his purpose, which is: "I introduce people to each other who together can do more than they can do alone." He went on to found one of the first companies to provide Internet payment services and electronic payment software as well as eight other start-ups. His decision back in 1985 to fire himself as breadwinner earned him way more bread. Following his passion has so far grossed him $100 million. Dan has recently started a camp to teach entrepreneurial skills to inner city youth and spends the rest of his time buying forests and preserving them.

LIVING YOUR PURPOSE AT WORK

The purpose of purpose is to help us navigate through life. If you lose your way in the busy-ness of work—and you will—your purpose helps you realign with what you find most fulfilling and gets you back on course. To discover the purpose you're actually living at work, look at your calendar. The gap between actual time spent and your stated purpose can feel like quite a shock. To understand the purpose you're living outside of work, take a look at your checkbook.

Taking 100% responsibility in your life means living your purpose as fully as possible at all times. The key question is: *How do you create ways to adjust work responsibilities to ensure that your mind, heart, and soul thrive—while getting your work done?*

To awaken the sleeping giant of your genius, pay close attention to the new questions that float to your mind as you do the previous exercises, then follow the thread of those questions as they lead you to your genius and your purpose. Listen carefully and generously to the answers your heart provides. Once you ask the questions, you awaken more than genius alone—you also awaken integrity, passion, and purpose.

Kathryn Sutton found a way to bring her genius to work and more than doubled her salary. Six years ago she was looking for a job, taking temporary assignments, and feeling discouraged. Some days she barely had the energy to answer the phone and go on assignments. Luckily for us, one day she did and landed in our office, scheduling 360° interviews. She had been a student of personal growth for some time and quickly realized how aligned she was with Worth Ethic's values and purpose. She knew she could flower in a company like this and looked for a way to create that.

After a month of working as a temp at Work Ethic, Kathryn persuaded me (Kate) she could learn to do the 360° interviews as well as schedule them. She proposed a risk-free trial period in which she'd continue to receive the same salary while expanding into the new role and made it easy for me to say yes. We also made a clear agreement about phasing in someone to take over her administrative work. Kathryn turned out to be a great writer and so friendly and outgoing that people loved working with her. She became a valuable contributor to our staff and our success and freed me up even more to operate in my zone of genius.

YOUR COMPANY'S GENIUS

Every company has its own zone of genius that ideally aligns with its business purpose. We've seen this very clearly at Dell. The area of genius Dell first recognized was a combination of directness and speed. Both reduce steps in the assembly process and therefore the cost to Dell and to customers. The Dell Model originated with Michael Dell when he visited that computer show at age 16.

Michael went direct to customers with catalog-based sales in the early 1980s. A few years later, the Internet allowed a further step in the direction of "direct." All these direct relationships with customers have yielded enormous data, allowing for a level of accurate analysis competitors have not had.

The second "direct" was to have suppliers ship stuff direct to Dell's factories, where within a day or two the parts became computers and were shipped out. Competitors, on the other hand, had their supplies shipped to warehouses, then shipped to their factories as needed. Direct shipping shaved a step in the process to allow Dell to take advantage of dropping costs of supplies.

In their work culture, we see two points to their genius of "Direct from Dell." They focus on "direct communications," and have consciously worked to create a culture where obstacles are seen quickly and "directly" communicated at meetings. Any hallway talk becomes a further, deeper discussion of decisions made in the meeting. Less gossip and complaining make the path to success even more direct.

People also get on board with decisions at Dell quicker than any place we've seen, not because it's an autocratic culture, but because they're comfortable speaking their resistance in meetings, then putting their contrary opinions aside. Sometimes speaking up also means their ideas get used in the decision.

MESHING OUR MISSIONS

In the October 2001 issue of *Fast Company*, Michael Hammer, author of *The Agenda: What Every Business Must Do to Dominate the*

Decade, asserted: "When you ask people to make changes—large, frightening changes—you need to enlist not just their minds but also their hearts. And possibly their souls. You're not going to get passion in your organization by talking about shareholder value. You have to give people a sense of transcendent purpose," he says. "In short, you have to make them believe."*

When the life purpose of the employee meshes with the company's mission, both benefit exponentially. Magic can happen when employees discover what they're here to do in this life, and if they can find a way to serve the company while serving their life purpose, they step into "passionate productivity." Organizations and employees who want radical results direct energy toward finding the right fit.

According to the *Workplace 2000 Employee Insight Survey,* corporate or departmental mission statements mean more to people when they've been involved in creating them, and one way to bring a mission to life—and to keep it thriving and evolving—is to make it a topic for ongoing dialogue. Relatively few companies follow either of these recommendations.

How fortunate, when bottom-line benefits are so tangible in companies where personal and company purpose mesh. Jim Kouzes and Barry Posner of the University of Santa Clara report that a clear understanding of company purpose improves commitment to the organization and the job by 10 percent to 15 percent, and understanding your personal purpose increases commitment by 50 percent. Connecting personal purpose to company purpose adds another 10 percent, for a total of 70 percent—a handsome return by any investment standard.

Here's a story from a company that seems to get it. For years, Carlene Ellis was VP of Information Technology at Intel Corporation. To be at that level in a techno-rich company like

---

*Hammer, Michael. *Fast Company.* October 2001.

Intel, you've got to be brilliant at technology, and Carlene certainly was. However, after many years of fulfilling this role skillfully, she became aware that her job was not using her full genius, nor meshing comfortably with her growing sense of the larger purpose of her life.

Carlene decided to hire and groom a replacement so she could take some time off to uncover her life purpose and discover ways to merge this purpose with her talents and skills. During her sabbatical, she spent time inquiring within, and it became clear that her real passion and genius lived in education rather than information technology. When she returned to work, bringing with her a deep sense of purpose, Intel found a brilliant and masterful way to marry her newfound clarity to the company's mission.

Carlene discussed what happened. "After many years of being the best chief information officer (CIO) I could be, at age 52 I wanted to make a bigger difference. What's amazing is that Intel was willing to give me the chance to make this bigger difference as an Intel employee. We all have a body and a brain and a heart and a soul, and we need to get everyone's to work. I feel unquestionable support for the initiative that has been handed me in this new role. It is an incredible marriage of my passion and the company's needs."

Carlene's experiences at Intel told her—and others—that the time was rapidly approaching when hiring technical geniuses was going to be extremely difficult. Businesses of today, Carlene says, require technical expertise not just from the computer core, but also from secretaries, front-line personnel, and every other employee in a company because companies are rapidly moving into a high-tech state of functioning on a daily basis.

"Intel needs to increase this pool of talent, and I'm going to go back into third-grade and sixth-grade classrooms to ensure that everyone, including girls and minorities, understands that they can go into science and technology. Giving money to MIT and Stanford won't solve this problem."

When the economy took a nosedive and Carlene's stock options at Intel plummeted, she reported that her "net worth is down, but self-worth is up, and I'd gladly do this job for free." Intel has married its future need for talented employees with Carlene's commitment, genius, and passion. Is this type of thinking—the thinking that found a useful niche for Carlene—widespread at Intel? You bet it is, and a look at the numbers testifies to this. Intel is one of the longest-running success stories in the high-tech world, with one of the lowest turnover rates.

Companies are better able to stay on course if they're not losing employees constantly. Although headquartered in Silicon Valley, with the astronomical turnover rates of 25 percent to 35 percent typical in firms based there, Intel's turnover rate is 5—yes, that's 5—percent. Can this be attributed to high salaries at Intel? No, because their salaries are below the average for Silicon Valley. We believe it's this kind of breakthrough thinking—the kind that married Intel's purpose to Carlene's—that has made Intel one of the top companies for the past 20 years.

You can create this vibrant atmosphere within your company and yourself as well. Start right now to call forth your genius. Genius is not simply a place at which we arrive. It's a place we access deep within and then nurture over time, all the while creating a richer, deeper, more heartfelt experience as we travel through our work day, providing value to our companies as we continue on our own path of personal discovery.

SUMMARY

- Each of us has a purpose that rests at the core of our being, and each of us has qualities and talents that are different from others. Our life purpose is the specific way we use our genius to benefit the world.

- Most companies focus their time and energy on improving employee weaknesses rather than capitalizing on their talents and strengths. People and companies that want radical results leverage those areas of noticeable genius and develop excellent skills so they blossom into genius.

- Truly successful people get "good enough" at basic skills and then optimize their natural gifts, their areas of genius, for maximum return.

- You are at your most productive when you spend at least 70 percent of your time working in your Excellent and Genius Zones.

- To uncover your life purpose, ask yourself, "What do I love to do so much that it doesn't feel like work when I'm doing it?"

- Another way to uncover your purpose is by recalling memories of events and activities throughout your life that brought rich feel-good experiences inside, then notice the underlying themes.

- Our challenge is to align our purpose and genius with our jobs and our company's genius. The result is a skyrocketing of efficiency, productivity, satisfaction, and joy.

TAKE ACTION

- If you think others can't work from their genius and get their job done, most likely this describes how you see your own job. Make a commitment to spend at least part of today operating in your zone of genius.

- In what ways does your company focus on developing employee weaknesses, rather than expanding strengths? What steps can you take to change this focus?

- How can your company best articulate its genius and keep it in the forefront of employees' minds?

- How does your company, as a business, focus on developing its own weaknesses, rather than expanding its strengths and its zone of genius? How might that change?

- How could your company's mission or vision statement be expressed as a deeper purpose?

- List the special qualities in your company. How do those qualities become part of the genius of your organization? How can you articulate these to your employees, so that they can better align their behavior and their work to what your company is really about?

CHAPTER EIGHT

APPRECIATION
Seeing Gifts Everywhere

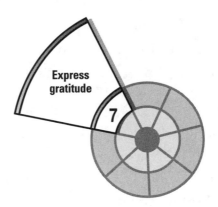

Express
gratitude

7

What leads me to express less appreciation than I feel?

How do I deflect appreciation from others?

What's the most meaningful way to express appreciation?

When you learn to express appreciation, everything increases in value: your employees, your company, and your quality of life. How many other things in life can you think of that take only a minute or two from start to finish, feel great for all involved, have a lasting positive effect, produce multiple, often surprising results, and are free?

When will we begin to tap the deep well of magic that appreciation brings to work? Remember Alfred E. Newman, the caricatured icon of *Mad Magazine,* and his motto, "What, me worry?" Sometimes I (Kate) get the feeling the motto of business is, "What, me appreciate?" The ironic ways in which we feel dumbfounded and confused by appreciation would make me chuckle more if I didn't feel so stunned by them at times.

As a psychologist fascinated with how we humans operate, I repeatedly observe that we usually wait for something to happen before we appreciate people at work. Our internal comparative systems then ensure that what's given to us is never quite enough to warrant appreciation, so we hold back. In other words, most of us have it on backwards: We wait to appreciate something until we have something to appreciate. It's like saying we'll water a rose bush once it produces a rose.

We know it's smart practice to express appreciation to the people who work for and with us. We know appreciation and personal acknowledgment motivate others because we know how it invigorates us. Nothing new there—except that we don't do it. I (Kate) recently overheard an executive I'm coaching express exuberance over another team member's performance. "Have you told him that?" I eagerly asked. "Oh, yeah, he just got a $75,000 bonus," explained the executive with slight bravado. I pressed him: "But have you *told* him that?" The executive responded with, "Sure, he just got the chance to work on *the* hot, new, dream project around here." By this time I saw how clearly he didn't understand the spirit of my question, so, one more time with feeling, I posed, "You mean you told him what a great job he's doing *in actual words?*" He hadn't.

Many of us have invented what seem to be valid reasons to justify withholding our appreciation of others. Do any of the examples below sound familiar? While at first glance they may seem reasonable, linger over the following a moment and consider how they stop the flow and limit a sense of forward movement and delight in your world:

- "If I tell him how well he's doing, he'll stop working so hard."

- "If I let her know how much I count on her performance, she might want more money or more stock options."

- "If I let him know how great I think he is, he might become arrogant and I'd lose the nice guy I get to work with."

- "If I lavish her with appreciation, she'll come to expect it, and I may not be able to keep it up."

- "If I start giving appreciative comments, I'm afraid I'll sound somewhat fake and insincere."

- "If I express appreciation, he might misconstrue it as wanting to start a personal relationship, which would be inappropriate."

- "This feels way too touchy-feely for a business setting."

Most of us would agree in a heartbeat that the world could use more appreciation, but we might argue that an entire chapter about why and how to express it belongs more in the realm of books for parents, kids, or feel-good guides to the 1960s, rather than in a business book.

I agree that if we *only* appreciated people, we'd handicap ourselves. And the same is true if we only compare, judge, and criticize. The issue isn't to replace all negative feedback with appreciation but to find a way to use both in an effective balance. I want to get your attention here and explore appreciation from all angles so it becomes a way of life.

I once had a stunning experience in a crowded executive strategic planning meeting at Dell. Michael Dell was being uncharacteristically critical of the ideas expressed by one of the SVPs as they discussed a business issue. And the SVP, who liked a good fight, was throwing gasoline on the fire, from my perspective.

My role was to observe, and even if I had felt impelled to give Michael some coaching, I couldn't physically get from my seat to his, the room was so packed. I felt frustrated. Michael spontaneously expressed his appreciation to the amazed SVP for having the courage to disagree with him. At one point, he even cracked a joke about his attitude about the particular business issue they'd been discussing, and everyone laughed, vaporizing the tension.

The exec hadn't been listening to Michael or building on his ideas, and they'd gotten very polarized in their thinking. Each became seriously "locked in." Michael's appreciation acted like magic, and suddenly the exec began listening. Instead of reinforcing his stubbornness, it opened him up to listening and to integrating info from Michael, a result contrary to what most people believe will happen when they express appreciation. Instead, the exec felt heard and appreciated for his noble intention to communicate his own ideas about what he thought was best for Dell. The group reached easy agreement about the issue less than 30 minutes later. The solution was a combination of the other exec's original idea with a decision-making process and timing from Michael.

APPRECIATIVE REALITY CHECK

A lack of negative feedback is not the same as appreciation. Because our satisfaction barometer measures episodes of discontent and negative feedback, if we don't hear positive feedback, we sometimes have a distorted view of the specific value others believe we provide. Take it from us; nearly everyone is hungry for more appreciation, an action that also breaks up the energy-dampening flow of criticism that infuses most companies.

You can recoup the cost of this book by a factor of several hundred if you'll practice this exercise every week. If you do it just once, you'll easily get a 100 percent return on your investment, and you won't have to clip any coupons or fill out any forms or mail in receipts or barcode labels. Think of four people with whom you work closely, or on whom your own success is dependent to a large degree. Next to each of their names, write down a few of their qualities you recognize as valuable.

Give it the thought it deserves—be as honest, authentic, and appreciative as you can possibly be. Once your list is ready, approach each person and ask them directly, "What qualities, traits, or behaviors do you believe I value in you?"

If you feel particularly brave, follow that question up with the real kicker: "What qualities do you value in yourself that *you* don't feel are recognized and appreciated by *me?*" If you head into this exercise with only the motivation to "be right," you will likely score high, albeit on the superficial side of things. If you head into the exercise with the full, ripe intention to learn something meaningful and important and listen accordingly, you may radically change two people's lives in the process—theirs and yours.

Appreciation has a profound impact. Done well, it not only nourishes souls and relationships, it demonstrates the relative impotence of criticism as a method of learning, growing, and problem solving. We are, many of us, starved for simple, basic appreciation. *If you're looking to add a meaningful new facet to your own life purpose, aspire to become a teacher of appreciation.* Apparently, there are plenty of slots waiting to be filled.

APPRECIATION AS ELIXER

Let's face it: Many companies and many work teams are cesspools of criticism, where appreciation and acknowledgment are the exception, not the rule. Criticism tends to automatically, reflexively put people into personas where they don't move as quickly to make changes. Appreciation works much faster than criticism if you want people to change behaviors that bother you. This also works well at home. The Hendricks Institute has data on over 400 cases in which a sometimes decades-long troublesome behavior decreased or disappeared when a rich flow of appreciation was initiated.

Think of appreciation as tonic for the corporate soul. Coming to a halt in the middle of an intensely busy day to appreciate someone momentarily dismantles the autopilot of our habitual behaviors and personas. Appreciation restores energy and emotional balance for both the giver and receiver. Work lightens up and becomes more fun when people feel treasured for their true essence and contribution.

When he was the psychologist at Vineland Training School in New Jersey, Dr. H. Goddard measured fatigue in children after criticism and after praise. When they were praised, there was an immediate upsurge of new energy that increased performance. When they were criticized, their energy plummeted.

On the other hand, laughter lifts it up. You could observe the power of laughter in addressing life's challenges if you lived in a small village in Venezuela familiar to anthropologist Jean Liebain. He watched villagers one day attempt to push a canoe up a muddy hill for four continuous hours. Without fail, each time the canoe came sliding back down the hillside, great peals of belly laughing ensued.

Contrast this with your own experiences doing a particularly tough job with a team of people. As our struggle extends and deepens, we tend to slip into silent criticism. Energy flattens, fatigue sets in, negative attitudes rise to the surface, we bicker, complain, criticize, and lose confidence. Sound familiar? We've all been there. Next time, maybe you'll invoke the canoe-up-the-hill and inspire everyone to do likewise. If you do, please call us. We want to join your team. And so will everyone else.

FILTERS, FEARS, AND FEROCIOUS RESISTANCE

No matter how hungry we are for appreciation, acknowledgment, and approval, we often receive these gifts through a filter that distorts, denies, edits, and modifies what comes to us. Remember the CEO we mentioned at the beginning of this chapter who was thrilled with his VP's work but hadn't used actual words to tell him? The CEO admitted he had paid the VP a big bonus but hadn't used words to express his appreciation of the man's work because he was sure the executive knew it anyway. I (Kate) asked the CEO to take the next step and express his appreciation with words. He went to the VP and said something like, "I appreciate the big difference you've made in the business you're leading. People feel more passionate about their work, and the bottom-line results of the business have dramatically improved."

And now for the punch line:

The VP's response was, "What's wrong?"

Have you ever reacted to appreciation with suspicion? Here's another story along the same vein: I worked with a CEO who was a maestro at deadly dull public speaking. Think of the most boring personality you've ever met, and he was ten times worse. Nevertheless, he insisted on holding quarterly meetings for all employees. His intention was to motivate them, and instead he motivated only those who were sleep deprived because napping through his meetings was such an organic response.

I worked with him, and six months later I saw him in action again. He sounded brilliant, and more importantly, people felt enthused and charged up. Several times I attempted to sincerely acknowledge his speaking skills and appreciate his transformation, but he deflected each one. Finally he grew impatient with me and said, "Look, I just need to know what it is that you're after today. Go ahead and tell me what you've got on your mind. I'm sure there is something that you want. Let's just have an honest conversation about it."

So if discounting hadn't shut me up, he was now subtly insulting me by implying that I was appreciating him as a manipulative act. The truth was that I didn't want anything of him and didn't have a single agenda. I just wanted to make sure he really took in how much he had changed.

This CEO is not an exception. Most of us have to clear away a lifetime of negative experiences and fears if the flow of appreciation and other rewards can fully enter our lives. Explore the following two questions and notice what comes up for you as you consider your own responses:

1. "If I shower someone with appreciation, I would be afraid that . . ."

2. "If people showered me with appreciation I would be afraid that . . ."

I frequently use those two questions in workshops. If you are like most people, you have some concerns about being seen as needy, gushy, sentimental, insincere, not being taken seriously enough, etc. We feel suspect of our own kindnesses and very human vulnerabilities, and that then leads us to suspect others too.

An unspoken set of beliefs, such as the one my grandmother always quoted, "pride goeth before a fall," keeps most of us from feeling the joy of being appreciated. Our Irish friends grew up with: "Don't make too much of yourself." Whoa! Who among us would open our hearts under such risky circumstances?

Following are a few other aphorisms that may feel familiar to you:

- "The higher I fly, the harder I'll fall."

- "I don't deserve praise and recognition."

- "If I take in this praise, I might stop trying to exceed my goals."

- "I don't want to feel too good about this. I might get arrogant!"

We have filters to fend off the appreciation we receive when, in fact, the radical act of a simple "thank you" can feel less painful, risky, and dramatic! In Figure 8.1, you'll find some of the most common deflective responses.

Some of us deflect appreciation because of some history of being manipulated or psychologically smothered by excessive appreciation. Here's a bizarre story that takes this to an extreme. At the height of the Roman Empire, the Romans had 192 holidays, one of which was to celebrate the emperor. More than 60,000 people filled the Coliseum to shower Emperor Leo Justine with blossoms that represented their appreciation. They threw flowers, shouted the emperor's name, and worked themselves into a frenzy, burying him in blossoms. He suffocated and died. We promise you won't die from too much appreciation.

FIGURE 8.1   Appreciation Filters

- **Discounting:** "Anyone would have done the same. You do what you have to do! I was only doing my job."

- **Deflecting:** "You shouldn't have!"

- **Putting yourself down:** "I worked hard, but I didn't do as well as I should have."

- **Explaining:** "I did the best job I could under the circumstances."

- **Distracting:** "Let's talk about our upcoming project. Last time I was in front of an audience . . ."

- **Joking:** "You should have seen this funny scene at the meeting."

- **Complimenting:** "You're so nice to say so. In fact, you're one of the nicest people I get to work with."

WOMEN WHO RUN WITH APPRECIATION

Even the most successful companies are filled with people who feel uncomfortable giving and receiving appreciation—and they're mostly men. Once, wrapping up an intense, multiple-day retreat for the top executives at Monsanto where the agenda was an impending, major culture shift, I (Kate) introduced the appreciation exercise. It goes like this: Find people in the room to whom you feel drawn to express appreciation, particularly those from whom you've withheld it up to now. Straightforward and simple, right? There were approximately 12 women in this room of 120 people, and they immediately began working the room with obvious ease, comfort, and joy. The men mostly stood around looking awkward and embarrassed.

Finally, I saw the delightful and warmhearted VC, Nick Redding, walk up to the CEO, Bob Shapiro. These two men enjoyed a very close relationship of ten-plus years, and I was eager to overhear what they would say. Nick looked Bob in the eyes, socked him in the upper arm, and said, "Working with you is great." Then he turned and walked away. I was dumbfounded. Next, I saw Robb Fraley, the president of one of the major business units, walk up to the CFO, Bob Hoffman. "Bob," he said, "You could have been a real asshole last year. I'm glad you weren't." And that was his appreciation. No wonder our workplaces are so full of criticism! Without it, we'd have very little to say to one another.

AND MEN WHO DO THE SAME

When Eddie and I first became a couple, we visited Fiji. One afternoon we went out kayaking, and though Eddie felt uncomfortable, I (who had more kayaking experience) assured him that kayaks were stable and that I had kayaked in 20-foot ocean swells without capsizing. As we neared some large whitecaps, Eddie said he felt uneasy continuing out to sea, but I insisted we'd be fine.

Five minutes later, our kayak caught on the shallow reef beneath the whitecaps and overturned. We were knocked underwater by the fierce waves and strong undertow and repeatedly jostled against the sharp reef. Eddie rescued me several times as I was pulled under. We finally freed ourselves and as we slowly swam over a mile toward shore, bloody and injured, I felt angry with myself for causing this life-threatening accident. I fully expected anger and blame from Eddie. What I got instead was uproarious laughter. He felt so delighted that we were alive! He told me how much he appreciated my stamina, my grit, and that I hadn't panicked. That was the moment I fell in love with him.

CULTURES OF CRITICISM

It's easy to find fault. Anyone can do that. But fault-finding is actually the lazy way because smaller effort is involved in pointing out what's wrong than in expressing what is right. In workshops I often give people five minutes in triads to criticize their work and the people with whom they work. The room quickly gets to a deafening din, as people get louder and louder in their "ain't it awful" stories. Next, I'll ask people to talk for five minutes to each other about what they appreciate in their jobs and in each other. There's usually dead silence as people take in what I've assigned. After 30 seconds, someone will usually say, "I don't get the instructions," which always surprises me because no one ever has any trouble understanding the instructions about the criticizing assignment.

As much as 80 percent of conversations at work contain critical comments. We think otherwise, but "constructive criticism" is almost never constructive. Researchers studying motivation found that telling a group of adults they did poorly on solving ten puzzles decreased their performance on a second try. Telling the group it did well, regardless of whether the praise was deserved or undeserved, improved performance on the second try.

How do you *start* from a place of genuine appreciation, when there's obviously (in your view) something different the other person needs to do? Let's say there's someone on your team who's a strong performer, but whose constant carping and complaining drains everyone else's time and energy. Don't bite your tongue and complain about them behind their back, or share your penetrating insights (i.e., criticisms). These often take the form of your story about them. For example, "James, your constant complaining about your peers and your manager grows out of your insecurity." Instead, start by capturing James's noble intention and expressing something like: "James, I appreciate your attempts to point out what's wrong in our team because I imagine that you are attempting to raise the standards for everyone. However, I notice that my own energy flattens when I hear your comments. I wonder if there's a more effective way for you to get the change you want from people?"

Having his true intention recognized, James may feel more open to hearing a *better idea* about how to infuse the team with commitment instead of negative energy. The tricky part of this is that you have to capture and express the person's noble intention, not with intent to manipulate them but rather as a way to acknowledge their deeper purpose, a first step in coaching them to become more effective.

OUR IMPOSSIBLE APPRECIATION STANDARDS

Not many of us received abundant appreciation as kids, so there are very few teachers of appreciation out there. A research study, in which children wore voice-activated microphones around their necks, found that 85 percent of the messages the children received were negative ("don't, stop, if you don't"). We become so accustomed to that 85/15 split that we tend to recreate the same patterns in our own lives at work and at home. This is equivalent to eating nothing but thin, watery oatmeal for 30 years and then beginning to add milk and sugar (let alone cinnamon, raisins, and walnuts!). Just as our body might go "Whoa!" at first before it got used to running on richer fuel, we throw up lots of barriers.

We picked up critical habits in our childhood when our parents and teachers felt it was their duty to point out our faults and mistakes, and we internalized them. This means we incorporated our parents' critical approach, and now, as adults, we talk to ourselves in the same way. In our work with hundreds of the highest performing executives in the world, we commonly hear them tell themselves they've messed up, aren't good enough, and ought to have done better. They aren't satisfied to simply notice what needs changing and to efficiently do it. Instead, they worry and criticize themselves. As we're sure you're aware, this behavior is not exclusive to the executive suite.

A huge body of research shows that self-approval improves performance. People who concentrate on past failures become less productive as they strive for unnecessary and unrealistic perfection. Andrew M. Meyers and his researchers confirmed that self-critical athletes perform less well than Olympic qualifiers, primarily because they set overly high, perfectionist standards, get trapped in an endless loop of worry, and have greater difficulty recovering from mistakes.

Similarly, people who focus on their self-worth and job satisfaction produce stronger financial results than those who primarily target financial objectives. A survey of successful insurance agents by David D. Burns of the University of Pennsylvania turned up a surprising, if not motivating fact. Agents who evaluated their success in terms of their self-worth, job satisfaction, and enjoyment of their work outearned by 25 percent agents who evaluated their success entirely in terms of making money.

THE PAYOFFS FOR NOT APPRECIATING

A common payoff for behaving critically of others is that you're seen as a *strong* manager, someone who requires excellence in your people. You may be proud of being seen as tough, as someone who's direct and straightforward, who's comfortable "telling it like it is."

Several years ago I (Kate) worked with an executive who, though warm and funny, was notorious for his barbed wit and his absolutely biting criticism. It seemed he walked around looking for things that were wrong in order to talk about what wasn't going well. His team probably would have locked him out of the building long ago, except that he was so funny that he managed to get away with his heavy criticism.

Because he'd been unwilling to buy into my perspective initially, he kept track of the number of times he criticized his people over the course of a few days. Once he saw how clearly, indisputably negative he was, he wanted to change and start over with a clean slate. He vowed to give up "pimple management" and substitute more supportive behaviors to help his team expand their performance. You might also find it an eye opener to have someone monitor your positive, negative, and appreciative comments at your next team meeting.

THE BIOLOGY OF OPTIMISM

Appreciation builds optimism, which reduces wasted time, improves work performance, and reduces stress. Based upon the results of a 30-year study, the Mayo Clinic concluded in March 2000 that not only do optimists live longer, pessimism actually shortens lifespans. In addition to reducing stress, appreciation appears to strengthen the immune system by increasing levels of wellness-contributing hormones, according to the Institute of HeartMath in Boulder Creek, California.

In one particularly fascinating HeartMath study, salivary immunoglobulin, heart rate, and mood were measured in 30 people before and after experiencing appreciation or frustration. The people imagined these states and also watched videotapes where these feelings were expressed. Positive emotions produced significant increases in salivary immunoglobulin, an important contributor to a healthy immune system, while frustration significantly inhibited it. The study also demonstrated that self-induced positive emotional states are more effective than the positive effects elicited by videotapes. HeartMath is teaching people to modify their heartbeats and generate steady, healthful calm within the body by focusing their awareness on the heart and on feelings of gratitude and appreciation.

BEING OUR BEST AT BRINGING OUT THE BEST

The verb, *to appreciate,* carries two meanings. The first is "to effortlessly grow in value," as in, "Our home appreciated $75,000 while we lived in it." The second involves "recognizing or assessing values and distinctions," as in "I appreciate your new ideas," as well as, "I appreciate the difference between apples and oranges." When we give appreciation, it transforms into a very potent, tangible noun. We know something specific has been given. In my (Kate's) experience, regularly expressing genuine appreciation for another's contribution helps that individual appreciate in personal value as they continue to grow and expand.

Appreciation is about realizing we're here to bring out the best in one another. I (Kate) fondly recall Suzanne's transformation from a less-than-stellar employee in my department working below her potential into a fulfilled, star performer. Despite many attempts on my part to inspire, cajole, criticize, and coach her into more effective job performance, and in spite of her obvious talents, her master's degree, and other qualities that told me she was more than equipped to do the job, she simply plodded along. After a year of this, when I hired a new employment manager, Mary, I moved Suzanne to Mary's group. The truly thrilling transformation only took about three months.

What generated it? I wondered myself until the day I happened into Suzanne's work area just as she was proudly telling Mary about a recent victory—she'd filled another open position for a Ph.D. programmer, which in Silicon Valley is a great win. Mary reached out, squeezed Suzanne's shoulders, and cried, "You did it, you're great, you persisted, you made umpteen calls, you got another hire!" With Mary's attention fully focused on Suzanne's blow-by-blow account of the success, I realized I was witnessing the genius of both women in full expression. Apparently what Suzanne needed all along was someone with Mary's capacity to genuinely, passionately appreciate her. Within six months, the corporate controller was advising the CEO and chairman to figure out how to clone Suzanne for our recruiting group. I wanted to clone Mary, too.

As a side note, this episode helped me appreciate myself for something I'd figured out previously—that I can only be successful if I surround myself with people who can do what I can't (a belief that in itself eliminates much of the negative self-talk that slows me down). Earlier in my career I might have criticized myself for not finding the key to transform Suzanne. This time, I was thrilled—with Mary, Suzanne, and myself.

What Mary knew so well, we all can learn to do. And even though the benefits are immediate and worth every ounce of energy it takes to generate those benefits, there's one requirement that may be the deal breaker for many of us: *The act of giving appreciation must be unconditional.* In other words, it's not appreciation if we are motivated by a payoff; instead, it's manipulation. The practice of mindful appreciation involves our commitment to make clear distinctions between half-hearted compliments, flattery, and manipulation, and the gesture of a generous spirit noticing and articulating a success pattern or a special quality that makes a useful contribution, no strings attached.

APPRECIATION VERSUS PRAISE

Appreciation means expressing, in unarguable terms, your positive thoughts and feelings for something or someone. "I really appreciate the speed with which you got that budget proposal to me." "I'm very enthusiastic about the sales potential of your new strategy." "I deeply value your enthusiasm and passion for work. I notice I feel more excited about my job when I'm with you." These examples convey the generosity and sincerity of true appreciation, without a hint of manipulation. It's a one-way transaction of openended giving.

Praise, however, is based on judging something: "You did a great job." "You're so smart and make such wise decisions." Praise requires an evaluation—the assessment of a particular outcome that implies one thing is better than another. For example, if you are taking golf lessons, the golf pro may show you a correction in your swing. Flawlessly, you perform your swing with the correction, and he says, "Great swing!" In the same instance, he may also add, "Your eager attitude to learn and improve inspires me." The first is praise, the second is appreciation.

This distinction between praise and appreciation may seem too subtle to matter, until you consider the pitfalls inherent in praise that you eliminate completely when expressing genuine appreciation. Praise is somewhat like a Trojan Horse. It can look like one thing—a gift—but it can be interpreted or experienced as something else entirely. And that something else is not always pretty. Consider these three examples: the praise sandwich, the praise biscuit, and puff pastry praise.

The Praise Sandwich. If we say anything positive at all, we typically say, "You did great, but next time . . ." We're more likely to serve up a praise sandwich as positive feedback because we've consumed so many of them ourselves. Many of us learned early in our lives that the purpose of praise is behavior modification. Over time, we learn to associate praise with its cousin criticism. The childhood version might have sounded like this. "Nice job making your bed. Now, let me show you how to make it even better." At the office, "Great first draft. But here's what I'd like to see more of." Elation is followed by a correction and a letdown.

The well-intentioned praise sandwich is sometimes appropriate if it communicates honestly the range of opinions and feelings you have. "I notice I enjoy the time we spend chatting at the beginning of a meeting and catching up on our personal lives. I like your jokes and the funny stories you tell about your family. But I feel frustrated at the end of our hour when we haven't covered everything I'd thought we needed to discuss." It can be useful, but it's not appreciation.

Here's an example of showing your appreciation and also supporting someone's learning: "I appreciate your willingness to edit and tighten that report until it's concise and to-the-point. I have an idea about improving the conclusion, if you'd like to hear it." In my experience, people will nearly always go for the idea you're offering, and they will experience it as a gift or help you're offering up that will minimize defensiveness and the feeling that you're using praise to manipulate them.

The Praise Biscuit. When you want to encourage creativity in someone, giving them praise is not the best approach. Why? If you've ever trained a dog, you know the answer. Dogs, we are told, want nothing more than to please their masters. Effective dog training involves rewarding desired behavior with wild and enthusiastic praise. Dogs can be trained to do amazing things this way, but they aren't necessarily creative problem solvers. (We mean no disrespect to you dog lovers out there. We're willing to allow that *your* dog is brilliant!) In humans, praise may generate a desire to please, to go for the delimited "good" answers, rather than for the flashes of brilliance and infinite possibilities that do not, by definition, involve yes/no, right/wrong, good dog/bad dog.

Puff Pastry Praise. Because praising always involves a judgment of some kind, it can be deployed as a way of gaining status over people, rather than reassuring them about their worth. "How did you manage to do such a great job on that budget proposal?" can easily imply a patronizing position of power for the praiser, or an inferior position of less power for the praisee. Praise can sometimes be given or received as intimidation because judgment or flattery both invite subtle power trips. What a shame, if appreciation is what you were honestly going for.

Here is yet another distinction. Notice the subtle withholding and potential power play between "What a sterling report." and "I admire the way you put your whole self into generating that report." In the puff pastry praise, the intention of the praiser is likely to be mistrusted because some level of authenticity is held in check.

Praise can get you in trouble, given its judgment and power potential. To create stronger connections and less confusion, stick with appreciation. Make it clean and make it count.

CREATING SUSTAINABLE RELATIONSHIPS

The ultimate laboratory for looking at relationships is marriage, and key research in this area brings valuable lessons we can apply on the job as well. University of Washington professor and researcher John Gottman studied 700 married couples, ranging from newlyweds to people who had been married 25-plus years. Using only the ratio of positive, appreciative behaviors to critical, defensiveness behaviors, Gottman was able to predict the likelihood of divorce after watching a couple interact for three minutes at a statistically significant level.

Here's the finding that got our attention: Relationship meltdowns occur with a ratio of only 1:1 positive to negative experiences and are a strong predictor of divorce. We tend to think that a "negative relationship" that would lead someone to leave our company would be nothing but criticism, but a *1-to-1 ratio of criticism to positive experiences is all it takes for someone to leave a marriage.* We bet people depart emotionally from their jobs with the same ratio. They may still be there physically, but they won't be working at their full potential. Instead, they'll live for those moments at home when they can criticize their managers, roll their eyes at their misguided focus, and balance the ratio with other negative behaviors of their own.

The most negative experiences for people are as follows:

- Blaming someone for something they did or didn't do

- Criticizing the person's work or their style or their being

- Complaining about someone or their work

- Showing disrespect for someone, their workspace, their life, what they value

- Getting defensive when someone gives you feedback or shares an opinion with you

- Stonewalling and shutting people out

Vibrant, sustainable, collaborative relationships have a ratio of 5:1 positive experiences to negative ones. Five to one! Do you see why it's so important to make appreciation a big part of your lifestyle and work style? Figure 8.2 describes the qualities in relationship meltdowns and strong relationships.

BASIC SKILLS: HOW TO EXPRESS APPRECIATION

Five to one may feel like a big assignment. How do we come up with so many valuing things to say? Most of us find it easier to

FIGURE 8.2   Differences between Relationship Meltdowns and Strong Relationships

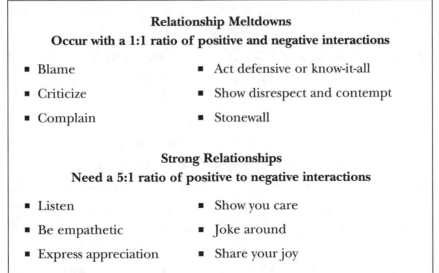

Relationship Meltdowns
Occur with a 1:1 ratio of positive and negative interactions

- Blame
- Criticize
- Complain

- Act defensive or know-it-all
- Show disrespect and contempt
- Stonewall

Strong Relationships
Need a 5:1 ratio of positive to negative interactions

- Listen
- Be empathetic
- Express appreciation

- Show you care
- Joke around
- Share your joy

joke around at work than to express appreciation and show in visible ways that we care. But we do care. We just need the skills to let our teammates know.

We're aware that false or exaggerated praise and appreciation may work with people who generally don't feel valued. That's because if we don't appreciate ourselves, we're more vulnerable to being manipulated by others' praise; we're a bit needy and trade our power for flattery and manipulation. Introducing an agenda, however subtle, implies a desire to control or direct an outcome and derails your efforts to express worth in the other person. If you do this, you've blown it.

You'll also notice that if you use appreciation to manipulate others, you'll expect the same in return—and probably get it. If you're in an open flow of giving and receiving appreciation, you'll register a benign feel-good experience when someone appreciates you. You'll have a wave of positive energy that will feel great, instead of thinking, "Wow, he really likes me. Maybe he'll promote me."

The moment you use appreciation as a *tool,* you become inauthentic and manipulative. It's far more powerful to appreciate someone in order to honor your own commitment to live in an appreciative state of being. Aspire to work and live so that giving appreciation is simply a reflection of your own commitment to integrity and to the quality of life you want for yourself.

Appreciating an "essence" quality in someone usually touches them more deeply than appreciating contributions, behaviors, or skills that anyone could provide. For example, appreciating someone for responding promptly to your e-mail has only moderate impact because many people are prompt in their e-mail responses. More meaningful appreciation is, "Thanks for your prompt e-mail. I'm touched by how deeply you understand my challenge." The first sentence, without the second, will deliver little effect.

Figure 8.3 reveals the qualities of authentic appreciation.

FIGURE 8.3   Appreciation

Characteristics	Description
Genuine:	Say only what you really mean.
Specific:	Describe your experience with clear details.
Benefit:	State how the person's actions supported you and the business.
Emotions:	Express your feelings about the experience.
Purposeful:	Restate your appreciation several times in different words to help the person "get it."

The following three tools from the previous chapters help us craft meaningful appreciation:

1. Speak in unarguable terms about your emotions ("I feel . . .").

2. Speak sincerely about your own, specific experience ("I've observed . . .").

3. Listen consciously to the other person's experience, emotions and intention ("You seem to be saying . . .").

THE APPRECIATION HALL OF FAME

We have witnessed the power of appreciation to change lives and transform companies. In one of our especially memorable off-site assignments, the CEO and founder of a large services company courageously took center stage during the closing appreciation exercise with the management team. He named each person in the room, one at a time, and publicly expressed his appreciation. Not only did he blow everyone away by his heartfelt recognitions, he was blown away by the impact it had on his own way of being.

As it turned out, those very tender and precious exchanges were sowing seeds of renewal for everyone. As this man, an analytical type of personality, connected more deeply into the giving of appreciation, tears of joy began to roll down his cheeks as he realized his role as the founder had been met by so many high-quality people, without whom his vision could not have manifested as it had done over the years. His voice cracked. He was dumbfounded that he had such emotion within him and that he'd never before shared it openly. He confessed to them all that doing so was also fueling a sense of larger possibilities that the company could, indeed, expand to its next level of growth and development.

The company had been stalled for a while, and he had begun to doubt his own leadership skills. It had been a personally painful period in his career, as self-doubt is an uncompromising teacher. His appreciation for his coworkers carried the real-time benefit of showing him he didn't "need to do it alone." It was a pivotal time for the whole team and for the company. They experienced 40 percent growth for the next couple of years, moving forward into new markets in a completely fresh way.

SUPER BOWL COACHING

Some years ago, I (Kate) had the good fortune to work with Jack Hart, the SVP of human resources at Impell, who was willing to invest a bit of time with me, even though I reported to one of his direct subordinates. Hart had heart and fed mine. I grew more then than at any previous period in my career, and he gave me a tool I use even today to keep growing. For about a year, he spent about 15 minutes with me once or twice a month when I returned from a weeklong business trip. I probably had about eight to ten meetings like this, or a grand total of one and a half to two hours over the year. Yet the experience was so profound for me that I consider Jack as the best HR mentor I had in my career. He taught me to lovingly evaluate and appraise my performance and also to appreciate my contributions, and he did this using a very simple process.

When I returned from a trip, he would stop by my office to hear my report firsthand. Jack always wanted me to tell him what I felt I'd done really well, and then, because he was a gifted listener, he offered his own summary of what he'd heard, weaving it all together in a way that clearly showed me what I had done that worked. He taught me to evaluate my performance from the perspective of what worked instead of what wasn't working. Simple and profound.

He never said, "Oh, it sounds like you really did a great job of public speaking." That would have been noise with a little cheerleading thrown in for good measure. Rather, he very specifically acknowledged, "Well, it sounds like the reason the talk worked is that you sensed the special needs of this group and slightly changed your opening to connect with them, and you were authentic in sharing a story from your own life that they could relate to." Or, "It sounds like you were able to get this training program to work so well because you listened through all of their initial resistance and helped them connect that resistance to how the problems had been created." He would help me see the vitality in my unique qualities.

Then he would ask, "Well, what's the one thing you would do differently?" And he taught me to look at improvements from the perspective of learning. Time spent with him left me feeling confident and inspired about improving when in less capable hands, I might have been inclined toward self-criticism and personal bashing.

He also taught me to focus. When I generated a laundry list of possible improvements, he'd respond with, "You know, you're probably only going to make one significant change, so why don't you just think about the one thing that would make the really big difference." And if I became overly critical, he would reflect, "Well, I don't want us to lose perspective because it sounds like there's some learning here, but hang on to the big picture, too. Overall, it went really well."

Out of my experience with Jack Hart, I developed the Three-Minute Coach process shown in Figure 8.4, and hundreds of managers have now used it. In three precious minutes, you can make a world of difference in someone's work life.

CALLING ALL APPRECIATION TARGETS!

We hope you now feel primed to integrate a generous dose of appreciation into your life, so let's take a deeper look at the

---

FIGURE 8.4   The Three-Minute Coach

Coach:	State a general improvement you've recently observed.
	Ask the person what he likes about this positive change.
Learner:	Comment on the improvements you notice in yourself.
Coach:	Ask the person to describe *one* improvement they want to make (within this same area of general improvement).
Learner:	Describe one thing you plan to do differently.
Coach:	Agree with the value of what they are suggesting, and if another change came to your mind, offer that too.
	Summarize the conversation and especially refer back to the positive change you've noticed.

possibilities for your new commitment. Call to mind the one person in your office who rubs you the wrong way, pushes your buttons, and annoys you even more than your kid brother or sister did. And while you're at it, generate a list of people in the last month who truly stirred up some "grief" for you. Sit with that list until you can see into an essence quality belonging to every single person. Continue to sit until you can articulate what you learned from the experience and therefore what you appreciate. Next, visualize what it would be like to share it with them. As you imagine it, don't focus on their response. Steer clear of any desire to control how they feel or how they respond.

Maybe you're thinking about a team member whose performance is slipping. Can you appreciate that she is making you a better manager by inadvertently requiring you to improve your coaching skills? What about the person who keeps missing your deadlines? He's teaching you a different approach to planning and anticipating problems. Perhaps we would wish it otherwise, but the truth is that people who push our buttons and trigger disappointment, anxiety, and frustration in us have something to teach us. By the conflict they trigger in us, they may be offering us opportunities to expand and change in positive directions. If you're dedicated to your own growth as a human being, appreciate! When resistance shows up, view it as a teacher and appreciate even the resistance. Become a student of your own resistance, and you'll eventually earn a Ph.D. in living in a state of appreciation.

FLYING IN FRIENDLIER SKIES

Appreciation can become a state of mind in which we live each day—*a way of being*—and goes far beyond acknowledging someone at work. Our business involves frequent air travel, and

I (Kate) once had the worst flight record of anyone I'd ever met in terms of late flights, missed connections, lost luggage, and drinks and food flying through the air onto me. My attitude became, "What will go wrong today?"

Before I learned how to travel in a state of appreciation, I experienced flying as combat duty, with the foxhole stories to prove it. The good news was that I had a great repertoire of flight nightmares to share, which I did with true glee. The bad news was that each of those stories cost me valuable time from my workday and added significantly to my stress level. I've found that making the radical change of living in a state of appreciation for all the invisible support I receive on every trip creates a happier space within me. Magically, I now have far fewer of the ain't-it-awful flight stories to share.

Because you may have to fly frequently, too, here's a sample of my personal approach to the runway. When I walk into an airport I'm already feeling appreciation in my body, mind, and full being for the effort and energy it took to make my flight day possible and the greater miracle of the ease I'm likely to have. As I walk from the parking garage to the airport, I smile as I think about the luggage check-in people and all the people buried in the bowels of the building who are managing the process of getting my luggage from the conveyer belt to the plane . . . the rep who checks my ID, the security agent who compares my boarding pass to my ID, and all those computer people who make it possible to verify that only passengers on the flight have luggage in the plane's cargo hold.

I bring a similar attitude of appreciation into my day after I land, knowing I can smooth out most of life's problems and challenges if I appreciate them head-on. In the past I attempted to squelch the resistance that sometimes (okay, usually) appears in teambuilding programs before it "infected" the entire group. But at some point along the line I began operating from the assumption that if one person were saying it, probably others were sitting in silent agreement. Maybe they didn't understand what I was communicating, their beliefs didn't align with it, or they were forced to show up when they didn't want to. I shifted into appreciating the resistor for his courage in communicating his truth, even if I didn't agree with it. By appreciating the value of the resistance, the degree of learning in the room increased exponentially and I became a better listener and communicator. I also had more fun and less stress, because my energy was focused on understanding and learning, not on the squelching and controlling that can burn up a lot of energy.

DEVELOPING YOUR APPRECIATION MUSCLES

How do we begin from a place of appreciation in life? How do we make appreciation second nature? By making it more of a habit. Habit-building takes practice. Figure 8.5 provides some practical ideas.

SAYING YES TO ALL OF LIFE

The most powerful use of appreciation is to appreciate life exactly as it shows up—somehow trusting that this is the path of learning and therefore has value. With this full bodymind embrace of what is, we instantly step into joy. We assume an attitude of attention and fullness that serenely meets the events, challenges, and opportunities of life and presents no obstacles to its many gifts. This is the fastest way we know to create a life you're happy to live and work you passionately love.

A great deal of work must often be done on ourselves before we can greet every moment of life with a grateful heart. Until

FIGURE 8.5   Twelve Ways to Make Appreciation a Natural Part of Your Life

1. Look around you and let your eyes rest on something you can appreciate. Say to yourself, "I appreciate _____."

2. Notice one of the major qualities you appreciate about your workplace. Say, "I appreciate _____."

3. Become aware of one of the things you most appreciate about the person you report to. Then say to yourself, "I appreciate _____." Share this appreciation.

4. Before you get out of bed each day, mentally list five things you appreciate about your life.

5. Make a list of 100 things you appreciate about yourself. Notice how long it takes you to come up with this list. Ask coworkers for feedback if you need help. Keep it on your PDA and read it at least once a week.

6. Begin each e-mail with at least one sentence of appreciation for the person receiving it.

7. At least once each day, express genuine appreciation to people you work closely with—your team members and your manager.

8. Keep a tally of how many times you express appreciation each day. When you reliably do it at least ten times a day for a week, you've probably made this into an operating mode.

9. Have someone else keep a tally of how often you express appreciation at your next departmental meeting.

10. At the end of each day, name five things you've appreciated about your day that you haven't already expressed that day.

11. Catch yourself in a mental or verbal complaint and counter it by noticing five things you appreciate about that situation, and the learning and change it's creating.

12. Whenever you are dealing with a problem, begin by genuinely expressing appreciation for whatever the problem is teaching you.

then, we may rise in gratitude for a while, then bring ourselves down by a challenge. If we handle the challenge successfully, gratitude may come to the fore again to lead the way.

A key move that opens the heart is to regard all of life's experiences as learning opportunities—as challenges to love some part of yourself that most needs acceptance. Some people greet life's events with an attitude that guarantees misery: "I refuse to accept that this is happening to me, and I will not rest until I find out who is at fault here." A major shift happens when we drop this attitude in favor of another: "I acknowledge this is happening, and I open myself to learning all the lessons I can harvest from this experience." The former attitude closes off possibilities with its cosmic ungratefulness. The latter opens the heart to the wonder of life itself.

With practice, the appreciation reflex happens more quickly. I (Kate) didn't appreciate getting fired from the San Francisco Mental Health Association when it happened in 1979. This event did, however, lead me to face the fact that I had found the nonprofit arena a frustrating place to work and further led me to explore corporate positions that used my talents and changed my whole career. Then the appreciation flowed in.

In early 1990, when I decided to cut back on work-related travel at the time my daughter was a college freshman at an expensive private college, I felt scared, not appreciative. I used the time to create one of the first computer-based 360° assessment tools, and this helped me differentiate my company and tripled my revenue. Major appreciation.

I began to notice that at each step the more quickly and deeply I was able to embrace a hurdle—to really take it in and experience it with gratitude as opposed to resisting it or wishing it were different—the greater the healing, the speedier my own career growth, and the happier I felt. And the more I could share this appreciation with the person who appeared to be my nemesis—you know, the person who appeared to be doing me wrong—the speedier my own growth and the greater the momentum I received from the experience. So, to me, *this is the highest art of appreciation—to appreciate those things you think you do not want,* and I mean *really* appreciate them, and to make this the pattern of your life.

When we learn to appreciate career hurdles in the moment, they're more likely to become blessings in hindsight. With the softening balm of passing time, I've come to know that most of life's big, ugly problems turn out to be invitations to learn to welcome change even more wholeheartedly.

THE APPRECIATIVE STATE OF BEING

Once you've learned the basic skills, make appreciation a conscious habit. Day by day, encounter by encounter, we make progress. And so, as we move through our days and consider our interactions with people, we stay alert to our intentions to stay out of autopilot mode. "Was that thought, e-mail, or utterance stingy or generous in its appreciation? Was that a stingy commitment intended to break up the flow of energy, or was it an appreciative thought to add energy? As we catch ourselves in a conflicted thought, we work at not staying attached to our momentary slip out of integrity. Gently, lovingly, we move on. Some days are better than others, but we have tremendous faith in the process that has led us to generate the following list of commitments I revisit regularly and offer for your consideration as well. See Figure 8.6.

A WALKING MEDITATION

Some day in the near future, we invite you to go on a walking meditation at your place of work. Don't make a big deal

FIGURE 8.6   My Commitment to Appreciation

- "I commit to a quantum positive shift in my ability to appreciate myself and others."

- "I commit to a quantum positive shift in my ability to receive appreciation."

- "I commit to expressing my appreciation in a way that transcends people's listening filters so they 'get it.'"

- "I commit to discovering new things about my work and my life to appreciate."

- "I commit to creating my life as an expanding flow of appreciation."

about it. Don't announce it. Just discreetly, quietly, gently, walk down the corridors, through the cubicles, into the conference room, the lobby, the supply room. Realize your heart has eyes, and invite it to see. For the few moments of time it will take, notice all of the life that is being lived in the margins, and bring it to the center of the page in your mind, where you shower it with appreciation.

Both feel and express appreciation as you walk. Notice the personal way someone has expressed themselves in their cubicle, with the warmth of a lamp they brought from home. Turn to the person and say, "Right now I'm appreciating how much warmth it adds to our office when people personalize their cubicles, as you've done." This immediately shifts you to an energy state that's a flow of appreciation. Enjoy the laughter coming from a meeting room. Say to yourself (or to those in the meeting, if appropriate), "Right now I'm appreciating your laughter and the reminder that work can be fun." Notice two people engaged in sorting out a problem and say, "I appreciate how fully you give yourselves to your work."

People may think you're a little different at first, because most people aren't used to someone who is genuinely appreciative. Initially people may not believe you're sincere because most people don't pause for those ten seconds through the day to truly feel appreciation for all the caring and beauty that surrounds us. But I know of no better way to create a workplace where people feel truly happy—and where *you* feel happy. It's the best antidote I know to tight shoulders and that complaining whine inside about too much work to do, or the distracting mind spin as you relive a recent blast of criticism, thinking of rebuttals you wish you'd said, while cringing in anticipation of the next barrage of judging remarks.

We can all be far more effective in a world where we all look for what's right as well as what's wrong, a world in which we speak the simple truths about what we appreciate about ourselves, our coworkers, our life. If you find the walk a pleasant one, make a vow to repeat it periodically. You may be sowing the seeds of your own radical transformation.

A FINAL NOTE OF APPRECIATION

I (Kate) want to close on a personal note and tell you about the power of authentic appreciation in healing old wounds. To do that I need to share a very personal story about my mother, with whom I had an ambivalent relationship most of my life. While meditating one morning, it flashed in my mind that my mother would die suddenly in a year and a half. I was age 38 at the time and she was age 63. She had attempted to be a good mother, doing all the *Ladies Home Journal* things a great mom should do, but somehow it never came off right for me. I got lots of homemade cookies and support for my various interests, but not nearly enough expressed love and genuinely positive acceptance of who I was.

We seemed to have so many arguments, conflicts, and hassles when I was growing up, and even as an adult I wasn't particularly close to her. I tended to spend the obligatory week at home around the holidays and to call her every month or so, but I certainly didn't live in a place of appreciation with her. In fact, I felt like I spent most of my time with her either preparing for or recovering from her criticism. (Notice all my "out there" thinking about her; I felt criticized by her and I blamed her for it. We lived in The Bermuda Triangle, as so many mothers and daughters do.)

I spent the week after this meditation thinking about her from the perspective of appreciation and particularly considered all that I felt anger, irritation, and regret about. Childhood images surfaced, and I reflected how she always wanted chores done her way, instead of the ways I found more interesting or challenging. We argued and I got angry; instead of listening and learning, I heard her criticism as a put down. The exchanges often turned ugly and personal as we deteriorated into attacking each other, which escalated into screaming and crying. My dad always wanted me to apologize. I never did.

From my adult perspective, I could see my parents never punished my challenging behavior. I was allowed to be quite disagreeable, very sassy, and certainly confrontive of authority. The seeds of my own professional genius were sown through my relationship with my mother, whom I suddenly saw as my first trainer. I passionately love my work, and yes, it does require that I regularly confront the top executives of companies, something I do with great confidence (and delight!).

So I sent my mother a very long letter appreciating all of these things that had been so difficult for me to accept and embrace until that moment, and sharing with her the positive learning and ultimate capabilities I had received from what, as a child, appeared to me to be hurtful. Although she never mentioned the letter to me (we didn't have that kind of openness in our family), I began for the first time to feel genuinely appreciated and acknowledged by her. She seemed to value my success. Our whole relationship shifted. Conveniently, I forgot about my foresight that she was going to die. Exactly a year and a half later, she suffered an unexpected fatal heart attack. As I was going through her papers, I found multiple copies of this letter. She had been so touched by it that she had shared with my aunts and uncles—her brothers and their wives.

So profound was this experience that I began wondering if all of life's difficult journeys are not the same way. I began looking back, and I thought about the time I'd been fired and how much there was to appreciate about that because it allowed me to redirect my whole career. I also appreciated the time I'd been laid off, in which I found a job that bumped me up two or three levels in my career and nearly doubled my salary at a point in life when I was still struggling financially as a single mother, and on and on. I began to greet the expected and unexpected events of life with genuine appreciation that came more quickly and felt it at a greater depth. The journey continues.

To me, the highest art of appreciation is the commitment and skill to appreciate those things that you think you do not want—and I mean *really* appreciate them, and to make that the pattern of your life. *Thanks, Mom. I love you, too.*

Appreciation, the oxygen that gives vitality to our interactions, energizes all of our relationships. I appreciate *you* for purchasing this book and for reading it and for taking in these ideas. I leave you with the words of Pierre Teilhard de Chardin, a twentieth-century Jesuit and celebrated archeologist, who wrote, "We will conquer for ourselves the energies of wind, gravity, waves, but one day we will harness for God the energies of love and then for the second time in the history of the world, we will have discovered fire." Go light up the world with appreciation.

SUMMARY

- Most people tend to criticize and notice what's missing, rather than what's working well. A common illusory payoff for being critical of others is that you're seen as a strong manager, as someone who requires excellence in your people.

- Many of us incorrectly assume our coworkers feel appreciated because they haven't received negative feedback from us.

- To express appreciation, clearly and specifically communicate your positive thoughts and feelings about someone. When you share your appreciation with people, describe the specific action or quality, state how the person's behavior touched you, share your feelings, and say only what you really mean. The act of giving appreciation must be unconditional. In other words, it's not appreciation if we are motivated by a payoff; instead, it's manipulation.

- We tend to hear appreciation through a filter that distorts, denies, edits, and modifies what comes to us. The most common ways we deflect appreciation are discounting our contribution, turning attention to work, distracting by making a wisecrack, and complimenting the person expressing appreciation.

- Extensive research by Gottman shows that a ratio of five positive experiences to one negative experience is required to create healthy relationships. Blame, criticism, contempt, and stonewalling are particularly destructive to relationships.

- The fastest way to create a life that you're happy to live and work you passionately love is to appreciate life exactly as it shows up and trust that any obstacles and apparent problems offer valuable lessons.

TAKE ACTION

- What hidden payoffs do you receive when you criticize or complain about other people or yourself? Find a better way, using more appreciation and less criticism.

- For one week, keep a count of how many times you express appreciation and how many times you criticize, judge, compare, and complain. Make a commitment to triple your appreciation the next week, and keep track until expressing appreciation becomes an engrained habit.

- What sorts of filters prevent you from fully *receiving* appreciation when it's given to you?

- Whose work do you value and appreciate but haven't acknowledged in clear and specific ways? Take time at your next team meeting to appreciate the members of your department.

- Find at least one thing to appreciate about coworkers you consider difficult to work with. Reflect on the value these people provide by stimulating your learning. At your first opportunity, express your appreciation to them.

- Find at least one thing to appreciate about something within your company that you don't like. If you feel stuck, ask yourself, "What can I learn from this situation?" Then notice if the problem becomes less troubling as you move forward to learn.

- Within the next week, take a walking meditation through your company. Express appreciation aloud to at least three people. Put this on your calendar as a biweekly event.

- How can the expression of appreciation become part of your company's regular business practices? What steps can you take to make this change in your team or department's work culture?

CHAPTER NINE

THE RIPPLE EFFECT

Change Your Life, Change the World

How can I stay motivated and sustain my commitment to change?

How can I create big results from these conscious choices?

How can I bring these results into the larger world?

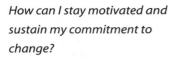

Making real change in life and at work is a challenge for most of us. Think of all the New Year's resolutions that dissolve into a faint memory by the time April rolls around. So what can you do—this minute—to ensure that the changes you've dreamed of and thought about as you've read this book come to fruition? One radical act might be to welcome the next change in your life and embrace it as the pathway for your next level of learning, instead of trying to "manage" the inevitable change.

People say they long for quieter lives and more personal time, without realizing that one of the most effective time savers is to eliminate their denial about the need for change and their initial resistance when directly confronted with it. Denial and resistance eat up valuable time and make life harder, slowing the pace of needed change in our companies, our personal lives, and our nations.

If we commit to shift our own consciousness and take visible, in-the-world action, we can unleash the power to change more than ourselves, more than our immediate work team, and more than our own personal lives. We *can* change the world. If you think about it, most of our personal problems as well as our global problems result from a failure to take the seven actions described in this book. The first step toward a shift is to catch yourself forgetting these practices—becoming defensive instead of learning, telling less than the whole truth, or fudging on an agreement.

We are often caught in paradoxes. Like a rock in your sock, paradox doesn't hurt much but it makes you limp a lot.

- We say we want more personal time, but we spend more money than we make and keep ourselves locked on a money treadmill like rats on a wheel. We ensure that future generations will do the same by allowing them to get credit cards while they're still in school, and we adopt our values from a media-driven culture.

- We complain about the high cost of medical care, but most people do little to keep themselves as healthy as they could. We starve ourselves by eating foods rich in sugar and fat. We eat when we're upset. We fail to exercise.

- We feel upset by illegal drug use in our country, yet we allow American tobacco companies to market to children and to export tobacco and cigarettes to third world nations, creating new generations of addicts and huge medical costs.

- We're eager to complain about our politicians and how they don't seem to be in touch with what's going on and how they fail to address the real problems. But half of us don't vote. And if we do vote, we base important political decisions on TV sound bites of information, choosing our politicians by their public personalities, not by their competence.

- We say we want peace on earth, but we wage subtle and not-so-subtle battles every day at work and at home.

Many people we work with feel impotent to change their companies and to change any of the big problems that plague the world. People want to make a difference in their companies and in the world, but they don't believe they have the resources to create real impact. They aren't personally wealthy, they don't have the enormous influence of major political players, and they have families to care for when they're not at work. Some people don't take a step until they know what to *do*. They believe there is something "out there" that they need before they can make the right choices to effect radical change. They want to make a difference—they really do—but because everything seems so big, they settle for complaining and making occasional donations to worthy causes instead of committing heart and soul.

Our only limitation in changing our companies and the world around us is the way we think. When most people spot a problem, they look first to identify who created it. Some people immediately start blaming themselves, while other people quickly look for the culprit and work industriously to deflect all blame from themselves. The focus is on "who messed up?" not "what can I learn?"

Instead, use the seven actions described in this book. A single act of awareness, curiosity, candor, or accountability starts those radical ripples.

These ideas aren't particularly new; most of them have been around for thousands of years in some form. They just haven't been universally applied in or out of business. Your decision to make these choices will ripple out and affect many others.

Imagine a world in which we all show up with the greatest version of who we are. Where each of us is willing to change inside to effect the greatest change outside. Where we learn on the run, dropping our defenses in a flash. Where we have access to our whole bodymind to make the wisest choices. Where we show up authentically and powerfully, taking 100% responsibility for whatever happens in our lives. Where we tell the truth 24/7 and operate in our zone of genius most of the time, appreciating all we have.

The people you've met in this book are just a few of the thousands who've been exposed to these ideas, then used them in their workgroups, with their customers, and also taken them home. Can you put these concepts to work? Can you start this week? Can you make a difference in transforming your culture and your world? Take the first step to change your world and change your own life.

These seven actions have completely transformed our lives and the lives of thousands of clients. They're yours now. Take action and realize your dreams. Your next decision determines the future of our world.

INDEX

Worth Ethic Corporation <www.worthethic.com> provides 360° assessments, coaching, teambuilding, emotional intelligence training, and culture change programs designed to create a high performance organization. Major clients include such companies as Adecoo, Dell, Motorola, Pharmacia, Special Olympics and U.S. Defense Logistics Agency.

Kate Ludeman, Ph.D., is CEO and founder of Worth Ethic Corporation and coauthor of *The Corporate Mystic* and three other books. She has coached more than 1,000 CEOs and senior executives on every continent.

Eddie Erlandson, M.D., is a Senior Vice President at Worth Ethic Corporation and a former hospital Chief of Staff and vascular surgeon. He delivers keynote talks, coaches executives on leadership, and delivers change management programs to middle managers and front line employees.

For more information please contact us at:

Worth Ethic Corporation
PO Box 550, Carpinteria, CA 93014
805-745-1210
info@worthethic.com